Covering Your Campus

Covering Your Campus

A Guide for Student Newspapers

MATT NESVISKY

ROWMAN & LITTLEFIELD PUBLISHERS, INC.
Lanham • Boulder • New York • Toronto • Plymouth, UK

ROWMAN & LITTLEFIELD PUBLISHERS, INC.

Published in the United States of America
by Rowman & Littlefield Publishers, Inc.
A wholly owned subsidiary of The Rowman & Littlefield Publishing Group, Inc.
4501 Forbes Boulevard, Suite 200, Lanham, Maryland 20706
www.rowmanlittlefield.com

Estover Road, Plymouth PL6 7PY, United Kingdom

Copyright © 2008 by Rowman & Littlefield Publishers, Inc.

All rights reserved. No part of this publication may be reproduced, stored in a retrieval system, or transmitted in any form or by any means, electronic, mechanical, photocopying, recording, or otherwise, without the prior permission of the publisher.

British Library Cataloguing in Publication Information Available

Library of Congress Cataloging-in-Publication Data
Nesvisky, Matt, 1942-
 Covering your campus : a guide for student newspapers / Matt Nesvisky.
   p. cm.
 Includes bibliographical references and index.
 ISBN-13: 978-0-7425-5388-0 (cloth : alk. paper)
 ISBN-10: 0-7425-5388-4 (cloth : alk. paper)
 ISBN-13: 978-0-7425-5389-7 (pbk. : alk. paper)
 ISBN-10: 0-7425-5389-2 (pbk. : alk. paper)
 1. Student newspapers and periodicals—United States. I. Title.
 LB3621.N47 2008
 371.8'974—dc22
                                                2007002200

Printed in the United States of America

∞™ The paper used in this publication meets the minimum requirements of American National Standard for Information Sciences—Permanence of Paper for Printed Library Materials, ANSI/NISO Z39.48-1992.

Contents

Acknowledgments vii

Introduction 1

1	Putting Policies on Paper	11
2	Staffing the Newspaper	27
3	The Newspaper Office	45
4	What's New(s)?	55
5	Reporting	77
6	Investigative Journalism	101
7	Opinions	119
8	Features	131
9	Arts and Entertainment	145
10	Sports	155
11	Photos and Graphics	167
12	Design	181
13	Copy Editing	193
14	Headlines and Cutlines	205

15	The Online Edition	217
16	Finances and Advertising	229
17	Student Press Law	241
18	Taste	253
19	Ethics	259
20	The Joy of Journalism	267

Bibliography	275
Index	281
About the Author	287

Acknowledgments

For their editorial and production assistance, my thanks go to Professor Aaron Barlow, Dr. Douglas Campbell, R. J. Corby, Brenda Hadenfeldt, Kayla Hockenbroch, Sally Jaskold, Professor Edward Lorden, Erica Nikolaidis, Steve Schmoyer, Bess Vanrenen, and the Kutztown University of Pennsylvania Faculty Professional Development Committee.

For their education and inspiration, my thanks go to Dr. James Applewhite, Alex Berlyne, Wolf Blitzer, Erwin Frenkel, N. David Gross, Mary Hadar, Alec Israel, James Nechas, Dr. Arnold Newman, Judy Peres, Ari Rath, Dr. Elaine Reed, Ruth Connell Robertson, Faye Bittker Rudnick, Sasha Sadan, Hanan Sher, Dr. Heather Thomas, all of my journalism students past and present and, last and first, Lin.

Introduction

Not long ago I received a phone call from one of the innumerable vice presidents of my university. Such a call not without reason sets many a student newspaper adviser atremble. The conversation went like this:

"Matt, this is one of the innumerable vice presidents of your university. I just thought I ought to tell you about the reporter for the campus newspaper who came to interview me this morning."

"Okay," I said warily. "Shoot."

"Well, the reporter had come by to ask me some questions about certain financial matters. As I was answering her questions, I noticed she wasn't taking any notes. She was just sitting there with her arms folded. So I remarked on that. I gently suggested something like, 'Maybe you'd like to write down some of these facts and figures . . . or some quotes . . . ? If you need some paper . . . or a pen . . .' But she just shook her head and said: 'Thanks, I have a notebook. And as soon as you say something interesting, I'll write it down.'"

Yeah, that conversation left me shaking all right.

Shoot was almost the right word.

As a student newspaper adviser I've had my happy moments: reading an especially well-written or insightful article, rejoicing at a genuine scoop, learning the newspaper has won a national award, watching a student editor graduate and get a promising entry-level job in journalism. I've also had my bad days: the cringe-inducing gaffe in the banner headline, the misspelling of the name of the college president's wife, the threatened libel suit. Which have I seen most often—the good, the bad, or the ugly? I don't know. Keeping count is a fool's errand, and it probably doesn't matter. But because producing a newspaper is a complex process involving numerous human hands, the finished product is always imperfect. (Not for nothing have newspapers been called the first draft of history. Think about *your* first drafts.) Those who care about their newspapers invariably wish they could have done yesterday's edition better. Reporters blame their oppressive deadlines, editors question their own decisions, publishers wring their hands—or the closest available necks. And the readers—ah, the readers. It's axiomatic in journalism that ninety-nine out of a hundred readers' letters, e-mails, and phone calls will be complaints, not compliments. If you're seeking expressions of appreciation for your work, you'd probably do better to pursue an altogether different profession. Maybe pet grooming. Or tattooing. Or delivering meals-on-wheels.

I know the editors and reporters of the student newspaper I advise aren't going to earn many handshakes and backslaps no matter how well they perform. That's why when I write my weekly critique of their newspaper I always try to give praise where praise is due. But in pursuit of excellence—of doing the job even better next time around—I don't let many errors go unremarked upon. I certainly try not to accentuate the negative; that's not good pedagogy, and it can earn one the reputation as a nitpicking, *gotcha!*-gloating old crank. That my students no doubt do think of me as a nitpicking, *gotcha!*-gloating old crank doesn't upset me. I merely point out that while the verb *nitpick* takes no hyphen, the modifying noun *nit-picking* does, that *gotcha!*-gloating is an awkward locution, and that as for being old, well, the university hasn't forced my retirement yet.

But in truth it's not the nits that sting me. My red pen may well circle typos, transposed lines of type, or clumsy photo captions, but that's only because my old editorial eye and hand operate as a sort of rapid response team. Technical slips certainly don't please me, but neither do they upset me. No, what upsets me is the kind of incident described by that vice president in the opening of this Introduction.

A typo you can always blame on the printers (those sabotaging illiterates!). Or on a sleepy-eyed proofreader (what do you mean you ran out of coffee?). But a reporter conducting an interview without taking notes—and then offering an impertinent explanation for not doing so—signals systemic failure.

The reporter clearly should know better—but who was responsible for teaching her to know better? The reporter deserves blame, but the editors who assigned her the interview without giving her proper training and instructions are even more to blame. And maybe there's a culture in the news organization that is even more blameworthy than any of the individual editors involved in this incident. That culture—that level of concern for doing the job right—probably explains why your newspaper is what it is. And why it earns the degree of respect that it does.

Are Eee Ess Pee Eee Cee Tee. Over the years I've studied hundreds of campus newspapers. They range from terrific to terrible. Some are considered indispensable by their readers. Others are hardly considered at all. How much respect does your newspaper receive? And if—worst-case scenario—like Rodney Dangerfield you don't get no respect, do you know why?

The university vice president mentioned above didn't get no respect, but he's not my concern. Rather, consider this: The reporter who acts like an airhead and makes lame remarks on the job surely makes herself look bad. The problem, however, goes far beyond the reporter. Her gaffes speak poorly for her editors. They also speak poorly for her newspaper as an institution. That reporter's dumb behavior even reflects on the innocent newspaper adviser: Why isn't that old crank doing his job? More important, her behavior reflects badly on the university: What kind of students are we admitting here? You may not be profoundly concerned about this last point, but future employers who weigh the value of your diploma might be.

This sort of pernicious ripple effect is why news organizations must strive each and every day to get the job done right. Because when a newspaper or a TV news broadcast screws up, the news consumers' faith and trust—which aren't all that solid these days anyway—are eroded yet again. Bear in mind, the readers or viewers lose faith not just in the reporter who goofed but in his or her entire news organization as well. Perhaps rightly so. But it gets worse. Because people tend to generalize, individual errors discourage the public's faith in journalism in general. ("Look, in this obit, they got Grandpa's middle initial wrong! That's the media for you!") And before you know it, readers are dropping their subscription to the local daily in favor of something more gratifying, like *Guns and Ammo* or *Cosmo*. And viewers are using their remotes to find a no-news-none-of-the-time channel—maybe the Cartoon Network.

Are you at all concerned about this? If you aren't, then I'm concerned about you.

Think of it this way: If you're involved with a newspaper—even a student newspaper—you're in the information business. And when you're in the information business, you're obligated to gather and disseminate worthwhile and accurate information, and to do so in a manner that will have your readers coming back next time for more.

Those tasks pose complex and difficult challenges. But if you're in the information business, you no doubt believe it's important for people to be informed. And so you want to do the job and you want to do it well. But to do the thing right, you have to do the right thing. (That may sound like rubbish, but remember who's giving out the grades here.)

This book is about doing the thing right. Yet it's not a rule book, because the rules of journalism are few and far between. It is, instead, more of a discussion of what experience shows works well and what works less well—and it attempts to illustrate and to explain why. The book will ask you to examine the principles and practices at play in your publication. It will urge you to evaluate these things, with the aim of determining if what you are doing is the best way to be doing it. Maybe it is. If so, I'm thrilled. But maybe the book can suggest better principles and practices. At the very least, the book hopes to inspire you to step back and take a critical look at your publication from a variety of angles. Finding time to do this is something editors and reporters typically consider a luxury they can't afford. But periodic self-examination is no luxury. Jeez, you find time to check your hairdo and your clothes a half-dozen times a day. Shouldn't you hold your newspaper up to the mirror at least once a semester? (I know, I know, how are you going to read your newspaper in the mirror?)

Let's take an example or two (I thought you'd never ask) of the kind of self-examination I'm talking about:

You, the editor in chief, tell me you publish your weekly campus newspaper on Thursday. I say cool. And then I ask, Why Thursday? After some hesitation, you probably mumble, Well, 'cause it's always come out on Thursday. And I say that answer's not good enough—and speak up, don't mumble. Then I go on:

Thursday might be the ideal day to publish your weekly. But maybe not. For one thing, your football games are among the biggest campus events of the week. And they're played on Saturday. You're publishing coverage of the game, complete with scoreboard, five days after the event—when everybody on campus already knows your team got creamed by its opponents. Meanwhile, your readers are already starting their weekend parties on Thursday night and by Friday morning many are leaving for home in droves with their bulging laundry bags—and leaving your newspapers bulging in their racks. And for the losers stuck on campus for the weekend, there's going to be all those interesting police raids at parties for underage drinkers on Friday night, those amusing fistfights on Saturday night, those picturesque collisions on College Boulevard on Sunday morning. And you're not going to present coverage of any of this until the following Thursday? What are you publishing, a newspaper or a history text?

Yeah, okay, you admit it, your newspaper does lack a certain freshness. So again I ask, Why Thursday? Has your newspaper in fact always been published on Thursday? Can you at least determine how the publication day was chosen? Investigate it—you're journalists. Maybe in terms of your production schedule—and your academic schedule—it's just the most convenient day. Or maybe it was chosen arbitrarily years ago by your university's administration. Or maybe it was decided because it best suited the timetable of your commercial printers (those sabotaging illiterates!). Or maybe the advertisers prefer appearing at week's end. Who knows? Well, you should. And you should also determine if perhaps you would be serving your readers better by publishing on a different day—say, Monday or Tuesday.

Or maybe not. Maybe after a close examination of all the relevant factors you decide Thursday is as good if not better than any other day. So maybe the question is not Why Thursday but Why do you keep publishing out-of-date news stories? Maybe it's simply a matter of emphasizing articles that look ahead to what's coming—in other words, newsier news.

Examining the rationale for your publication date is an example of looking at a newspaper practice and evaluating the principle behind it. But sometimes this book will ask you to do the reverse: to weigh principles in order to determine the practice. Here's an example of the latter:

As editor in chief you've had a team of reporters working throughout the spring semester on what you consider a major investigative story: homophobia on campus. Your reporters have conducted a comprehensive and well-designed survey. They've interviewed numerous students, faculty, administrators, and campus clergy. They've done abundant research on the Internet and in the library. They've elicited information on the subject from other campuses. They've reviewed relevant state and federal laws. Now they've written a terrific story. And it's one that has stunning news: Antigay attitudes on your campus are deep and widespread—indeed, far more endemic than at many comparable colleges. The gays on your campus really feel intimidated. And despite their pleas, the university has pretty much ignored the situation.

You're confident that you have a carefully researched, well-written, and important story here—with news that might even get picked up by the mainstream press. You're set to publish the first week of May—lead story and jumping to a full page inside.

Then just before your story is to appear you suddenly get a phone call from the dean of admissions. He's aware of the story you're poised to run—he was even interviewed for it. But he's concerned, because the story is to appear on Parents' Visitation Day—when over a thousand parents of prospective freshmen are to spend the day on campus. The dean suggests that it is hardly good for the university's image to have all these potential paying customers (sorry, "parents") exposed to a student newspaper with a banner headline screaming: "CAMPUS HATES GAYS." The dean isn't asking you, God forbid, to suppress the story. "But for the good of the university, couldn't you, like, just delay publication for a week? Meanwhile, you could run another exciting article. How about, er, a piece on all those students who volunteered over spring break for Habitat for Humanity . . . ?"

Because the dean is a good guy (not long ago he helped your newspaper get funding to upgrade its software) you want to give his request a fair hearing. And because you're not a dictator, you convene your editorial board to discuss the issue. And man, do they discuss it.

Your news editor, who headed the investigative team, says they worked long and hard, did the job well, and want that story out now.

Someone else says that delaying the story by a week won't kill us—and after all, it's not like we're being asked to kill the story.

Another editor says there's a principle of administrative interference involved: The dean was out of line even to suggest holding the story, and that's enough reason to print immediately.

"Yes," says another voice, "but after all, we must always consider the consequences of what we print. Running the story this week could turn off a lot of parents. And the university, like so many institutions of higher learning these days, needs all the freshmen it can get. Don't we have an obligation to our university community's well-being?"

"Well-being shmell-being," says your Op-Ed editor. "Give in to the dean's request and we take the first step on the slippery slope of administrative control of our news columns."

"We're having a thousand parents visiting campus?" says the business manager. "Let's increase the print run by a thousand."

"Don't be provocative just for provocation's sake," says the sports editor.

"A lot of people are counting on this story," says a reporter. "The Gay-Lesbian Alliance has suffered in silence long enough."

"We don't publish stories for the benefit of any individual or group," snaps another reporter.

"*Veritas odit moras*," intones one of your geekier grinds. "Truth hates postponement. Or so says Oedipus."

"Right," says your news editor. "Let's not forget the readers here. Our obligation is to get the story first, but of course first to get it right. Well, we got it right. We uncovered the truth, and the readers deserve to have the truth without delay."

"Since when does Oedipus speak Latin?" your arts editor asks.

"Since Seneca translated Sophocles," sniffs the geek, a comparative lit major and a major bore.

At about this time you're wishing you were in fact a dictator. But it seems to me that consulting your staff members was the right thing to do, because look what they did: They articulated a half-dozen or more worthwhile journalistic principles. And by placing these principles on the table and debating them—something the staff probably rarely does—the editors should come to a reasoned, defensible decision on the practical question: whether or not to hold that homophobia story.

This book encourages you, as another antique Greek put it, to live the examined life—or more precisely, to examine the life of your newspaper. Granted, reconsidering your publication day is the kind of thing you can do at your leisure; deciding whether to print or not to print an article might be something you have to do under the sweaty pressure of a deadline. Nevertheless, the habit of mind should be there to subject all aspects of your journalistic activity to critical scrutiny. (All scrutiny all the time!) This book aspires to help you develop that habit of mind.

I'll put it another way: If you're putting out a campus newspaper, there's little point in doing it half-heartedly. Unlike, say, chairing the chess club, publishing a newspaper is a high-profile campus activity, and it certainly affects more people than the chess club does. So with your whole world watching, you have every reason to put out the best paper you can. That means not just going through the motions for each issue just to get the pages filled; that's a recipe for mediocrity. It's so easy to get hung up on the mechanical steps of the production process, which admittedly often involves racing the clock. But doing the job well requires analyzing and evaluating what you're doing. This book is designed to get you thinking in that direction.

In the ensuing chapters, this book will discuss numerous aspects of campus newspapers—writing them, editing them, designing them, managing them, improving them. I'll review what they contain and perhaps what they should not contain, how they look, how they are financed. I'll consider nuts-and-bolts issues, like what makes for good and bad headlines. And I'll get into philosophical matters, like what makes for good and bad journalism. I'll examine legal matters, ethical concerns, and crossword puzzles. And I'll focus on problems, because the exercise of publishing a newspaper is riddled with problems—and because problem-solving is what life is all about. And in case you're worried, I'll also discuss sex, drugs, and rock and roll, because of course that's what life is all about, too.

Above all, this is not a how-to manual. It's more of a what-should-we-do-and-why book.

My strategy here is to advise more than to instruct. You certainly don't have to buy everything I suggest (but you'd better have something better to sell me). My purpose is not to tell you what to think but what to think about. I don't have all the answers as to what makes for the best possible newspaper. Or rather, I like to think I have, but I know other advisers and journalists likely have answers that are different but just as valid. That's why I draw greatly on their collective wisdom as much as on the shreds and patches of my own. But if we all agreed on everything, then I suppose all campus newspapers would be exactly alike and equally excellent. That, however, ain't exactly the case. Some campus papers are more perfect than others. (And if you don't know what's wrong with that last sentence, you'd better drop everything else and get going on chapter 1.)

TWO NOTES

In the following chapters when I refer to "the student newspaper" or "the campus newspaper" I am normally referring to the campus's official, or semi-official, or at least main, student newspaper. Many colleges these days have in addition to a recognized student newspaper an "alternative" campus paper. While it is directed at the same readership as the "official newspaper," the alternative newspaper most likely is edited and printed off campus, is unsupervised and unsupported in any way by the college, and may be distributed only in an unofficial manner on campus. I'm all for competition. I'm all for alternative newspapers. I'm even for outlaw publications. Nevertheless, because alternative newspapers are under no obligation to listen to advisers or to any campus officials, I consider such unofficial publications outside of my purview here and therefore am not really addressing them. Still, many of the points I make about covering the campus should apply to the alternative press as well, so it can't hurt if they listen up.

Second, I tend to use the terms *college, university,* and *campus* interchangeably. This isn't always as precise as it might be; I recognize that a university is not a college and a college is not a campus. I'm simply trying to avoid lengthy and repetitive locutions like "your university or college or community college" or "institutions of higher learning." So sometimes I'll refer to "your university administration" or to "a college newspaper" or to "campus media," with each of those modifying nouns encompassing the others.

Now, can't we all just get along . . . to chapter 1?

1

Putting Policies on Paper

You're all familiar with the venerable news lead formula of the five Ws and the H. (If you're not, man, are we in trouble.) What I'm suggesting here is applying those interrogatories not to a spot news story but to the newspaper itself. To wit: *Who* are you? *What* is your purpose? *Where* are your parameters of news coverage, market, and advertising? *Why* do you do those things you do? *When* must you do them? *How* do you get them done?

Now these questions are as tough as they are broad, and I wouldn't expect you to answer them off the cuff. And you shouldn't have to. That's because I'm a firm believer in having things in writing. Well, I'm a journalist, so that shouldn't come as any great surprise. But in this instance I'm referring to a newspaper's basic policies, principles, definitions, and the like. Having these things spelled out on paper (or in electronic files) won't solve all your problems. But they just might help you get a better fix on problems as they arise—and therefore save you the task of reinventing the wheel each time another wheel falls off.

KNOW THYSELF

Let's start from the top: Just who exactly are you?

A student newspaper more often than not is a recognized, sanctioned, university activity or organization, like the student government or the Environmental Club. Such official recognition typically earns the organization certain

11

rights and privileges, such as office space in the student union building or elsewhere on campus (and maybe after-hours access to that office), office equipment, financial underwriting by the university or the student government, and so on. To gain recognition as an official campus organization, such groups customarily must formulate a document spelling out their raison d'être in the form of a constitution or a set of bylaws. This defines the organization, indicates how it chooses its officers, swears fealty to all university rules and regulations, and all that sort of stuff.

If your newspaper is indeed such a recognized entity, then it probably already has such articles of confederation. If it doesn't, I think it would be a good thing to have one. (I picture editors asking themselves if such a document exists and frantically pawing through ancient file cabinets.) At the very least, bylaws should spell out what you're all about—the organization's objectives—and should list your staff positions and the responsibilities of each. Your operating manual should also indicate how those positions are determined—appointed or elected—and by whom. The bylaws might also lay down whether or not staff members are to be compensated for their work and how and by how much. And it's good to have on paper how a person may be removed from office and for what reasons.

The reasons for all of the above should be obvious—and if they're not, they will be the first time one of the staff questions how a position got filled, or queries the compensation, or challenges his or her removal. Sure, you can manage these things based on oral tradition ("We'll do it this way this semester 'cause I think this is how they did it last semester")—but that's no way to run a railroad (I mean a newspaper). Think of having your basic principles in written form as a sort of contract—if only a contract with yourselves. If all you have is an unwritten contract, bear in mind what the wise old movie mogul Samuel Goldwyn allegedly said: "No verbal agreement is worth the paper it's written on."

If your newspaper does have a constitution or a set of operating and business rules or whatever, that's all to the good. I suggest it's equally good to know what's contained therein. This means it might be fruitful to dust off the old yellowed document periodically and subject it to a review to see if it's still meeting your needs and aspirations. If it's not—if your contract needs renegotiating, if your constitution needs adapting and updating—then you should call a constitutional convention to see if any amendments are in order.

Alternately, if you discover your news organization does not have such a founding document, you'd probably be wise to find one. I mean that literally. You don't have to draw up a constitution or a set of bylaws from scratch—nobody does that. The standard practice is to locate an organization that has such a constitution and . . . rip it off. (I suppose they all go back to the Magna Carta.) Your student government most likely can help (although that may be a first). If the student government can't supply a template then you can no doubt find some other student organization, a faculty organization, or even a professional group that has a set of bylaws you can use as a model.

Here's an example of a campus newspaper constitution. It's not terribly original—it's based on a template provided at a university for all official student organizations—and it's not perfect. (Even the U.S. Constitution has needed amending from time to time . . . to time . . . to time.) But consider something like this:

TEXTBOX 1.1.
Sample Campus Newspaper Constitution

THE SLAVERING NEWSHOUND STUDENT NEWSPAPER
J. P. SLAVERHUNDT UNIVERSITY
CONSTITUTION

ARTICLE I: NAME

Section 1: The name of this organization shall be The Slavering Newshound, the student newspaper of J. P. Slaverhundt University.

ARTICLE II: PURPOSE

Section 1: The purpose of The Slavering Newshound newspaper shall be:

a. to report and comment on news and issues pertinent to the university community in accordance with fair and professional journalistic practice and ethics

b. to provide an open forum to members of the university community for the exchange of ideas and opinions

c. to publish creative and entertaining essays, reviews, feature stories, artwork, and other editorial matter of interest to the university community

d. to provide practical journalistic experience to J. P. Slaverhundt University students

ARTICLE III: MEMBERSHIP

Section 1: All J. P. Slaverhundt University students who have paid their student activities fees shall be eligible for membership in The Slavering Newshound newspaper.

Section 2: Active membership shall consist of staff members who have attended three consecutive meetings.

Section 3: Members of The Slavering Newshound staff shall include writers, reporters, editors, designers, artists, photographers, business and advertising personnel, and anyone else otherwise engaged in the production of the student newspaper.

ARTICLE IV: OFFICERS

Section 1: The governing editorial board of the newspaper shall consist of editorial and business managers of the newspaper.

Section 2: The board members shall customarily comprise the editor in chief; the editors of the news, feature, sports, opinion, photography, and art departments; and the business and advertising managers. The precise number and designation of governing editorial board members, however, shall be determined according to need by the board.

Section 3: Members of the editorial board shall be responsible for determining the contents and character of the sections of the newspaper for which they are given responsibility.

Section 4: The board shall be headed by an editor in chief, who shall have ultimate responsibility and authority in regard to the contents and character of the newspaper.

Section 5: Neither the Student Government Association, faculty, or administration of the university shall have any role in determining the content or character of The Slavering Newshound newspaper; nor shall the Student Government Association, faculty, or administration of the university share in any liability arising from material published in the newspaper.

Section 6: Decisions on administrative matters regarding membership, meetings, elections, scheduling, and the like shall be determined by a simple majority vote of a board quorum.

Section 7: The editorial board shall constitute the sole executive committee of the newspaper.

ARTICLE V: MEETINGS

Section 1: Venue, time, and frequency of meetings shall be determined by the board.

Section 2: Board members shall be informed of all meetings at least one week in advance.

Section 3: Quorums shall be established by the attendance of a simple majority of the active membership (one-half plus one).

ARTICLE VI: ELECTION OF OFFICERS

Section 1: All J. P. Slaverhundt University students who have paid their student activities fees may stand for office in The Slavering Newshound newspaper.

Section 2: Officers shall be elected during the final month of each semester.

Section 3: Elections shall be advertised to the university community at least two weeks before the election date.

Section 4: Officers shall be elected for terms of one semester but may stand for re-election.

Section 5: Officers shall be elected by a simple majority vote at a meeting of the editorial board.

Section 6: Nomination and balloting procedures shall be determined by a majority vote by the editorial board.

Section 7: Board positions that fall vacant during a semester shall be filled by election at the next regular board meeting.

Section 8: Elected replacement officers shall serve in their positions until the next regularly scheduled elections.

ARTICLE VII: REMOVAL OF OFFICERS

Section 1: Officers may be removed from office if they fail to fulfill their duties as set down in this constitution and in its amendments.

Section 2: Cause for removal of an officer shall be brought before the board meeting, and if the accused wishes, the accused will be permitted to answer the charges.

Section 3: Officers may be removed by a vote of three-fourths of the board members present at a board meeting.

ARTICLE VIII: BUSINESS MANAGEMENT

Section 1: The Slavering Newshound business staff shall sell advertising space to advertisers approved by the editor in chief.

Section 2: Billing, expenditures, records, and accounting shall be overseen by the business staff according to guidelines determined by the editorial board.

Section 3: Advertising revenue shall be distributed to the appropriate Slavering Newshound accounts according to regulations determined by the Student Government Association and by the appropriate university administrators.

ARTICLE IX: ADVISER

Section 1: The adviser of The Slavering Newshound newspaper shall be a member of the J. P. Slaverhundt University faculty.

Section 2: The adviser to the newspaper shall be a nonvoting member of the editorial board.

ARTICLE X: RATIFICATION

Section 1: This constitution shall be ratified by a majority vote of the members of the editorial board and upon approval of the Student Government Board, the Student Affairs Committee, and the president of the university.

ARTICLE XI: AMENDMENT

Section 1: This constitution may be amended by a vote of three-fourths of the board members present at a board meeting.

Section 2: Amendments to this constitution shall become effective upon subsequent approval by the Student Government Board, the Student Affairs Committee, and the president of the university.

ARTICLE XII: ORGANIZATION COMPLIANCE

Section 1: The Slavering Newshound student newspaper shall comply with all of the rules and regulations of J. P. Slaverhundt University and with the laws of [YOUR STATE HERE].

This sample constitution touches on a number of what seem to be technical matters but which in fact are quite important, such as liability and editorial independence—matters that will be discussed in subsequent chapters. But for the moment I'd like to focus just on Article II, which talks about what you're all about. In a broad sense you know what you're all about. But I think it's good to have it spelled out, both so editors can remind themselves of their objectives (it's so easy for the eye to wander off the ball) and so cub reporters and other newcomers to the staff can be educated as to your reason for existence (and maybe even to get inspired).

YOUR MISSION

Article II is akin to a *mission statement*. Mission statements are often criticized, and rightly so, both because they are so ubiquitous (even trash collectors, I suppose, have them) and because they are so often expressed in such a high-flown and idealized manner as to be utterly meaningless. So, okay, keep it low-flown and harshly realistic.

Can you write a mission statement? Do you really need one? Consider also this very mysterious and yet very meaningful sentence, which has been attributed to at least half a dozen writers: "I don't know what I think until I read what I've written."

Get it? Got it? Good. Or not. See, the very act of writing out your ideas focuses the mind—almost as much as coming under automatic fire does. Nothing squeezes you to think when you're just ruminating. That's why daydreaming is so relaxing. But composing words means composing thoughts. Writing it out forces you to think—that's why writing is so grueling. So don't sleep on it. Write it down, and who knows what you'll dig up.

Here's what I suggest: Get the posse together and have yourself a brainstorming session. Have everyone individually write down what he or she thinks should be the objectives of your publication. Then put them all in the hopper. Weed out all the rude notions and sarcastic witticisms, the glib and the goofy. See what you have left. Then hold up the last several issues of your newspaper and see how they measure up to what your editors think or wish they were doing.

Let me suggest something further: If you eventually find you can't create a statement of purpose, or if you conclude it's too much trouble to draft one, then, Houston, we have a problem. By that I mean you're putting out a newspaper on automatic pilot. Which may work, sort of. But is that pilot truly aware of where it's going—and why?

Here's a little secret. People in the news business—reporters, editors, publishers—are usually thought of as a hard-bitten, maybe even cynical, breed. But in fact more than are willing to admit it see themselves as carrying out a mission, one that is impelled by no small measure of idealism.

So when it comes to formulating the purpose of your newspaper, don't be afraid of expressing a little idealism. (After all, your mission statement most likely will remain safely in-house and classified.) I won't suggest a model mission statement beyond what's found in the model constitution above. Work out a statement for yourselves that expresses your individual hopes and dreams. Meanwhile, a number of other newspaper practices can benefit from having a written formulation.

WHO HAS ACCESS?

A *submissions policy* or *contributors policy* deals with who has access to your columns. Most of your editorial matter presumably is written by staff members, but there are occasions when outsiders seek to have something printed in your paper—or when you solicit a non–staff member to do so. So, who qualifies to appear in your pages? Anybody? That's possible. Only students? That's possible too. But consider the ramifications of each scenario.

First of all, readers picking up a student newspaper reasonably enough expect the publication to be student-edited and -written. But what if a faculty member submits an Op-Ed piece to you? Well, you might want to extend your range of contributors to all members of the university community. Cool. But what if the university provost submits one of her periodic diatribes against drugs to your editorial page? That might also be cool. You might consider printing her article a good public service. But because the provost represents the university administration, running her article might cross a line in your readers' minds, raising the question: Hey, is *The Slavering Newshound* the independent voice of the students or an organ of the administration? By printing "the official line," are you endorsing it? Doesn't the administration, moreover, have its own means of disseminating information? There's a further consideration: When you allow an administrator to publish in your columns, you might be sending a message that the administration enjoys easy or even automatic access to those columns. With this in mind, you might conclude you'll soon have no more editorial independence than *Pravda* did under the Soviets.

It gets even more complicated. A college administrator or a prima donna faculty member might offer you a worthy article that you wouldn't mind publishing, but such writers may take the attitude that their words are so exquisitely nuanced that they don't want anything edited. Oops—now you're faced not only with opening up space in a student newspaper to nonstudents but also with surrendering your duty and privilege of editing.

Then you might get articles submitted from persons who have no connection with your campus. You might think that highly unlikely, but you'll be surprised at the number of scribes out there—politicos, religiosos, wackos, whateverosos—who hope to direct their screeds at what they consider the tender and vulnerable minds of students. Cool again. So what's your policy on accepting articles submitted by the Society for the Prevention of Racism Among Fur-Bearing Animals?

Obviously one way to handle this matter is on an ad hoc, case-by-case basis. That might work. But there's also an argument for hammering out a policy on outside contributions—maybe one that sets your limits but also allows for the extraordinary exception to be determined at the editors' discretion (you don't want to become a prisoner of your own rules). Having a written policy has two practical advantages. First, it focuses your own thinking and provides some guidelines to fall back on; second, when you want to turn aside an unwanted contribution from an administrator or faculty member or some other outsider, you can point to that policy and say: Sorry, but this is the policy as established by the newspaper's editorial board.

Will this tick off the administrator, professor, or other outsider? Maybe. You don't want to tick off people unnecessarily—but sometimes it's unavoidable. (The editorial page editor of *The New York Times* on occasion rejected articles submitted by the publisher—the man who signs the editor's paycheck!—and was respected for doing so.) And you always have other options you might draw on. You might, for example, suggest that the contributor write a letter to the editor rather than an Op-Ed piece. Or you might say you prefer not to run the piece, but how about if a reporter interviews the contributor? That way the wannabe columnist gets his or her views across, and you run a student-written article.

At the very least, a policy on submissions should state that all articles are subject to editing for accuracy, clarity, brevity, and style. No one should expect to have unfettered and unedited access to your pages—and that of course includes staff members as well. (It's good practice to show the edited piece to the contributor before publication, but I wouldn't swear to do so, as time constraints may not allow for this.) In any case, having a submissions policy printed in the paper—say, under the masthead—might save you a lot of grief. You might run an abbreviated form of the policy on the editorial page and have a fuller statement of policy in your office files or stylebook for additional reference.

YOU HAVE MAIL
Pretty much the same holds true for letters as for articles. Do you print letters only from members of the university community, or do you accept them from off-campus sources as well? (Bear in mind that a lot of loony tunes out there are indiscriminately gang-mailing and mass e-mailing letters and other stuff to campus newspapers.) Also, would you run a letter from a person who wants his or her name withheld? (Common practice is to permit this if, in your judgment, circumstances warrant it, but the name should not be withheld from *you*. Indeed, common practice is to check back with the writer of every letter before publication to confirm that that person actually wrote the letter—and not someone else using that person's name.)

Letter writers should likewise be informed via a policy statement on the editorial page that their epistles are subject to editing. You might also suggest letters should be kept brief (everybody overwrites). Finally, before you rush to print you should read every reader's letter, like everything else you print, with an eye for defamation and other legal transgressions. Contrary to popular belief, your newspaper can be sued for libel expressed in a reader's letter.

TAKING ISSUE
An entirely different issue, but one you might also do well to have spelled out under your masthead, is a *circulation policy*. This refers to a situation that has arisen in recent years and affects student newspapers that are distributed free. What is to prevent someone from scooping up hundreds of copies of your freebie publication—or in fact the entire press run? But why, you ask, would anyone be so daft as to collect all those newspapers? Two possible reasons. First of all, the United States has seen scores of incidents where someone—an enraged reader or group of readers, a fraternity or political group, or even the college administration—has seen fit to confiscate all copies of a student newspaper to keep them out of others' hands. They do so because of something the

paper-snatchers find objectionable (maybe an animal modesty squad objects to that photo of a nude horse). Alternately, we also have trash-picking freelance recyclers who have emptied distribution boxes. In either case, as they're loading their pick-up trucks, the confiscators might thumb their noses at you. After all, ha-ha, the papers are free, aren't they?

Courts have intervened in a number of instances on the side of the newspapers, but your case will be strengthened if you modify your free-for-all policy. That's why many otherwise free newspapers have taken to publishing a circulation policy under their masthead—something to this effect: "One copy of *The Slavering Newshound* is made available to each reader free of charge. Additional copies are 50 cents each, payable at the newspaper's business office." Such a statement effectively turns legally scooping up newspapers by the batch into theft. (And what about that cub reporter who pinches ten copies of the issue carrying his first byline to send to all his relatives? Threaten the little miscreant with the full force of —! No, of course not. But that illustrates the point about being flexible even when you have policies carved in stone.)

COPY THIS

Okay, you've dealt with legal possession of individual copies of your newspaper. Now what about ownership of the articles, photos, and graphics appearing therein? In other words, is the material in your newspaper—and your Web site—*copyrighted*?

While you're scratching your head and going, "Duh?" I'll tell you that the quick answer is yes. U.S. copyright law, unsurprisingly, is fairly complicated, but, essentially, since 1976 your intellectual property is copyrighted the moment it is created—even before it is registered with the U.S. Copyright Office. Two questions logically follow:

First, if the above is true, why should you bother to register your publications with the U.S. Copyright Office? Well, according to the relevant bureaucratic gnomes beavering away in Washington, "Registration is recommended for a number of reasons. Many choose to register their works because they wish to have the facts of their copyright on the public record and have a certificate of registration. Registered works may be eligible for statutory damages and attorney's fees in successful litigation. Finally, if registration occurs within 5 years of publication, it is considered *prima facie* evidence in a court of law" (U.S. Copyright Office, www.copyright.gov).

Okay then, to your second question: Why the heck should you expect a lawsuit regarding ownership of the material in your newspaper or online edition? Well, you shouldn't—but for any number of reasons an ownership conflict could occur. A reporter might want to use his or her article again in another publication. A book publisher (*Best College Writing*, perhaps?) might want to reprint something that appeared in your pages. Someone else may be inclined to rip an article or a photo from your Web site for his own nefarious use. Who owns this stuff? (Sometimes it's the newspaper; sometimes copyright is shared between the publication and the writer, sometimes some other arrangement is in effect). So, should permission, payment, or at least acknowledgment be required of those seeking (or appropriating) secondary use of your stuff? Having a policy on these matters determined in advance is a good thing. The policy need not be printed in the newspaper (simple indication of copyright should be sufficient) and the policy need not be inflexible—but it's wise to have one.

Finally, those federal gnomes in the U.S. Copyright Office have mounted a very thorough and user-friendly Web site that will answer more of your questions in detail. Check it out at the above-mentioned www.copyright.gov.

IT ALL ADS UP

All of the policies discussed so far refer to the editorial matter of your newspaper. But there's still that large portion of your pages—half or more, if you're lucky—that isn't produced in the newsroom. So—what about an *advertising policy*?

Ooh, I thought you'd never ask. Although I do hear a few of you in the back of the room muttering, "Why do we need a policy on ads, of all things?" Well, if you'll quit your mumbling for a minute, I'll explain.

An advertising policy mainly deals with what kinds of ads your newspaper and Web site will or will not publish. On the one hand, especially if your publication is at a state institution, state or local laws may forbid you from advertising some products and services (this might include booze or even restaurants with liquor licenses, or messages that could be construed as hate speech). On the other hand, there may be ads you prefer not to run simply because, like Bartleby, you prefer not to. These might include ads for (a) cigarettes, (b) gun shows, (c) abortion clinics, (d) bongs, (e) massage parlors, or (f) all of the above and a whole lot more. A whole lot more might include the increasingly common political or public-issue ads. For example, would you run a paid advertisement that argues against affirmative action? Do you accept an ad from the Young Republicans as well as one from, say, the Old White Power Party? Are you willing to allow the World Wildlife Fund to solicit support from your readers for orthopedic surgery on humpbacked whales as well as to allow the Institute for Historical Review to suggest "debate" on the "myth" of the Holocaust? Alternately, are there outfits for whose ads you might be willing to reduce or waive costs, like certain charities, women's shelters, or other social services?

Such specific instances most likely should be determined on a case-by-case basis. But that's all the more reason at least to have a general policy in place. First of all, you should know what state or university regulations exist concerning your advertising content and language. Second, you would do well to articulate a policy that affirms that you reserve the right to reject any advertisement your editorial board deems "unsuitable" for your publication. That's basically all you need. From there you can judge an ad unworthy for any number of reasons—for example, you oppose abortion, you believe the ad offensive to members of the community, you think the ad likely to stir conflict and hatred, you think the ad misleading or untruthful (yes, you can be held accountable for a libelous advertisement).

Above all, do not be taken in by the false argument that by rejecting someone's ad you are abridging that advertiser's freedom of speech. You are never obligated to publish anything, and therefore you are not trampling on anyone's First Amendment rights just because you decline to let him sell his sex toys or her anti-Semitism in your newspaper.

THE E-WORD

Ethics? Did somebody mention *a code of ethics*? Not really, but okay, now that you've brought it up, let's talk ethics. Well, we were just alluding to the ethics of advertisers. (Honestly, that credit card deal just sounds too good to be true.) And like most newspapers, you may well find yourself at some point examining the ethical conduct in some corners of your (university) community. So okay, Mr. and Ms. Slavering Watchdogs of the Campus, how 'bout your own ethics?

The number of ethical dilemmas journalists face on a daily basis wouldn't pass through the eye of a camel, or whatever the metaphor is. What I mean is, the number is big. Ethics are discussed in more detail later in this book, but here are a few sample problems off the top of my head: (1) Should your reviewers accept free theater tickets or CDs or meals? (2) If you can't get hold of someone for her response to a serious accusation made against her, may you report the allegation anyway? (3) Should a sports reporter cover a varsity sport if the reporter is good friends with one of the star athletes on the team?

Deal with such issues case by case? Possible—but hardly desirable, especially if an ethical decision must be made under pressure of a deadline, which is often the situation. Much better if the guidelines are already spelled out in print for your staff members; then staffers can't claim they didn't know that a particular practice was unacceptable. Sure, you can assume people should know they can't raid the petty cash drawer to support their cigarette habit. But you can't assume all staffers are going to be alert to all of the problems involved in reporting fairly, accurately, and comprehensively.

As with several of the other policies mentioned above, you needn't draft an ethics code from scratch. Most news organizations have such codes, and most are either inspired by or adopted from the code drawn up by the Society of Professional Journalists. Even though the SPJ guideline on plagiarism is exceedingly blunt ("Never plagiarize"), ripping off the SPJ code isn't exactly a rip-off. First of all, if you do model your code on the SPJ document, be sure to credit your source. Second, it wouldn't hurt if your newspaper supported the SPJ by becoming a member of the organization. Third, you may very well wish to rewrite, amend, or otherwise adapt the code to your needs. And fourth, for heaven's sake, the SPJ didn't draft the code for itself: It *wants* news organizations to heed its guidelines. (By the way, the SPJ's forerunner organization, the Sigma Delta Chi honorary society, admits it originally "borrowed" its code of ethics in 1926 from that created by the American Society of Newspaper Publishers.)

Anyway, the full SPJ Code of Ethics, most recently overhauled in 1996, may be found at www.spj.org. It doesn't cover every conceivable ethical problem, but its lists of what journalists should and should not do are pretty darn good. And of course you're free to consult other news organizations, student or otherwise, to look at their codes of ethics—on the optimistic assumption that they have them.

NEWBIES TO NEWS

Every semester you're likely to have some new reporters and photographers who don't know the newspaper's operating procedures, traditions, routines—and maybe don't know much about journalism in general. The more guidance you have down on paper to hand them, the better. Such help might include things like names and phone numbers of editors and regular contacts; the newspaper's schedule and deadlines; tips on interviewing procedures and etiquette and on otherwise dealing with the public; suggestions on writing leads, striving for accuracy, and using quotes and the like; and, for photographers, news photo principles, regulations concerning use of cameras and other equipment, information gathering for captions, and so on.

RETREAT? HELL, YES!

Okay, okay, by now you're saying, "Jeez, what is it with this guy? He's got us writing constitutions and position papers and policy documents on every damn thing except how many times the employees must wash their hands. Give me a break. If we spend all our time writing out policies, when are we going to write the news? Just when does he expect us to do all this—late at night after we've put the paper to bed? Or at our normal editorial meetings?"

I hear you. And, no, I don't expect you to get your policies drafted and crafted during your normal workweek. I don't even expect you to get the job done over the course of one semester. But hey, that's why God invented winter break, spring break, and those long, lazy days called summer. Seriously, I recognize it's nearly impossible to find the time during your regular publication period to discuss and draft policies. That's why you should do your best to arrange an off-hours and maybe even out-of-season time to tackle these chores. Hopefully you already have some of my suggested policies in place, so you don't have to face tackling the whole bunch. Even if you do have eight or nine such projects confronting you, you don't have to take them on all at once. Prioritize the list and get on it. Probably the best way to do this is to have a *retreat*—out of your offices and maybe even off campus (I hear Maui is nice year-round). But really—spend a little of that petty cash, find a room, supply lunch and dinner for the crew. Then focus on the subject at hand; don't make formulating a policy one of a dozen things on your agenda. In the end, you'll hammer out a policy or two—and I promise, you'll feel better for doing so.

Of course you're not done yet. You finally get a constitution, a mission statement, an advertising policy, a code of ethics, the whole package mentioned above. Congratulations. Oh, and lots more things, you'll be thrilled to know, are good to have down on paper, like job descriptions, flow charts, budgets, assignment sheets, and calendars; I'll get to those later. But for now, two things: First, collect all these documents, print them out in multiple copies, and store them electronically as a sort of newspaper operating manual. (I know of at least one newspaper that had a neat set of documents and guidelines in exactly one copy—and sure enough, it eventually got lost.) Second, don't forget to set aside time periodically to review all this stuff—once a year or whenever you get a new editorial staff. Hey, work things right and you can be on retreat more often than you're in class.

Now that you have your basic policies in place, we can consider your practices, which are the subject of the subsequent chapters.

2

Staffing the Newspaper

Whenever I meet with a new crop of student reporters—say, at the beginning of a semester—I always make it a point to point out that reporters are the most important personnel at a newspaper, for without them there would be no stories to print.

At the same time, whenever I meet with a new crop of editors, I point out to them that they are the most important members of the staff, for without them there would be no printable stories.

Do I contradict myself? Yea, I contain multitudes. But in a sense both statements are true.

The public generally has some idea of how reporters go about doing their jobs. Few outside the profession, however, have much understanding of an editor's role. At best, most people have an image—provided largely by movies and TV—of the editor as an overweight, overwrought figure planted behind a desk and alternately barking orders, tearing out what little remains of his hair, and swigging Pepto-Bismol. Not too far off the mark, as far as that goes. But let's go further.

An editor—and I'm including all section editors as well as the editor in chief—is arguably first and foremost a manager. That's precisely why becoming an editor can be such a challenge for students. You have enough trouble managing your own time and your own life. As an editor you're suddenly being asked to oversee other people's schedules and productivity and the like.

Unless you've somehow moved up the food chain from burger flipper to burger manager or have done some coaching or been responsible for some organizational work, you probably haven't had much experience in the world of administration. Well, welcome to your seat behind the editor's desk.

The first mental adjustment required of the reporter who graduates to an editorship is to acknowledge that, alas, this is not an opportunity for that person to beef up his or her portfolio of bylined stories. As an editor you may well find yourself writing articles occasionally—but if you find yourself regularly churning out news or sports coverage or film reviews, then you really aren't doing your job. What you should be doing is helping others beef up their portfolios. That may require a major change of mindset, but there it is.

What the editor does more specifically may be divided into two categories or stages. The first deals with generating story ideas. The second deals with developing and processing the stories. I know this is going to sound terribly conventional, but let's take the first one first.

GENERATION J (FOR JOURNALISM)

News happens—and it doesn't. That is to say, certain events occur—a water main explodes in the library, the dean drives his car through the glass doors of the student union—and you have a news story. But reporters and editors can't afford to sit around and wait for spot news—spontaneous events—to occur. After all, you have a paper to fill and you can't count on happy accidents to fill it. Hence you are constantly seeking to develop story ideas. This doesn't mean you sabotage the water main or drive through the student caf yourself (no thanks, but we appreciate your creativity). No, what an editor does is stay constantly on the alert for legitimate story ideas—and the editor encourages the reporters to do the same. A good editor will be a fount of story possibilities, and so will a good reporter. It's a team effort; the editors can't count on reporters to come up with sufficient stories, and the reporters can't just sit back and wait for assignments. I'll talk more about this in the chapter on reporting, but for now here's how it should work:

The news editor sits down with a reporter, either at your regularly scheduled reporters meeting or individually, and says, "I understand the university administration is considering increasing the parking fees for students. How about looking into that?" Or the features editor says to a reporter, "Have you noticed this new fad—everybody seems to be wearing leg warmers on their arms? Would you like to talk to these people, maybe work up a picture story?" Or the sports editor says to a staffer: "I hear the captain of the hockey team has a 4.0 grade average. How about doing an interview?" And of course the editors should be encouraging reporters to do the exact same thing—constantly pitch story proposals. Or, for that matter, at an editorial meeting, the editor in chief might say, "Hey, some wacko congressman is making noises about a reintroduction of the draft. What say we conduct a poll among the readers, get their views?"

Okay—you get the idea. Ah, but you ask, where do you get the ideas? Right. That's precisely the difference between what a textbook can spell out for you and what is actually going to work. Which means that good creative editors have to bring a lot to the job, namely a curiosity about how things work and why, an alertness to what's going on around them, and a sensitivity to what's interesting—not interesting just to themselves but to others. (André Malraux once asked: "Why am I interested in only what I'm interested in?" which I hope you recognize as a profoundly interesting question.)

In other words, editors have to have a highly developed news sense, or nose for news. This is an attribute that no book can provide for you. As with any set of skills, you simply have to develop it through practice. But don't despair, because, presumably, you already have some degree of intellectual curiosity and an interest in what's going down and why or you wouldn't have been attracted to journalism in the first place.

LET'S HOLD HANDS

Beyond generating or encouraging the generation of stories, an editor's other major responsibility is shepherding stories into print. This involves a number of tasks and talents. First is giving guidance to the reporter: What kind of angle or tone do we envision for this story, what questions need to be answered, who should be contacted for information, how might the Web or the library be useful for research, what are the parameters of the story, what size story, tentatively, are we talking about, when should the story be turned in? Note that these matters are listed here as questions, or as talking points for discussion, not as orders or commands. Yes, the reporter is the legman on the story, but you shouldn't treat him or her as an underling or a servant to carry out your wishes for the simple fact that people don't like to be treated like that. The reporter is a member of your team, and while you may be the captain, what you're engaged in is a team effort.

I can't stress this team attitude enough because, as you will quickly learn, you are going to have to deal with your reporters' peculiar personalities, and everyone's personality is peculiar, present company excluded. Some reporters are self-starters and go-getters, and some need lots of guidance; some are energetic and enthusiastic, and some are lazy and lethargic; some are insecure, and some are confident, and some are overconfident; some are outgoing, and some are introverted; some are great at interviewing, and some mumble over the telephone; some are driven by the goal of informing the student body of the latest news, and some are just hanging around the office for the pizza. In short, there are all kinds out there, and sooner or later you're going to encounter them all.

The fact is, though, whether it's your most talented staff member or your most inexperienced cub, all of your reporters at one point or another are going to need your help—whether they know it or not. That's because nothing can or at least should be downloaded directly from a writer's head to print; every writer needs that extra set of eyes—in this case, yours—to determine if the job has been done as best it can. Here we're talking about the ABC's of journalism—accuracy, brevity, clarity—and a whole alphabet of other concerns that editors are required to monitor in their reporters' copy.

Now, the reporters who are aware of their flaws and weaknesses and know they need help and are grateful for it are in some ways your best reporters; they will be the easiest ones to work with. It's the prima donnas who think they know it all and can do it all by themselves and who resent being edited who will make your life miserable. In my professional experience as an editor and in my years as a student newspaper adviser, I think I can count the former on the fingers of one foot. Sadly, there are far too many of the latter. Or maybe I'm exaggerating, and you'll be lucky and not have any divas on your team. If so, good for you. In any case, be prepared to give reporters at the outset of each story the most comprehensive and comprehensible instructions; be ready and able to consult as the reporter does the fact gathering, making sure he or she is on the right track, covering all the right bases, asking the right questions, and collecting the right answers; then be prepared to go over the story with the writer, looking for holes, sniffing out unanswered questions the reader might have, and checking that the writing is clear and vivid.

Let's look at an example of how an editor might go over a brief news story with a reporter. So this eager young member of your staff comes up to you and says excitedly that she's heard about a mugging on campus the previous night and she's written up the story for you. Here's what she offers:

> A female freshman had her purse snatched last night as she walked from the library to her dorm, campus police confirmed this morning.
>
> The victim told police the robbery occurred in an instant after a male dressed in running clothes came up from behind her, ripped the purse from her shoulder and raced off in the direction of College Avenue.
>
> The student used an emergency phone to report the incident, and a police cruiser was immediately dispatched to the area.
>
> No suspects have yet been apprehended, police said, but the investigation continues. Police cautioned students about walking on the campus alone at night, and asked that anyone with information about the attack should call campus security at ext. 1234.

The young reporter can't conceal the fact that she's proud of getting a story that is already a much-talked-about incident on campus. She also points out that she crafted it with a proper lead (the five W's and the H) and in accordance with the AP stylebook and that her paragraphs are crisp and short and that she checked and rechecked her spelling and grammar and sentence structure.

Indeed, the first thing an editor should do is praise the young reporter both for her enterprise and for her clean writing. You should also applaud her use of lively language, like "ripped" and "raced off." Then, ever so gently, the editor should point out how the student failed to get the story.

First, you ask, who was this mugging victim? Well, the reporter says, the campus police wouldn't release her name. But that's silly, you say; that's the cops, they always like to hold information close to their chests, and anyway the student didn't do anything wrong, she's a victim, and it's not as if she'd been sexually attacked. You should have wheedled the name out of the cops. I know, the reporter sighs, but the cops for some reason would say only that she was a freshman, which is kind of dumb, really, since everybody in the dorms knows who it was anyway.

Oh, you say, that's interesting. So did you talk to the victim herself? Well, no, the reporter says, but I got the official version of the incident from the cops—isn't that good enough? It's the official version, you agree, but the cops weren't there at the robbery and the victim was. Wouldn't it have been a good idea to speak to her? By doing so you might have gotten a few more facts—was she knocked over by the thief, or at least knocked aside? And you might have scored a quote on how she felt about this mugging, which would add an emotional element to a story that at present doesn't have one.

The absence of the victim's name, you might point out next, is only one example of a lack of specifics in the story. There are simply too many things the reporter apparently didn't ask about. For example, the story says the theft occurred last night—but in fact how late was it? Was it 9 p.m. or 2 a.m.? That could be significant, and at the very least fixing the hour helps the reader get a fix on the story. The article also says the incident occurred as the victim was walking from the library to her residence hall—but that's a distance of nearly a mile. Where exactly did this happen? And is the lighting adequate in that area? Was anyone else around at the time? And gosh, you say her purse was stolen, but we don't have a clue as to what was in the purse. Credit cards, cash, books, a cell phone, an iPod? Readers naturally wonder about such things, and the contents of the purse clarify the seriousness of the loss.

And that's just the first paragraph. Other questions arise. The cops say a cruiser was dispatched "immediately"—but is that a fact or is that just the cops making themselves sound efficient? After all, they may not be the most objective judges in this regard. It would be good to get from the victim an idea of how long it actually took the cops to arrive on the scene. Note, too, when the cops say the investigation continues, well, would you expect them to say anything to the contrary? Sounds like they're just blowing smoke because they have no leads in the case. Did the reporter in fact ask if they had any leads? Were there any witnesses? Did the reporter ask if such incidents have been reported before? How common is this sort of crime on campus? Any trends—up or down—in regard to such crimes? You might not get answers to all these questions, the editor tells the reporter, but they should be asked, and if the cops decline to answer, you report that. Note, moreover, that the cops warn students about walking alone at night on campus. That might be good advice—but the reporter might have followed up on that. Why do cops advise this? Is the campus unsafe at night? Alternately, are the cops in this instance blaming the victim for the crime?

I could go on in this vein—and while I wouldn't want to see this story blown up to sensational dimensions, it should be clear that the story as it stands is underreported. This is where the editor's guidance is required. But bear in mind what's also important here: The editor must never come down on the reporter like a ton of bricks. The editor must consider the reporter's sensitivities. Praise where praise is due ... and then work with the reporter on improving the story. Trust me, compliment reporters for something done well and they'll remember it and you forever; stomp them and they'll eventually crawl off to find some other campus activity that doesn't involve journalism.

One of the least productive things editors might do, tempting as it might be, is to gather more information and rewrite stories themselves. This is not a proper use of an editor's time, and it doesn't much help the reporters. The planning, strategizing, editing, and so on should be a team effort. Still, sometimes a story has to be updated, shortened, or otherwise altered at the last minute—even when the reporter isn't available for consultation and the minutes until deadline are ticking away. In such instances editors exercise their judgment in editing and they are within their rights to do so; they are, after all, the team captains.

Be aware, however, that despite their reputation for callousness journalists in fact are easily injured creatures with very tender egos. So you have to be prepared to hold hands and to stroke egos throughout the reporting and editing process—and quite possibly to soothe savage beasts and to kiss boo-boos afterwards. It's all pretty icky, but as you should have figured out by now, an editor serves somewhat like Mama or Papa (or both) to these unruly children called reporters.

Reporters, meanwhile, shouldn't be springing stories on editors like so many jacks-in-their-boxes; perhaps the first mistake our young reporter made on the mugging story was failing to contact her editor before embarking on the reporting.

Finally, in regard to reporters, editors have yet another duty: talent spotting and nurturing, with the objective of training new editors. You should always be aware of time's winged chariot (huh?). By that I mean semesters tend to fly by, and before you know it you're graduating on to another position on the paper—or maybe (at long last) graduating from college. It's one of your responsibilities as an editor to see that good candidates, most likely from your pool of reporters, are in line to replace you when you depart from your desk. You may not always succeed in finding such candidates, but for the sake of the newspaper as an institution, you should always try to find new replacement blood, so that your departure won't leave a gaping staffing hole.

A MATTER OF BOOKKEEPING

But hold on, you're not done yet. Another major part of the editor's job is keeping track of everything. This means an editor must maintain date books, flow charts, news budgets, assignment sheets, phone listings for reporters and contacts, and so on. However you choose to designate or design these battle plans, your main function here is to record for yourself such matters as who is assigned to what, when their copy is due, and whether or not photos need to be assigned for their stories. It's also a good idea to create and regularly update a master list of all staffers and regular source contacts, with phone numbers and e-mails; make sure every staffer has access to that list, and maybe post a large version of it on the office wall. This can save a lot of time when you're trying to get hold of someone just before deadline.

Managing such information reflects what I was saying in the first chapter about the importance of getting things down on paper. Don't try to keep all these things in your head, because heads are notoriously unreliable archives and customarily have such irregular business hours. Keep your operating notes instead in whatever fashion suits you, in a notebook or in your computer, and constantly update them; thus when the editor in chief asks the features editor what's cooking for next week, Ms. Features can point to a budget or chart, on paper or on screen, and handily reply. Likewise these charts will prompt you to remind reporters of their deadlines and record when your next team meeting is being held and when the university senate is scheduled next to meet. This last is the kind of thing you should definitely have in your date book: No editor should suddenly discover that Valentine's Day is next week or that the rugby playoffs are being held this Saturday. If such events take you by surprise, you're not doing your job as a manager.

So, in addition to possessing the requisite language skills and managerial abilities, being a good editor requires a lot of qualities, among them intelligence, alertness, patience, and such people skills as a talent for educating, being a good listener, having good judgment, and being a good psychologist. In other words, editors need all sorts of things normally not written into job descriptions.

EDITORS ON PAPER: JOB DESCRIPTIONS

Somebody mention job descriptions? No, it is not mandatory to write out a list of duties for each editor, but it certainly can be useful. At the very least, when an editorial board is being appointed or elected, persons being considered for positions deserve to know as accurately as possible what is expected of them. Having written job descriptions also helps everyone to appreciate and to focus on a news organization's overall mission. Job descriptions, moreover, can help avoid conflicts later, such as when the sports editor claims he never knew he had to write captions for photos. Or when the features editor insists she doesn't do windows, because that's not in her contract. The following are some sample descriptions, based on ones I drew up for the student newspaper I advise, for common positions on student publications; not all may apply to your newspaper, but in some fashion most of these will.

Editor in Chief

The editor in chief has overall responsibility for the editing, management, and production of the newspaper. Oversees all departments of the newspaper and consults with and mentors all department heads. Helps to develop story ideas for the newspaper. Encourages professionalism; maintenance of high journalistic standards of balance, fairness, accuracy, and taste; and adherence to the objectives of the newspaper's constitution. Is expected to read everything that is prepared for the newspaper before it is published, giving special attention to fairness, accuracy, balance, taste, and social awareness. Is responsible for establishing and maintaining guidelines for editorial and advertising policies. Monitors the entire newspaper for libel and defamation, racism, sexism, and offenses against community standards of taste and fairness. Works with the business manager and the advertising manager to determine the annual budget and to monitor the financial concerns of the newspaper. Represents the newspaper in regard to the student government, the university administration, campus organizations, the faculty, and the university community at large. Maintains liaison with counterparts at other student media on campus and on other campuses. Conducts regular staff meetings and convenes special meetings concerning policies and elections.

Managing Editor

The managing editor serves as the assistant editor in chief and is the liaison officer between the chief and the staff. Is largely concerned with helping to execute the instructions of the editor in chief to the rest of the staff. Is responsible for communicating the concerns, plans, problems, and the like from the staff to the editor in chief. Serves as an assistant to all and is therefore required to have a high degree of knowledge and expertise in all aspects of producing the newspaper. Should be equipped to fill in for any other editor in the event of that editor's absence. Helps to recruit and assign reporters for all departments and helps to develop story ideas for all departments. Is expected to participate in all staff meetings.

News Editor

As head of the newspaper's news division, the news editor is in charge of recruiting and training the news reporters and determining their writing assignments and beats. Prepares the news budget for each issue, assigns the stories to be written, edits the news stories, and helps lay out the news pages. Is expected to consult with the editor in chief in all of these matters and to keep the editor in chief apprised of all developments in the news editor's division; in this regard, it is incumbent on the news editor to remain at all times on top of the news by monitoring developments on campus and by keeping pace with the relevant news media, wire services, Internet news sites, and the like. Also works closely with the photo editor to determine photo assignments for news-related stories. Strives to achieve fair, accurate, balanced, objective, and wide-ranging coverage of news events of interest to the university community. Is expected to participate in all staff meetings. The position of news editor is often shared by co-editors.

Copy Editor

Unless individual sections of the newspaper have their own copy editors, the copy editor is charged with editing all copy and with consulting with other editors on text, headlines, and picture captions. Is the newspaper's arbiter on style, grammar, punctuation, and the like. Reads content with an eye for thoroughness, completeness, fairness, balance, and accuracy. Is alert to violations of media law, taste, and ethics. Often has an assistant; if there is more than one assistant, the copy editor is known as chief of the copy desk. Is expected to participate in all staff meetings.

Features Editor

The features editor is in charge of all editorial matter that does not fall naturally into another editorial section, such as sports, arts, Op-Ed, and so forth. Feature material may range from "soft" news stories, sidelights, and personality profiles to cartoons, advice columns, and crossword puzzles. The features editor is in charge of recruiting and training the features reporters and determining their writing assignments and beats. Works closely with photo and design editors to graphically enhance the features pages. Prepares the features budget for each issue, assigns the stories to be written, edits the stories, and helps lay out the features pages. Is expected to consult with the editor in chief on all of these matters. Is expected to participate in all staff meetings.

Sports Editor

The sports editor is in charge of recruiting and training the sports reporters and determining their writing assignments and beats. Prepares the sports budget for each issue, assigns the stories to be written, edits the stories, and helps lay out the sports pages. Is expected to consult with the editor in chief on all of these matters and to keep the editor in chief apprised of all developments in the sports editor's division; in this regard, it is incumbent on the sports editor to remain at all times on top of the sports news by monitoring developments on campus and by keeping pace with the relevant news media, wire services, Internet news sites, and the like. Also works closely with the photo editor to determine photo assignments for sports-related stories. Maintains liaison with the university's athletic department and sports information office. Strives to achieve accurate, colorful, and wide-ranging coverage of sports events of interest to the university community. Is expected to participate in all staff meetings.

Photo Editor

The photo editor heads the newspaper's photographic division. Is in charge of recruiting and training staff photographers and determining their picture assignments. Is responsible for realizing the photographic needs of the various editorial divisions, and to this end consults with the various editors on their picture requirements. Is responsible for the acquisition, maintenance, and security of all of the newspaper's cameras, photographic materials, and other equipment. Is responsible for monitoring the newspaper's photo budget. Keeps the editor in chief apprised of photo assignments and pertinent equipment and budgetary matters. Is expected to participate in all staff meetings.

Arts and Entertainment Editor

The arts and entertainment (A&E) editor is responsible for the newspaper's arts, culture, and entertainment features. Is in charge of recruiting and training the section's reporters and reviewers and determines their writing assignments and beats. Prepares the A&E budget for each issue, assigns the stories to be written, edits the stories, and helps lay out the A&E pages. Is expected to consult with the editor in chief in all of these matters and to keep the editor in chief apprised of all developments in the A&E editor's pages; in this regard, it is incumbent on the A&E editor to remain at all times on top of cultural news by monitoring developments on campus and by keeping pace with the relevant news media, wire services, Internet news sites, and the like. Also works closely with the photo editor to determine photo assignments for the A&E pages. Maintains liaison with the university's offices that sponsor cultural programs. Strives to provide informative and interesting coverage of campus and off-campus arts, culture and entertainment news, reviews, previews, and other features of interest to the university community. Is expected to participate in all staff meetings.

Literary Editor

The literary editor selects and edits the creative writing contributions to the newspaper with the aim of providing the readers stimulating poetry, short stories, and essays. Solicits and encourages contributions primarily from the student body. Prepares the section's budget for each issue, edits the material, and helps lay out the literary pages. Is expected to consult with the editor in chief on all of these matters and to keep the editor in chief apprised of all developments in the literary editor's pages. Is expected to participate in all staff meetings.

Editorial Page Editor

The editorial page editor is in charge of the newspaper's opinion and editorial (Op-Ed) pages. Since these pages are partly the forum for non-newspaper staff members, the editorial page editor suggests, solicits, and encourages contributions from readers. In consultation with the editor in chief, the editorial page editor then selects editorials, opinion pieces, editorial cartoons, and letters to the editor for publication. Prepares the Op-Ed budget for each issue, edits the material, and helps lay out the Op-Ed pages. Strives to provide a section that features a diversity of views from all parts of the university community. While cognizant of the right of free expression for contributors, the editorial page editor remains vigilant about such matters as fairness, accuracy, and balance. Remains equally alert to writing that is inflammatory, divisive, prejudicial, offensive, or ill informed. Works on the principle that while everyone has an equal right to express views, not all views are equally valid, and no newspaper is under any obligation to facilitate anyone's expression of opinion. It is incumbent on the editorial page editor to remain at all times on top of current issues by monitoring developments on campus and by keeping pace with the relevant news media, wire services, Internet news sites, and the like. Is expected to participate in all staff meetings.

Business Manager

The business manager is the newspaper's chief financial officer. As such, the business manager keeps the newspaper's financial books and records, administers purchase orders, oversees such operational activities as expenditures and payment of bills, and is largely responsible for the preparation of the newspaper's annual budget. Works closely with the advertising manager and with appropriate financial offices of the university. Is also required to keep the editor in chief and the adviser of the newspaper informed of all pertinent matters regarding the newspaper's budgets and finances. Is expected to participate in all staff meetings.

Advertising Manager

The advertising manager sells advertising space in the newspaper and/or the Web site or coordinates the advertising sales staff. Processes billings with the business manager and keeps the advertising revenue accounts. Is responsible for monitoring advertising copy for adherence to principles and policies established by the newspaper, by the university, and by local or state regulations. Maintains vigilance to avoid publication of misleading or otherwise undesirable advertising. Consults with the editor in chief, the business manager, and the newspaper adviser on matters of questionable advertising. In coordination with the design editor, the advertising manager helps design and lay out the advertisements. Is expected to participate in all staff meetings.

Design Editor

The design editor, alternately known as the production editor, layout editor, or art director, coordinates all of the design and graphic elements of the newspaper. Working in consultation with all of the other editors, the design editor creates, selects, and executes those elements of design required by the various departments of the newspaper; these elements include typography and layout, as well as photographs, drawings, graphs, and other display devices. The design editor's main objective is to develop a graphic harmony for the overall newspaper while creating specific and defining graphic characteristics for the various editorial sections. Along with working with the editor in chief toward that objective, the design editor also assists the advertising manager in the creation of display ads. Advises the editorial and advertising department on the appropriate computer software applications required for the newspaper's publishing and graphic needs. Is expected to participate in all staff meetings.

Online Editor

The online editor, or Web master, is charged with overseeing the electronic version of the newspaper. In consultation with the other editors, the online editor selects and edits text and graphic material for the online edition and sees to it that the online edition is properly updated. Is also responsible for overseeing such Web-only features as surveys, polls, links, blogs, and video and audio elements. Is expected to participate in all staff meetings.

Subsequent chapters will deal in detail with the conventions and requirements, operating procedures, and whatnot regarding these various editors, their sections, and their staffs. But for now—say, wait a minute! Enough about you, what about your adviser? Shouldn't there be a job description for him or her? I thought you'd never ask:

Student Newspaper Adviser

The main objective of the student newspaper adviser is to encourage professional journalistic standards in the writing, editing, and management of the student newspaper. Promotes dedication by the newspaper staff to publication of fair, accurate, well-prepared, and wide-ranging news and feature stories of interest to the university community. To this end the adviser encourages standards of responsible editorial judgment, taste, ethics, and sensitivity to the needs and interests of all constituents of the university community, as well as a commitment to the principles of freedom of expression and inquiry. As a nonvoting member of the editorial board, the adviser helps the staff formulate policy guidelines on such matters as editorial content, style and tone, news coverage, advertising, internal structure, and management. Beyond his or her role as mentor, the adviser is an advocate of the students' right to self-expression through publication of the student newspaper. As a representative of the university, the adviser strives to communicate and to promote university principles, policies, and ideals to the newspaper staff.

Specific duties of the newspaper adviser include: helping to recruit newspaper staff; attending editorial staff meetings; conducting training seminars for staff members; advising on editorial, design, technical, and business matters; suggesting story ideas; enhancing the staff's consciousness of racism, sexism, and other offenses to the community; advising on such legal matters as defamation and invasion of privacy; preparing detailed written evaluations of each issue of the newspaper; helping to prepare the newspaper's annual budget; monitoring and approving operational expenditures; facilitating communications between the newspaper and the university's administration, faculty, and campus organizations; encouraging staff involvement in regional and national student newspaper conclaves and competitions; maintaining liaison with counterparts at other universities and membership in relevant professional associations; and overseeing the nomination and election process or appointment process for editorial staff positions.

CHOOSING THE CHOOSERS
The job descriptions above are hardly comprehensive in their definitions or delineations and are of course open to your individual tunings and tweakings. Bear in mind, however, that it likely doesn't pay to make them overly specific; allowing for a little creative ambiguity in these descriptions is probably better than providing terms that you may later find too confining.

Having said all that, you should now have some guidelines on the qualities each editor should have, and these things should figure in your thinking when editors are appointed or elected. Former *Washington Post* executive editor Ben Bradlee once defined an editor as "one who chooses." Cool. But how do you choose your choosers? The editorial boards of student newspapers may be assembled in a variety of ways. Editors may be elected at the end of a semester by the outgoing editors or by the entire newspaper staff. (This is the model used in our sample constitution in the previous chapter, but it's worth noting that many student newspaper advisers believe students electing students is the least desirable method of choosing a newspaper staff—too much personality and politics involved.) Alternately, editors may be chosen by a panel of student journalists and faculty and administration, usually called the Student Media Advisory Board or something to that effect. Editors may simply be appointed by journalism professors; they may be selected by some other means. Whatever the mechanism that obtains on your campus, after students are nominated or self-nominated for editorial positions, their selection shouldn't be determined by their popularity or by their computer skills ... or by their grade average or by their major ... or their year or their height or their weight ... or their CD collections. Editing talents and people skills are what count.

SOME SUMMING UP
I'll conclude with a few observations that should apply to all editorships, no matter how you determine or define them:

First, it is traditional for editors to bitch and moan about their reporters. It's traditional, but it's also fruitless and ultimately unhelpful. You can blow off steam cursing this reporter because he doesn't know how to spell or that reporter because she overlooked pertinent information for her story or the other reporter because his sentences seem to come out of *Finnegans Wake*. But grumbling about such things is a waste of grumble. And it's not very professional. You have to work with what you have, and if the reporters don't quite gather the facts or write as they should, it's your job to help them shape up.

Look at it another way: If the reporters were all of Pulitzer Prize quality, then there wouldn't be much need for you, would there? And, at the risk of repeating myself, do you recall the little anecdote I recorded at the beginning of this book's Introduction? Oh, you always skip introductions, do you? Well, I'll just make the point once more: When I learn of a reporter doing something really foolish, or when I read a really lame story in a student newspaper, I don't fault the reporter—I fault the person in charge of the reporter. If reporters fumble their news gathering or writing, it's the editors' job to do the unfumbling.

So, yeah, riding herd on reporters is tough. Yet that's only part of this demanding job. Another large portion is this: As an editor, you have to know more about your journalistic turf than anyone else on your staff—and maybe more than the editor in chief as well. That means if you're a news editor you have to be a news junkie; a sports editor should be a walking encyclopedia of sports; an arts and entertainment editor better be on top of everything that's happening in movies, theater, music, dance, art, dining, architecture—the whole nine muses; an Op-Ed editor has to stay current on all current events, controversies, trends, and the like. You constantly have to be up on your beat, to feed the monkey.

Hey, nobody said it was going to be easy. Or if they did, they were fibbing through their fangs.

Oh, yeah, and one last point. The editor is supposed to be the person who knows that *i* comes before *e* except after *c* or when sounded like *a* as in *neighbor* and *weigh*.

Well, maybe that popular image of a harried editor alternately barking orders, tearing out what little remains of his hair, and swigging Pepto-Bismol isn't wrong. But there are rewards, too, not the least of which is seeing an important job well done and a public well served.

3

The Newspaper Office

Theoretically, a newspaper no longer needs a newspaper office. Using e-mail, BlackBerries, PageMaker, uploads, downloads, and whatever's coming next, newsies can sit in their own dorm rooms—or on the lawn in front of the dorm, or in their nearby Starbucks, or in their cars on their way to Starbucks—and produce a newspaper. (Yeah, it can be done that way, but how do you share out the pizza?)

In other words, just as the computer age has yet to fulfill the promise of the paperless office, so we have yet to see the officeless paper. News organizations still find it necessary, not to say convenient, to maintain headquarters, and no doubt yours does as well.

HERE'S LOOKING AT YOU

The first thing to consider is that you can never have enough room. I've visited student newspapers, such as Harvard's daily *Crimson*, that are housed in their own buildings, which is ultra cool. If, however, as is most common, your university makes space available to your newspaper in the student union or in part of some other general purpose campus building, that's cool too. Be grateful—but always keep pressing for more space or additional rooms, because the more options you have, the better you'll be able to function.

Not, however, that we want to separate or balkanize the various departments of the newspaper. Here are some operating principles to consider:

First, since the production of a newspaper is a team effort, journalists and their support staff should not work in isolation. You want people to be within hailing distance of each other—literally. This is why the most notable feature of the classic newsroom was the horseshoe- or U-shaped copy desk. Such a furniture arrangement dates back to the days before the introduction of computer workstations, and yet some computerized newspaper offices still find the horseshoe useful. The original idea was that rewrite people, page designers, headline writers, and copy editors or any combination thereof all seated themselves around this big, staple-shaped configuration of desks or tables. Sometimes reporters found it congenial to work right there as well, or at least very close by. On the one hand, people could see and interact with everyone else at fairly close range; on another, a senior editor could sit inside the U and deal with everyone encircling him or her.

Such configurations meant there was no privacy, but there wasn't supposed to be privacy. (Management always liked this sort of setup because staffers could not, without detection, sleep in front of their keyboards, or write poetry, work on their novels, polish their resumes, or compose article proposals for *The New Yorker*.) To the contrary, the arrangement allowed for the kind of interchange whereby one journalist would freely ask another for the capital of South Dakota, or for the phone number of that expert on volcanoes over at the natural history museum, or for, as the comic Steven Wright once pondered, "another word for *thesaurus*."

Most reporters, of course, as well as feature writers, columnists, section editors, and so on, had their own individual desks or cubby holes. But people still tended to cluster around or near that central horseshoe configuration. Sure, you can shoot e-mails from one side of the building to another, but many observers believe sending e-mail proves more disruptive to productivity—and is certainly less desirable—than maintaining the human contact. The only real downside to having everyone in the same living space is that it can get cacophonous when everyone is on the phone or shouting questions or requests at one another. But hey, what's a little cacophony among friends? A happily humming newsroom seems preferable to me than those high-tech cloisters where everyone is hunkered in silent meditation behind ranks of personal computer screens. To me those places always look more like insurance offices than newsrooms. Someone once said you can judge the vitality of a publication by the noise level in its newsroom. If it sounds noisy, it sounds good to me.

Anyway, ask yourself how efficiently you're using your main office space and its furnishings. If you have only one room, try to determine if your staff is arrayed in that room in the best possible way. Are workstations arranged so as to encourage solitude, congeniality, or conflict? Is everything lined up in rows? Why do the desks face the directions they do? You don't want your people crammed on top of each other, but neither do you want them all working in splendid isolation. Newsroom writers and editors should have easy access to each other—so as to be able to help each other. Don't feel you have to stick with whatever setup you've inherited. Get creative.

GIMME SPACE

Even better if you have additional rooms, because for all the joys of clamorous close living, it's good if you can have at least one quiet place as well. Sometimes the editor in chief will have his or her own office. That's not simply an imperial perk. A private space, even if not much more than a glorified cupboard, is eminently practical. First of all, the editor in chief is responsible for everything that appears in the paper and therefore should read everything before it goes to press; to do so, the editor in chief certainly benefits from a quiet place in which to carry out this task. Secondly, the editor in chief frequently needs to speak to a staffer in private—say, to read the riot act. Third, a separate office is the best place to deal with those irate outsiders—the angry reader, the outraged faculty member, the upset advertiser—who are forever invading the newspaper office. Dealing with individual complaints or other problems is normally not the entire staff's business; both the editor and the visitor will appreciate a private place in which to work out their dispute. Fourth, depending on the size of your available rooms, the editor in chief's office might be better than the newsroom for your regular editorial meetings. Finally, a separate office for the editor in chief needn't always be considered that person's sovereign space. For example, let's say an interview is to be conducted in the newspaper office. Perhaps you have only two rooms, a general office and a chief's office. Rather than trying to interview someone in the noisy newsroom or stepping out into the hallway, it would be good if you had an established practice whereby the editor in chief will vacate his or her office in favor of some on-the-spot news gathering.

It's also desirable if the newspaper's business staff has its own office. This not only reinforces the notion of the firewall that is supposed to exist between the editorial and business sides of a news organization (something I will talk about later), but it simply keeps reporters and businesspeople from tripping over each other. The business of the business staff is business; the business of the editorial staff is editorial. Reporters shouldn't have to deal with telephone callers or people dropping in who have billing or advertising matters on their minds. The businesspeople likewise shouldn't have to struggle to carry out their duties while reporters are gathering facts over the phone and readers are bursting into the office to threaten libel suits.

To recapitulate: If you've been struggling along with a single office, I'd suggest (through negotiation with the authority that provides your space or by hosting regular rent parties or by whatever other means) trying to expand to two offices. If you have two offices, I'd urge pushing for three. Four is even better. That fourth office might well be a general purpose room. This could be a space for some occasional editorial business like meetings or interviewing, but it could also be the place that has the TV for monitoring news, the small fridge for yesterday's calzones, and your Mr. Coffee machine. (It's great if you can confine the staff snacking and caffeinating to a room away from your computers; that minimizes the mozzarella in the keyboards, but now I know I'm dreaming.) Your all-purpose rumpus room is also ideal for the racks for those essential publications like *Entertainment Weekly* to which the newspaper subscribes, file cabinets for clips and archives and back issues, maybe even a sofa for an emergency crash.

Now you may be currently carrying out all of your functions—editorial, business, TV monitoring, archiving, pizza microwaving, and sofa romances—in a single office, and maybe that's the way it's been since Abraham herded sheep and you may well think that expanding to a suite of offices is beyond the realm of possibility—yours or that of your university landlord. But here's another idea:

If you are in a building that houses other like-minded student organizations—say, a yearbook staff, radio station, literary magazine, or who knows what else—you might well look into consulting with those students to see if you have space problems in common—and to see if you might have common solutions. You may rarely have contact with these other students, especially those geeks over at the lit magazine, but it might well be a good idea to do some ex-

THE NEWSPAPER OFFICE   49

ploring. For example, if you have your editorial and business staffs in one office and the yearbook has the same, maybe a separate office housing all those businesspeople would be beneficial to both organizations. Alternately, if you're maintaining your own photo lab and the arts magazine is doing likewise, a marriage there might free up space for something else from which the two publications might benefit. It may be that such consultations will yield no new and improved office configurations. But you never know until you give all the floor plans a critical look and seek out some new and creative possibilities.

REFERENCES

So much for space considerations; now let's discuss what you're putting in that space. Beyond desks, chairs, computers, printers, and such necessities as a mini-fridge, Mr. Coffee, and Ms. Poland Spring Water, every newspaper office should have a number of things peculiar to such headquarters. The first is a reference library and archive.

Admittedly, those are fairly grandiose designations; we might be talking here about merely a shelf or a metal closet. But whatever the option, the principle holds. In terms of a reference library, you should maintain for everyone's use a number of basic tools, including at least one full-sized dictionary, grammar books (Fowler's *Modern English Usage*), stylebooks (*The Associated Press Stylebook, The New York Times Manual of Style and Usage*, or whatever else you might be using), atlases, almanacs, telephone directories for the campus (and for the local community and nearby communities), and sundries like city directories, ZIP code directories, and any other oddments you've managed to accumulate, such as biographical dictionaries, *Who's Who*, journalism texts, books on media law, and maybe some anthologies and classic works of journalism to inspire staffers in their slack moments. It also wouldn't hurt to have on hand such documents as the university budget, course bulletins, and program descriptions, and, hey, while we're at it, why not a directory of local and state agencies and a copy of the U.S. Constitution? Most of these things of course are accessible via the Internet, and that's cool, but it certainly can't hurt to have dead-tree versions in the office as well.

You needn't have an official newspaper reference librarian on your staff, but it might not be a bad idea to designate someone at least semi-officially to oversee the library—that is, to keep the shelves in order, to report missing items, to purge outdated material, and to suggest additions to or replacements for the collection. It also wouldn't be a bad idea to have a newspaper bookplate or rubber stamp or some other means of identifying the items as property of the newspaper that just might possibly deter someone from walking off with your *Rand McNally.*

NOW READ THIS
Following on the notion of a collection of books is a notion of a collection of periodicals. You should have in your operating budget money for subscriptions to a variety of publications. These include, first, news publications: your local daily newspaper and maybe the local rags of surrounding communities; any alternative weeklies that might be published in your area; national newspapers like *The New York Times, The Wall Street Journal, Time, Newsweek,* and *U.S. News and World Report.* Add political journals like *The Weekly Standard, The New Republic, The Nation,* and *The Economist.* Add professional publications like *Editor and Publisher, Columbia Journalism Review,* and *American Journalism Review.* You should also subscribe to or otherwise be on the mailing lists for campus newspapers from your area and beyond. Then, of course, there are your paramount essentials like *People, Entertainment Weekly, Rolling Stone, Spin, Us Weekly, Sports Illustrated,* and while we're at it why not *The Chronicle of Higher Education* and—Whoa, whoa, I can hear you yelling, do we really need all these magazines filling the office? And how could we possibly pay for them?

To your first impertinent question I'll say, yes, you need all of them and more, because you editors and reporters are obligated to be on top of everything. You're in the information business, and who, if not you people, should be expected to have all the information? Your professors? Forget that. Second, in terms of cost—hey, maintaining these subscriptions should be a sacred part of your standard operating expenses. Okay, for budgetary reasons you'll have to make choices. That's fine. But one choice you shouldn't make is cheating yourselves on good sources of news, cultural affairs, and other information. If nothing else, how else are you going to steal story ideas? More seriously, individual reporters and editors should be knowledgeable at least in regard to their beats, but you can't rely on everyone to be a dedicated autodidact. At the very least, the newspaper as an institution should make available the most essential publications for everyone's use. There is a direct relationship between how well informed your staff is and how good your newspaper is. So you can't afford to stint on sources of information. Bottom line—if you have to make choices in terms of your bottom line, pare back on the Perrier and pump up the subscriptions. (At the very very least, circulate among the staff a list of Web addresses of pertinent publications and make sure your editors regularly check them out.)

A TRIP TO THE MORGUE
The final category of paper with which to fill your office has to do with your archive, or, as it is also so charmingly referred to, the newspaper's morgue (so called because it contains dated, and therefore dead, news). Of course, you likely keep your archive electronically, and that's how it should be, but it's surprising how many times, either for editorial or advertising purposes, there's a need to access back issues of the actual newspaper. These copies should be kept in a secure place, and the use of this archive should be monitored in some fashion. There's little sense in having an archive full of gaps because people have thoughtlessly walked off with copies of the paper and never returned them. The same holds true with clips files, although I can't imagine anyone is still clipping and filing individual articles. Still, individual student journalists might be feeding their scrapbooks. Just make sure they don't feed their scrapbooks from the only copies of the back issues you have in the office.

SAFEGUARDING
Monitoring your archive brings up another area of concern—office security. Most mainstream newspaper offices these days maintain fairly strict security; visitors practically need CIA clearance before they can enter the building. Your office presumably doesn't need such controls. But for several reasons you should evaluate and possibly upgrade your security situation.

The first reason is to guard against theft. What, you may snort, do we have worth stealing? Answer: plenty. When was the last time you made an inventory of all the items in your office? If you haven't done so recently, it's a good idea to get on it—and to get your inventory down on paper. First of all, when you add up the value of all your possessions—computers, printers, scanners, software, cameras, voice recorders, CD burners, TV, fridge, popcorn maker, CD collection—you may very well be surprised at the total. If only for insurance purposes, your business manager should have a record of everything you collectively own, and in regard to electronic equipment, that record should include serial numbers, date of purchase, and other pertinent information. Keep that inventory updated on a regular basis. This inventory, along with your software and other valuables, should be kept under lock and key. Speaking of insurance, the university may cover you against theft but it just as well may not. You should know your insurance situation, and if it's not good, take care of it immediately.

At the very least, you should do your best to fasten down whatever is fasten-down-able. Call me a paranoid, or call me a grump (or call me a paranoid grump), but I've seen far too many objects disappear from newspaper offices. Well, no, I haven't actually seen them disappear. It's not like a magic act. It's more like yesterday you see it, tomorrow you don't. You get the idea—so get those computer locks and cable staples and bicycles chains for the cabinets and save yourself some grief.

You should also think about access to your office. Can just anyone enter the office at any time? That might be an overly friendly operational policy—especially after you discover your petty cash box is missing or that Mr. Coffee has suddenly and mysteriously grown legs (must be all that caffeine). But controlling access to the office is wise not just to prevent theft. All sorts of people might have all sorts of unwelcome reasons for visiting your premises. A fraternity might not like something the paper printed about it, and the frat decides to trash your office. The star of a campus musical production resents your paper's review and wants to trash the reviewer's face. The campus cops arrive, seeking your photos of a recent campus demonstration. Some student who tried out unsuccessfully as a reporter returns to wreak havoc on your computer system. Someone else drifts in just because she's curious about what's coming up in the next issue—or more specifically to make sure if her environmental club will be getting the coverage she thinks it deserves. Some nutter meanwhile keeps showing up demanding to be interviewed because he's intercepting secret phone messages between al-Qaeda cells via the fillings in his teeth. Reporters' significant others keep dropping by to chat, or worse. Athletes demand to discuss their careers with the sports editor. Some dean or vice president or representative from the university's public relations department keeps horning in to suggest what they think are wonderful story ideas. Pitchmen drop in trying to sell you crossword puzzles or astrology columns. Advertisers stop by with queries or suggestions. A freshman reporter brings in her parents to show off where she's building her journalistic career. The pizza guy barges in, mistaking your office for the radio station.

Some of these intrusions I've listed may sound unlikely or absurd or even paranoid, but believe me, I've experienced them all and more. I've seen newspaper offices, which can be boisterous enough places to begin with, that resemble a cross between a circus and a mosh pit. Especially if your space is limited—and if you're trying to get some work done against deadline—you really should have some means of controlling traffic into the office. And since you don't occupy the premises 24/7, some system of authorizing access—possibly via electronic keys—makes a lot of sense. (Otherwise, I might drop by unannounced and tell you about the messages I've been intercepting via my fillings.)

4
What's New(s)?

People shouldn't make assumptions (I assume you know that), and people (such as journalists) whose business is gathering and disseminating facts especially shouldn't make assumptions. But in the following discussion of news I'm going to assume the reader has already had some sort of involvement in journalism, either in a classroom or as a student reporter or editor. Therefore I'm assuming (oops) that I don't have to define *news* other than to say that in the most general sense news stories should be inspired by and built on information that is (a) new, (b) interesting, and (c) relevant to your audience. According to this overview, it's not exactly clear why we all want to publish (and read) stories about Madonna breaking a toenail, but hey, nobody said journalism in all its many glorious manifestations is all that easy to explain.

Anyway, rather than reiterate a whole bunch of stuff about news you most likely already know or can find in an introductory journalism textbook, I'm just going to share some observations about news for you to consider.

OF SPECIAL INTEREST

My first observation is that you should focus on what you are. So what are you? Well, you are not a general circulation newspaper but rather *a local, special-interest, community-oriented newspaper, and the more you focus on providing special-interest, community news and features relevant to your particular readership, the better you will be carrying out your mission.* (Whew. Those italics really take it out of a guy.)

Where was I? Oh, yes. Keeping in the forefront of your collective journalistic consciousness the notion that you are a community-oriented newspaper should help you fulfill your mission of serving your market to the best of your abilities. For one thing, it means that your newspaper should be full of stories and pictures not only *relevant* to your readers but *of and about* your readers. You're covering a community, a relatively small one at that. Your first priority is to cover that community—so cover it. The fact that people love to read stories and see pictures of themselves and their friends may sound . . . I don't know . . . small-minded, but it's still a fact, and your reporting on your readers' lives and concerns is going to be one of the primary things that impels them to grab up the paper each time a new edition appears.

Small-mindedness aside, the campus community is not a typical small town; in some ways it's something much bigger. Considering the range and variety of people and activities found at even a modest-sized college or university, there's quite a lot going on there—which means quite a lot of news. Once, after the editor of the campus newspaper I advise moaned that "nothing newsworthy" had been happening lately, I sat down and in short order composed a list of eighty-five potential "news-generating points" on campus. The list comprised everything from the academic departments to the libraries to club sports to the food services division to the grounds and maintenance department. I then leafed through the newspapers of the past two months and calculated that of my eighty-five "news generators," over sixty had had no mention in the news columns. That absence likely resulted from one of two possible causes: (1) either nothing newsworthy was happening in those parts of the campus, or (2) the news staff hadn't bothered to seek any news there.

When I confronted the editor with the results of my stunning statistical analysis, she toed the dust for a moment. She was silently doing some calculations of her own, or so I hoped. Let's see, we have about ten reliable reporters. If each one was assigned to contact around eight of those news-generating points every week . . . She mumbled something, then sped off to her office.

What else could I do in response but pat myself on the back and give myself a raise? I did both. Then I had a good lie-down.

Point is, any news organization worthy of the name should have on any given day more news than it can possibly print or broadcast. There's never not any news. Some days or weeks obviously are going to be newsier than others, but there's always news. And at a location like an institution of higher learning—which is full of intellectually active individuals, has a dynamic administration (even if the that dynamism is dedicated largely to staying financially secure), and houses everything from athletes to animal labs—don't tell me there isn't news. If you think your campus is moribund, better ask yourself just who's moribund around here. It's your campus; get out there and cover it.

WIDER HORIZONS

Right, cover your beat. But being a special interest, community-oriented news organ does not mean your publication must be as narrowly focused as a neighborhood throwaway or as parochial as a church bulletin. It simply means that even when you're covering wide-ranging news and issues, you must keep your eye on the ball—the ball here being your readership, its character, and its needs.

So what happens when big news occurs that isn't based in your community? A hurricane wreaks major damage on a city (say, oh, I don't know, maybe New Orleans). This is a national news story that will dominate the media for weeks. Fine. Yet the city is thousands of miles away from your campus. So how much coverage and of what kind can or should your newspaper give to this event? The answer, my friend, is blowing in your aforementioned self-definition and mission.

Well, ignore a big national news story like the hurricane that just wiped out a city on the Gulf Coast and you signal you're locked in your own little world and either don't care about or are oblivious to what's happening outside of your little patch of campus green. Okay, so cover it. But how do you report such a story? One way, which many college newspapers rely on, is by running copy supplied by the Associated Press or by some other wire service. This certainly isn't wrong, especially if, as at the University of Illinois or at Texas A&M, your campus newspaper also happens to a large extent to serve your surrounding community as well as your campus. But in most cases, whether you're in competition or not, your town's general circulation newspaper will be supplying its readers that same AP news coverage.

LOCAL EYES

So where does that leave you with your hurricane? That leaves you with your campus community's special interests in regard to this news event. This means beyond reporting the basic facts of the news event, which is obligatory but which your readers are going to get elsewhere, you should be seeking out the aspects of the hurricane that have a particular resonance with your audience. This is called localizing a story. But how can you possibly localize a hurricane in, say, New Orleans if your campus is in, say again, New Hampshire? Good question, and your job is to find a good answer. You might think this is a mission impossible—until you stop and think. For example, have you any students on campus who hail from Louisiana? How could you possibly find that out? Impossible? Or does your admissions office have records that might be useful in this regard? You don't know until you ask—and you should ask. Who knows, you just might track down students who can give you insights or human interest stories relevant to this hurricane that your paper and no other will publish.

We're not finished. What about the faculty and administration? It would not be surprising that a sizable campus might well have professors or administrators who come from, or perhaps at one time either studied at or worked in, our hurricane city. Track them down through faculty-staff directories, from bios on file at the public information office, via the library or other campus resources, and—viola! You may get nothing—or you may get a great interview. Point is, you'll never know unless you sic a few reporters on the job.

Still not done. Relief efforts for the hurricane victims are getting under way across the country; what about on your campus? Check with the student government organization and your campus volunteer, charity, and religious groups—and if nobody has yet set up a relief drive maybe the student newspaper can seize the initiative and do so itself.

Still not done. Those professors on campus are generally a useless lot, we all know that, but they are rumored to have some expertise in the areas in which they were hired to teach, and there just might be something useful to exploit there. Like the guy over in the Environmental Sciences Department who teaches meteorology and who might be able to give you an insightful interview on the nature of hurricanes. And oh, yeah, what about that woman who teaches oceanography and who might be able to explain the hazards of the gulf? And wait, didn't that guy from the Economics Department give a lecture just last month on the oil market? Might it not be a good idea to talk to him about this hurricane's impact on the gulf refineries? And hold on, didn't someone say your American Literature professor wrote her dissertation on

New Orleans novelist Anne Rice? And didn't that music professor spend a lot of his summers down in the Big Easy working with the Preservation Hall jazz ensemble? And didn't the assistant basketball coach once mention to the sports editor that he serves as a volunteer fireman and has done a lot of rescue work during floods? And on and on and on. There just may be some great sources on campus with great stories, and your job is to find them. Ask, inquire, probe, push, investigate.

What's the point here? I've suggested a number of avenues of inquiry, from the general (like searching for campus people who might have New Orleans connections and contacting campus organizations) to the specific (like seeking out professors who might have relevant information or insights to share). If your editorial team exhausts these possibilities and others, you might end up with no stories. Or nine stories. *But even if you find only one, that's one original campus-based story related to a major news event that's an exclusive for your publication* (puff puff). And because you found a local angle to this national story, your readers are going to read it.

IRAQ, YOU RAQ, WE ALL RAQ

Let's take a fresh example. At some point during the first decade of the Iraq War it occurred to me I hadn't seen any references recently in my campus newspaper about that conflict. Hello, I said. What's that all about? So I buttonholed the editor and asked, "Hey, there's the biggest and longest-running national and international news story: why nothing in the campus paper?" To which the editor replied, "Well, gee, the war is covered all over the media. What could we possibly add?"

What indeed? So I asked a few questions. Um, how many of our student reservists have been called up to serve in Iraq? How many haven't been called up yet but still face the possibility of mobilization? Have any faculty or admin people served in or anticipate serving in Iraq? How many students have dropped out of school to enlist? Do these folks include both men and women? Do students have parents, brothers, sisters, spouses, significant others (or what we quaintly used to call "sweethearts") serving in the desert? Are political groups on campus campaigning for or against the war? What do the ROTC people on campus have to say about Iraq? How do students feel about the possibility of the reinstitution of the military draft? Has the university made any plans to deal with special problems that the military service might cause students? What do Middle East experts on campus (teachers of history, political science, marketing, economics, arts, etc.) have to say about the war? What do Muslim students have to say? Have we in fact any Iraqi students among the student body?

In about twelve seconds I had fired off a baker's dozen of questions. Give me another twelve seconds and I'd fire off thirteen more. This is not because I'm particularly deft at inventing questions. No, I'm merely articulating the kinds of things the student body is likely thinking about. The kinds of things the student newspaper hasn't been reporting on.

The editor hung her head in shame. Oh, good, how gratifying. "Gosh," she said, "and just the other night we were complaining we didn't have much of anything to write about. . . . Gee, professor, you're just wonderful. . . ."

Okay, you caught me. I'm writing the dialogue here and I may not be reporting with strictest accuracy. (You sort of suspected that when I quoted the editor saying "gosh" and "gee.") But I trust you get the point. There are a dozen and more routes to a fresh, original, exclusive take on an ostensibly off-campus or national story. Of those twelve ways maybe ten won't pan out. But whatever does pan out helps fulfill your mission to service your target audience.

There's another value inherent in the kinds of localized stories I've been describing. These stories are essentially news features. Such articles have news value, but they are not breaking news stories. They are secondary reportage, offering sidelights and human interest related to current news. As such, these stories are especially suitable for newspapers that do not publish daily but come out on, say, a weekly or twice-weekly basis. As you no doubt know, when you don't print every day it's darn difficult to stay on top of the news and produce what looks like a fresh front page. If that hurricane has the bad grace to occur on a Thursday, which happens to be the very day you publish your weekly edition, you won't be able to print a story about it until the following Thursday. Your objective, therefore, should not be to inform readers about a week-old hurricane. No, but a fresh, original, localized story related to the event might well make a fine lead to your paper.

I cannot stress enough the importance and the value of localizing. Journalists develop and hone the instinct to localize—and not just in regard to national breaking news. Another popular area of fruitful mining is in trend stories. This is why, doggone it, you must scour *The New York Times, The Wall Street Journal, USA Today,* and all the other major news sources and their Web sites—every day. So, for example, when the *Times* runs an interesting story on the trend of students who for a variety of reasons are dropping out of four-year institutions of higher learning and enrolling in two-year community colleges, a student journalist shouldn't just lean back and say, "Gee, wasn't that an unusual story in the *Times*?" No, what student reporters or editors should think is, "Gee, I wonder if anything like that has been happening on our campus? I think I'll check it out."

Trends range from the frivolous (young people branding their lovers' initials on their tongues) to the serious (meth mouth). The neat thing about trends is (a) we always have them, (b) they're newsworthy, (c) they're interesting, and (d) there's usually some way or other to localize them (interviews, polls, local expert opinion).

The result of all this is this: If you read globally but think locally, there are plenty of ways to fill your newspaper with solid stories that will interest your readers.

INFORMATION PLEASE

I've already alluded to the notion that if you're in the newspaper business you're in the information business, but I want to return to this because from my observations too many student newspapers are too heavy on non-news. This non-news chiefly takes the form of feature story material like CD reviews, astrology charts, cartoons, sex-advice columns, football pools—all that entertaining stuff that's so much fun to write, and to read. In no sense do I minimize the significance of features (which will be discussed in subsequent chapters). Indeed, there's a persuasive argument that readers turn to newspapers primarily for the non-news material and not for the news itself (which, after all, they can monitor 24/7 on their TVs, in their computers, in their cars, with their iPods, with their cell phones, in their showers, etc.). But let's leave that argument aside for the moment. My point is if you call yourself a newspaper, and not an entertainment weekly, then you are obligated to devote some proportion of your newspaper to news.

How sizable should that proportion be? I wish you wouldn't ask such tough questions. There is no formula. The space devoted to news in print journalism ranges from very heavy, as in such heavy-hitters as *The New York Times* and *The Wall Street Journal*, to moderate, as in *USA Today*, to virtually nil, as in, say, Britain's wildly popular but nearly newsless daily tabloids.

None of that, however, helps you very much in determining how much of your newspaper should be devoted to news. Let me just say that, yes, readers do *want* to be entertained; this is why so much of the so-called news media in recent years has been bleeding over more and more into the fields of entertainment. Yet, in addition to being entertained, readers also want and *need* to be informed. (They may need this whether they know it or not.) I'll come back to the matter of wants and needs in a moment, but first consider that if, as I have observed above, news is available outside of your newspaper all over and all the time, so too is entertainment. If you take it for granted your publication cannot out-news *The New York Times* or *USA Today*, well, that's reasonable. But that doesn't mean you should throw up your hands in terms of news and then in response try to replicate *Rolling Stone* or *Entertainment Weekly*, because that will be equally fruitless.

In other words (what was wrong with the first words?) I'm suggesting that you focus on your self-definition and your mission. For one thing, you are not, or you should not be, primarily a publication devoted to entertainment. Think of it this way: Britain's top band-of-the-moment brings out a new CD. That's exciting, and it's news, and you want to share your opinion on this new offering with your readers, so a reviewer writes a piece on the new disk. Cool. I'm not saying you shouldn't do this. Rather, I'm asking, what are you giving the readers that they aren't already getting elsewhere and in great abundance? Equally significant, even if your readers want their campus newspaper's take on that new CD, how important is meeting that desire in respect to how much space you have in each edition of your paper—and in respect to your overall mission?

Cover the new release of that band-of-the-month? Quite possibly. But prioritize. A much more relevant, important, and interesting story for your readers is the one about the band from your campus that has just produced a demo or got a recording contract. In terms of international impact this may be less newsworthy than the Brit band—and in fact the local band in your opinion may not sound terribly special. The point, however, is that this news is happening on *your* campus and therefore it's *your* news. Yours, therefore, should be the news outlet that's covering this band.

SNICKER SNICKER

Localizing the nonlocal, however, is only one way to get the news your readers want and need.

Wants and needs? Say, didn't I promise some pages back to discuss this? Never let it be said I don't keep my promises:

Some news executives have taken the view, largely inspired by the dire economic straits of many newspapers, that print journalism should be dedicated to giving readers solely what they want. One publisher (namely William Dean Singleton, CEO of the MediaNews Group) has even gone so far as to compare a newspaper to a candy bar, theorizing that if it tastes yummy it will sell.

Well, Mr. Singleton isn't exactly an idiot, since he runs over a hundred newspapers. Yet such a marketing strategy makes sense only until you ask yourself what happens if your diet consists of nothing but candy bars. You're going to die, that's what's going to happen. Your teeth will decompose, your skin will break out, you'll be a sugar addict, you'll have all fats and carbs and no vitamins or minerals and hang on while I finish this Snickers bar. Okay, you get the point: Man cannot live simply by consuming what he wants. Man lives by absorbing what he needs.

Ergo, if your newspaper is providing only the confection, you will contribute to your readers' brain rot, and you don't want to do that. Which means that above and beyond attracting readers with some tasty ingredients, your newspaper should also be supplying the nutriments your readers need.

In terms of your campus community, what do your readers need? Well, at the risk of suddenly sounding somewhat lofty, I suggest that they need what all people need: They need to know how the world works, and they need that so as to better make their way in the world.

Catering to this need should be a direct result of one of the chief impulses of a journalist. Anyone who enters the business of providing information to others should have a curiosity and an appetite for acquiring information. Newsies are people driven by a desire to understand the world around them. This means that as student journalists walk about campus, they're asking themselves: Why do we have a parking problem on campus? Gee, the grounds crew is putting in tons of new shrubs and trees; I wonder who decides on such things and how much that costs and does that come from our tuition money? Oops, I almost walked into one of those emergency telephones. Say, do those phones really work—and what's the response time of the campus cops to a call? And oh, look at that—someone has chalked messages on the pathway. I've heard some campuses have banned such graffiti; is anything allowed here, or does the administration have guidelines on sidewalk messages? And check that out, two kids in wheelchairs almost collided. Say, doesn't it seem that we have more wheelchair-bound students than ever before? And I wonder if every campus building is wheelchair accessible? Oh, and look, that dork just threw a paper bag into a glass recycling bin. I wonder how problematic such contamination is, and for that matter how much the university spends on collecting recyclables—and where does all that stuff go?

What happened here? We walked with an alert student journalist for a few minutes across campus between classes and came across a half-dozen or more ideas for articles—stories that relate to things the readers might very well be wondering about and that they might benefit from reading about in their campus newspaper. In other words, you'd be doing nothing less than helping your fellow students comprehend their university environment better. Now ain't that a grand and noble achievement?

Yes, and achieving this isn't rocket science (it's something more complicated and subtle than rocket science). But by developing the right sensibilities and habits, you can enrich the news content of your paper immeasurably.

BOASTING, BOOSTING, BUSTING

Having discussed both a student newspaper's noble and ignoble ways of filling its columns, I'd like to turn to another aspect of campus news coverage, and that is: To what degree if any is the student-run newspaper representative of the university? Is it the newspaper's role to be part of the institution's overall educational mission? Should the student newspaper serve as a booster or cheerleader for the institution?

Truth is, I'm not sure how to answer these questions. It may well be that the student newspaper performs some of these functions whether it wants to or not. That is to say, the college might be so proud of the newspaper that it readily distributes sample issues to alumni and includes the newspaper in its recruitment materials. The administration also may well consider the newspaper, whether the editors see it this way or not, as a fine component of its educational mission. Or not. Who knows? But this subject is worth thinking about, especially in regard to certain sensitive stories the newspaper may find itself dealing with.

For example, what happens when the news staff finds itself facing a story that is potentially embarrassing to the college? On the one hand, you judge it as you would any story: Does it have news value? Is it interesting? Is it relevant to your readers? However, it may meet all those criteria and yet not be something the readers need to know. Example: You have it on good authority that the college's vice president for finances is being treated in a clinic for alcoholism, that he's also in a 12-step program run by Gamblers Anonymous, and that, oh, I don't know, the Internal Revenue Service is scrutinizing his tax returns. Now all this, to go back to our criteria, is certainly newsy and interesting, and you can argue that since the guy handles university finances the story is relevant to your readers. But since there's no evidence that the man has mishandled finances or otherwise not performed his job well, is this story necessary? In other words, even though you may be able to justify running such a sensational story, you also recognize that doing so is not going to make the individual, not to mention the college, look very good.

Deciding whether or not to run such a story is a judgment call, and different judges will make different calls. At some point or other, however, every student newspaper will be faced with a story that does not reflect well—or indeed may reflect very badly—on the college. The question is, how protective should you be of your institution's good name?

The journalist's normal impulse is to seek the green light, not the red light. The traditional view is that you're in the news business, not the suppression-of-news business. Fine, but every news organization finds reasons now and again—good reasons or perhaps not such good reasons—to withhold a story. A local newspaper, for instance, may withhold a story about a local teen getting busted for drugs (possible valid reason: save the kid and his family some embarrassment; possible less justifiable reason: the druggie's dad owns the largest auto agency in town and is the newspaper's biggest regular advertiser). In any event, you make your judgment calls. Moreover, bear in mind that you are certainly not obligated to print everything that comes across your desk, and if in your considered opinion a story should be withheld, so be it.

The question remains, however: In terms of the college as an institution, whose side, if any, are you on? Again, there's no easy answer. Consider it from another viewpoint. Your staff is busy every week running around trying to dig up news from every corner of the campus. In doing so you're helping to publicize this professor's research project, that administrator's development plans, this team's strategies for a winning season, that club's fundraiser. How much of this "publicizing" serves as public relations? Answer: Whether you intend it as such, a goodly amount. So what happens here—have you become a branch of the institution's public relations office?

Well, yes and no and maybe. But if you wish to avoid being perceived as such, you must maintain a steady fix on your mission and goals—and even on your language. It's one thing, for example, to announce an upcoming dance party; it's quite another to promote it ("Come on, shake your booty, get your tickets now!").

Drawing the line between informing and promoting, however, is not always as simple as the simple example I just gave. Even the mainstream media lose their grip to some degree on their mission. Indeed, some news organizations promote their hometowns with regularity. This is probably most evident the smaller the town, where the local press and electronic media tend to openly celebrate their localities ("a great place to live and do business!") and its citizens. This makes the audience (and advertisers) happy. Even *The New York Times* is not above some boosterism, regularly publishing articles that make fashion and Broadway and dining out in Manhattan sound so very exciting and glamorous. (Again, this pleases both readers and advertisers.) On a much lager scale, news organizations traditionally find it difficult to cover a war in which their nation is engaged without being, well, pro–home team.

And, sure, your student newspaper most likely supports the varsity footballers, boosts campus organizations (otherwise why all those editorials thundering against student apathy?), and in general probably sends a message, either by design or not, that your campus is pretty cool and you all made a good choice of where to burn your parents' money.

That's fine. But be careful not to lose sight of your mission—which is to be an information organ, and not a public relations tool. Of course, maintaining a studied objectivity won't always win you friends—and it might earn you some hostility. Some segments of the campus—the Greeks, the football team, clubs, or other organizations—may interpret your objectivity as unfair, unjust, or uncaring. That can be very hard for journalists to deal with. But you must remain faithful to your mission. Show undue favor toward any individual or group and you've not only tipped your hand, you've tipped your canoe.

WOOF WOOF

Here's another way to think about your role vis-à-vis the rest of the campus: What breed of dog are you? We like to think of newspapers in their noblest sense as watchdogs, doing guard duty for the public. Thus you don't want to be the student government's lapdog or the administration's cute little puppy. But neither do you want to be a Rottweiler or a pit bull. Be a friendly dog, sure, but a watchful one. Wag your tail? I don't think so. Pee on someone's tree now and again? I think that's only to be expected.

THE NEWSPAPER AND THE PUBLIC RELATIONS OFFICE

Ah, yes, the Media Relations Department, the Division of Public Information—whatever they euphemistically call it on your campus, it's public relations. You probably have some regular contact with this office—or it contacts you. Quite likely you've come to rely on the public relations office for a variety of things—news releases, faculty biographies, photos, statistics. Fine. I hope you have good relations with your public relations office. But watch out.

Why the warning? Because public relations and journalism, while not exactly enemies, have very different agendas. Too often students are not sensitive enough to these different agendas—and to how they can conflict. And herein lies one of the most common of student journalism problems.

PR people often as not like to think of themselves as having a journalistic role, or at least some role complementary to journalism, but I don't see it like that. Indeed, I am hardly alone in maintaining that journalism's job is disseminating information, while PR's job is controlling information. To this end PR may well distribute lots of accurate and useful facts, but it just as likely is spinning, hyping, or shading those facts. Sometimes, in the name of damage control, it even does its best to withhold the facts.

This is one reason why the public relations office is usually eager to be of assistance to student journalists. This is not to say the efforts of public relations people are dishonorable—they are not. PR people have a worthwhile mission: promoting their clients. But pursuing that mission customarily results in inflating the positive or minimizing the negative, and neither of those things suits your objectives.

Nevertheless, I've found student journalists all too reliant on college public relations services. The latter are eager to help, which is nice, but the former are all too acquiescent in being helped. Too often, this translates into student journalists being manipulated—used, if you will—by PR. Without knowing it, the student newspaper may become accustomed to being spoon fed by the PR staff—being advised on what's newsy and maybe being steered away from what PR has decided is not newsworthy.

You can see the dangers there. Yet far too many times, student journalists will contact their campus public relations office *first* for information on a news event or other story. My advice is to contact the PR office *last*, if at all. Turn to the PR office to confirm or perhaps to fill in information gaps, or to get a copy of the commencement speaker's speech, or maybe to obtain a photo if you can't get one on your own. If you must use a press release, rewrite it, purging the puffery and retrofitting it to your newspaper's style; not to do so is dishonorable. Above all, before you run to the PR office, do your reporting first.

This may sound a bit strident on my part, but really, it's common sense. Yes, the PR office is eager to assist you. But as you should do with any source willing to help, you must always consider the source's motives. Sometimes sources readily supply information because that's their job, or because they are just naturally helpful. Cool. That describes PR people, too—up to a point. That point is where PR hopes to contain or to spin information in the best light.

This problem is particularly acute when the PR office has been institutionalized as the sole or official source of information on campus. I've seen just that, where everyone from the groundskeeper to the campus cops refuses to be interviewed, directing student reporters instead to the PR office. Where this really creates problems is in news stories that deal with especially sensitive subjects, such as racial conflicts or crime.

IT'S A CRIME

Let's take crime, for example. There's some sort of criminal activity on virtually every campus. It may be common or it may be rare, but it's there. Even though your campus police force may be compelled by law to publicly post its arrest reports every week, your PR office would like to pretend there is no crime on campus. At the very least, the PR office seeks to minimize news accounts of crime so as not to harm the college's image as a safe place. Therefore, the college may have arranged that all inquiries regarding criminal activity be directed to the PR office. The campus cops are happy with that, being relieved of having to talk to student reporters; PR is happy, because it gets to control the info.

So consider what happened not long ago over at Slaverhundt University. A coed was walking from the library to her residence hall one Friday at 11 p.m. when a car pulled up alongside her and the motorist asked for directions. The young woman began giving the requested information when the driver suddenly wrenched open the door of the car and began hauling the student inside. The woman struggled. As the car began pulling away, she managed to free herself and flung herself to the street. The car roared off. Shaken and weeping, the coed ran to the closest emergency telephone and summoned the campus police. A squad car soon arrived, and as she described the incident the officers took the student to the campus medical center, where she was examined by a nurse. The student was treated for a few light scratches but was otherwise declared unharmed. The police, meanwhile, had alerted additional units of campus police and the local town law enforcement agency to be on the lookout for the attacker. The student was returned to her dorm.

By next morning, accounts of the attempted abduction, partly accurate and partly distorted by rumor, were the buzz of the campus, and a reporter for the student newspaper was duly assigned to get the story. The reporter phoned the campus police chief, who declined to impart any information, directing the reporter instead to the campus public relations office. The head of the PR office, let's call him Mr. Warren Fuzzi, received the reporter and supplied pretty much the information given in the preceding paragraph. Fuzzi then added a few statements. Knowing not to rely on a single source for this story, the reporter solicited comments from the head of the campus Women's Center and got a few additional observations. Finally, the reporter got a quote from a coed. Now let's consider what the reporter wrote:

Abduction attempt reported
By Joe Jones, Slavering Newshound Reporter

OURCAMPUS, April 7 — Campus police have issued a crime alert due to an attempted abduction that occurred Friday, April 1, at approximately 11 p.m. near the parking lot behind the main library building. The victim, a female student, reported to campus police that a man in a small, dark sedan had pulled up next to her while she was walking and asked her for directions. The man then opened the passenger side door and attempted to force her inside the vehicle, according to media relations spokesman Warren Fuzzi.

The woman managed to free herself. As the car raced off, she used an emergency telephone to alert campus police, who arrived promptly on the scene. An examination at the health center determined the student had suffered a few scratches but was otherwise unharmed, Fuzzi added. An investigation is currently under way by campus police, and no further information has been released on the incident. Police departments in "sizable areas" have been notified, and two additional Rape Aggression Defense classes will also be offered before the end of the semester, according to Fuzzi.

More police officers will be patrolling the campus, as well as more officers on foot, according to Fuzzi. "Our campus is safe," said Fuzzi, "but everyone needs to be careful and not take risks walking at night by themselves."

There are currently 15 campus police officers in the department, all of whom are sworn officers of the law and have undergone thorough training, said Fuzzi.

Asked to comment on the incident, Prof. Gloria Mundy, coordinator of the Women's Center, said, "The university is doing as much as it can, but the fact that an abduction was attempted shows us that there is a danger. We provide information on how to help people who have survived [violent crimes] and how to support them. The Women's Center puts out an ongoing effort for getting this information out."

Susie Kew, a third-year Communications major, told this reporter: "This was a scary incident. You start to wonder if you can trust anyone around here."

First of all, consider the time line of this story. The abduction occurred on Friday night. The news account was turned into the paper the following Tuesday evening, just before the weekly was put to bed. That's four whole days—Saturday through Tuesday—during which the reporter had time to assemble and write a story. But the article hardly reflects all that reporting time. Ouch.

Now the central problem with this story is its sourcing. The primary figure of the story is of course the attack victim, but she's totally absent. When I asked the reporter about this, he pointed out that PR spokesman Fuzzi had said that she didn't want to talk to the press. I said that might well be true, but had the reporter verified this? No, but the reporter assumed the woman wouldn't want to be identified. The reporter and I then discussed the role of assumptions in journalism. So, had the victim done something wrong or shameful? No, the reporter allowed, but still, she might not want to talk to the press about the incident. You're right, I said, she might not want to, you might have got nothing. Or you might have got a gripping, firsthand account of the attack. But you don't know what you might get until you ask, and you didn't ask. Whatever the case, the main source for the story is not quoted in the story. And is the victim satisfied with how these secondary sources told her story? We don't know. Equally important, is the reader well informed by this story? The answer to that we do know.

(Just to compound matters, it turned out that since the attack had become "the buzz of the campus," the victim's name was in fact well known to many students, including the reporter. Yet the reporter had simply taken Mr. Fuzzi's word that she did not wish to speak to reporters.)

As a relevant issue, I pointed out that if the victim had been molested or raped, she may well be reluctant to speak publicly, and her privacy should be respected. But was the victim molested or raped? We have no suggestion of that in the account of the events—although Mr. Fuzzi rather provocatively mentions rape defense courses. The reporter might have asked him why he was invoking that topic. And the reporter might well have pointed out to both cops and the PR office that withholding the victim's name perhaps suggested the worst had happened. It was all quite unclear, and wasn't it the reporter's job to clarify the who and what and so on of the attack? The reporter nodded.

Readers likely wonder if the victim had been sexually assaulted. Readers shouldn't be left to wonder. This is a serious attack, and worried readers have the right to know just how serious this incident was. The reporter should have at least asked the police if the victim had made a claim of sexual assault—or if there was any suspicion of such assault. Whether the police confirm or deny or decline to comment, police response—or nonresponse—should be part of the story. But the best source, of course, would be the alleged victim herself.

"But how could I ask her about such a serious matter?" the news editor whined. "I mean, could I just go up to her and ask her if she'd been raped?"

I agreed that this was a delicate and difficult situation but added that journalists often face such challenges. I myself had once had to interview the parents of a teenage suicide, and it was among the most difficult things I'd ever done. How did I justify my intrusion on this family's private grief? I suggested that publicizing their son's story might prevent similar tragedies. The reporter said this sounded sleazy. I agreed. It was sleazy. It was true—but it was also manipulative.

I moved the discussion back to my main point: sourcing. The primary source is the victim, and we don't have her. The secondary source would be the cops, and we don't hear them. So the story relies on a tertiary source, a thirdhand account. The victim reported to the police, the police reported to the PR office. (There may well have been further steps in between: the cops who arrived on the scene reporting to the duty officer, the duty officer reporting to the chief.) Anyway, how good can a story be based on a thirdhand account? And look what you got, I said, from that thirdhand source. No arrests yet, investigation continues, area cops alerted. All that is very general information, indeed the sort of things readers would assume anyway. But further questions: Attack was very rare? How rare—verify that. Cops and health center did their jobs in exemplary manner? Check that out. Campus is safe? The attack seems to contradict that. And if the campus is so safe, why is the PR officer announcing patrols will be increased and warning women not to walk the campus alone at night? Indeed, doesn't that last remark smack of blaming the victim?

"Okay, okay," said the reporter, "I know what I was told was all spin. And maybe I made a mistake in not trying to talk to the victim. But the cops wouldn't give me any information; they insisted I speak only to the PR guy. What else could I do?"

Lots, I said. First of all, why had the reporter phoned the police, rather than dropping by the police station?

"Why waste time doing that?" he asked. Then he added, brightly: "I was working the phones."

I appreciated the reporter's familiarity with the jargon, but what the reporter did not appreciate is that working the phones often doesn't work—and usually doesn't work as well as a one-on-one, knee-to-knee interview. I went into this matter further. Was the reporter in fact familiar with campus police headquarters? After all, the headquarters was the equivalent of a few short blocks from the newspaper office. Equally important, were the campus police familiar with him? What exactly was his relationship with the head of campus security? Well, he knew his name and had met him a few times. I asked if the police chief knew the reporter's name and would recognize him if they ran across each other. The reporter glumly allowed this was unlikely.

Humph, I said. Crime reporters should establish their physical presence among the cops on a regular basis. In other words, covering campus crime is more than a matter of copying the weekly police blotter off a bulletin board or Web site. Campus cops—like other primary sources on campus—should be accustomed to regular, friendly inquiries from the student press. The reporter, the news editor, the editor in chief should make themselves known to the police chief and to any other relevant staff—other cops, desk clerk, and so forth. A face-to-face interview, while not always possible to arrange, is always more desirable than a phone interview—or an e-mail inquiry. It is infinitely easier for a source to terminate an interview, avoid your questions, or otherwise blow you off on the telephone—or over the Internet—than it is when you are right there across his or her desk. Just coming to the source's office is a demonstration of your urgent desire and need to get information. Do whatever you have to do and you're likely to get at least *something* of value from the source. In any case, asking intelligent, well-informed questions, batting your eyelashes, or using whatever other devices you might have at hand to work the source will work better when you are face-to-face, and not at the end of a telephone or DSL line.

Still more: Student reporters should try to establish a concurrence of interests with their sources or—better yet—establish that sharing information can benefit the source. Reporters should not send the message that they are simply there to extract information for their own greedy purposes. For example, asking an ambulance service how soon they arrived after receiving an emergency call gives the EMS crew a chance to show how prompt they are. Asking police if students should feel confident that sufficient night patrols occur on campus gives the cops the opportunity either to boast of their activities or to complain of overworked manpower and the like. Asking the maintenance staff if the university is supplying it sufficient resources and equipment needs gives the staff a chance to make their pitch for increased funding. Meanwhile, by asking such questions the student reporter might gather some worthwhile information.

Most important: When sources like the police say the student reporter should consult the PR office for official comment, reporters should point out that some questions can be answered properly only by the cops. Examples:

Regarding the woman who claimed abduction—did her story seem credible and consistent? Were there any witnesses to the alleged abduction, and are any efforts being made to locate witnesses? Did the police find tire marks from the alleged perpetrator's car? Did the victim show any signs of physical abuse? Do the police believe the student might have been assaulted or molested or raped? What kind of medical exam did she undergo? Have there been any other instances of abduction or attempted abduction on campus before? Do the police have any solid leads in this case? The PR office says local township police forces have been notified—which ones, and what do campus cops hope for in this regard? The PR office says police patrols will be beefed up—by how much? How many exist now, and is that considered adequate? Do campus cops have enough vehicles, radios, other equipment? Are there enough campus emergency phones—and do they work?

That's a quick dozen or more questions, and I'm sure we can all think of additional ones. But notice what's happening here. First, I'm asking questions the PR office most likely cannot answer—or certainly cannot answer as well as the cops can—and I make certain to point that out to my police source. Second, I'm peppering the source with questions. Not bombarding the source, and not challenging the source, but asking plenty of good, pertinent questions—prepared in advance—to which my readers deserve answers. The source may not respond to all of my questions, but even if the source answers only a few, that's more police info than what appeared in the story. Even when a source says, "We're not at liberty to confirm that," that's a quote that should be used in the story. It at least shows the reader that the reporter questioned the police, and that the police are being tight-lipped. That's not much, but it's something.

As a last resort, I advised the reporter, try a little emotional blackmail. "Jeez, you're not giving me information . . . my story is going to be thin and the readers are howling for information here . . . they're alarmed by this reported abduction, rumors are flying about, and they might well imagine the situation worse than it actually is. . . . They might even perceive the police as uncooperative or uncaring because you're not giving me any facts. We're going to have a story, we have to have a story, I don't want to run a story full of inaccuracies and innuendos and unsubstantiated reports and rumors. Gosh, you're the expert on this matter, that's why I came to you . . . so you'd really be doing everybody a favor if you could just . . ."

Well, we hope it doesn't get to such an adversarial, whiny, or weepy point. But if you ask your questions respectfully and earnestly, you should get something of value. And when you finish the interview, thank the source. And when you have to get back to the source later for clarification or for further questions, the source should be receptive to you.

To summarize: Know and cultivate your police sources and other sources, and make sure they know you; that gets your foot in the door when you need information—and put your foot in the door, not just your fingers on the phone. (Work your sources—not your telephones.) Ask specific and pertinent questions configured specifically for your source, and do so in a way that your source feels flattered by your seeking out his or her expertise.

Okay, we've discussed what the reporter didn't get from the PR office, and what the reporter might have gotten from the police. Let's look at that third source, the head of the Women's Center.

Ms. Mundy was a reasonably good choice as a source—not firsthand or secondhand, of course, but still someone who might have something worthwhile to say about the abduction incident. So it's commendable that the reporter sought her out. But what does Ms. Mundy have to say? First, she asserts that "the university is doing as much as it can." Oh, really? The reporter should not have allowed this assertion to go by unchallenged, because there is no evidence that the university is "doing as much as it can." Similarly, when Mundy says, "I am glad to see that they are addressing it," we can be glad she's glad, but so far from what we've seen the university is not so much addressing this issue as skirting around it.

Then we get the clincher to the story, when Mundy says: "The fact that an abduction was attempted shows us that there is a danger. We provide information on how to help people who have survived [violent crimes] and how to support them. The Women's Center puts out an ongoing effort for getting this information out." What's happening here? Instead of examining and evaluating Mundy's three assertions, the reporter has turned into a tape recorder. Look at those three statements. The first: "The fact that an abduction was attempted shows us that there is a danger" is not exactly the most insightful of observations, and its information value is zero. Second sentence: "We provide information on how to help people" tells us nothing about what the Women's Center actually does regarding victims of violence. Third sentence: "The Women's Center puts out an ongoing effort for getting this information out" should be recognized, on the one hand, as likewise devoid of specific information, and on the other hand as self-congratulation or self-promotion. Or public relations. Important point: It's not just the PR office that engages in PR; lots of folks have an interest in making themselves or their offices sound good.

To get something solid here from this source, the reporter might have pushed for some specifics on victim aid and counseling. To perform a public service, the reporter might have included the address, phone number, and hours of operation of the Women's Center. Or to serve the readers better, the reporter might have concluded that the Women's Center had nothing useful to say regarding the attempted abduction and burned his tape. Any of those three options might have been acceptable. Instead, the reporter exercised a fourth option: to act as a stenographer, recording useless verbiage in a vain effort to flesh out his admittedly anorexic story.

Same holds true for the padding provided by our coed-on-the-street, Susie Kew. Sorry, but grabbing a quote from one student at random is unacceptable filler. We have no idea if her view is typical—or just a reflection of her particular mindset. Poll a hundred students on campus safety? Sure, that could be useful. Quote one student who fears "trusting anyone"? Dubious in the extreme. Burn it.

Our analysis suggests a number of lessons. One is that not all sources are of equal value. Another is that not all sources are equally available and that those that are harder to access—like police officials—most likely are more valuable than those—like PR spokesmen—who are paid to welcome reporters with open arms. Yet another lesson is that pseudosources result in pseudo–news articles.

Maybe there's an even larger lesson here: You students have reportedly come of age in an Age of Irony. You've been described as marked by cynicism. Yet what many seem to be lacking is a healthy sense of journalistic skepticism. When dealing with professional information providers—like PR officers or other official spokespersons—student journalists should not be ironic or cynical or suspicious—but they should exercise skepticism.

Finally, for all the flaws of the story, I ultimately don't blame the reporter, because reporters are only as good as the guidance they get from their editors. So news editor—ouch.

5

Reporting

The very first anecdote I related in this book—way back there at the beginning of the Introduction—dealt with a Reporter Behaving Badly. Indeed, I used the incident of the RBB to explain why I was moved to write this book. Accordingly, in this chapter I hope to outline the essential elements that will help reporters do their jobs properly.

Reporting encompasses a number of activities and skills that we can broadly place under the rubrics of news gathering, researching, and writing. I'll discuss all of these in this chapter. (News gathering includes interviewing, which will be discussed here, but in this chapter I'll focus on speaking to sources for news. Interviewing for the personality profile will be discussed in the chapter on feature writing; still, much of what is said here will apply to all kinds of interviewing.)

THE BASIC TOOL KIT

To begin with, a good reporter needs certain basic tools, and the most important of these tools is the appropriate brain. By this I mean a mind that is intellectually sharp, curious, questioning, sensitive to the nuances of others' behaviors and actions, alert to the weight and rhythms of diction and sentence structure, and a whole lot of other things I can't provide; for all this you'll have to turn to one or more of those innumerable self-help books or maybe enter some sort of mental 12 step program. Or maybe you just have to be born right.

Put another way, we can say a good reporter is a smart reporter. A smart reporter isn't someone who knows everything. (That would be desirable, but it's a bit utopian.) No, but a smart reporter is one who knows how to find out everything. More about that later. For the time being I'll just have to assume (uh-oh) you're brainy enough. Now on to the physical tools you need to do reporting.

Take Note

Since reporting largely consists of gathering information from people—either in a prearranged sit-down interview or while chasing after the fire chief—your cardinal piece of equipment is a reporter's notebook. Truman Capote said he never needed to take notes, but if that were true he was a rare bird indeed. Even when he was receiving a mere Ten Commandments, Moses had to get them written down. I suspect you too will do well to take notes, and experience shows that what we call the reporter's notebook is the most sensible choice. A reporter's notebook is a stiff-backed, spiral-bound, and pocket-sized affair, not too large and not too small. You don't want some tiny little black address book type of thing in which to take notes—(too cramped and too easy to misplace)—and you don't want to interview somebody using a three-ring binder—(too awkward). Your notebook should be easy enough to carry about, and if you call yourself a reporter you should be in the habit of always having such a notebook at hand. This holds even when you're not on an assignment, because news can happen anywhere and at any time. Your newspaper office should supply these notebooks, and if it doesn't, insist that it does.

Your next piece of equipment is a writing instrument, about which I will say only one thing: always have two. Why? Simply because when you're on the job you don't want to run out of ink or lead.

Of course, if you are adept at taking notes electronically—in your PDA or cell phone or BlackBerry or whatever the tech-fad is at the moment—go for it. Which brings up the more common mechanical reporting device, the voice recorder.

On the Record

Students are forever asking me if using a recorder is necessary. My answer is: not necessary, but certainly useful. The advantage of recording, say, an interview, is that it records everything. The disadvantage of recording, say, an interview, is that it records everything. Fact is, you don't want everything; you want only the interesting and the usable, and that presumably is what you would record with your pen in your notebook. You certainly don't want every ah, er, um, digression, tangent, evasion, and chunk of baloney thrown your way. That's what your recording device is going to gather, and that's why in one sense the notebook is superior to the recorder. Of course, that little tape cassette or flash drive that stores the complete record may well contain some important things your cramped fingers failed to grasp. So it seems a circular question. Personally, I do just as Columbia University Graduate School of Journalism professor and former *New York Times* reporter Samuel G. Freedman says in his *Letters to a Young Journalist* about the recorder versus notebook conflict: "I almost always take notes, because something in the physical act of listening that closely and writing that rapidly seems, paradoxically, to open all my senses wider." And believe me, a reporter needs wide senses. Still, when I conduct an interview I normally don both suspenders and belt: I set the recorder on the table in front of the subject—and I take notes. Afterwards, when I'm back at my workstation, I'll usually work from my notes, and I'll refer to the recorded interview only if I detect something illegible or otherwise deficient in my scribbled pages. Early in what passes for my career I used to type up entire transcripts of recordings, only to discover I'd pretty much wasted my time. What I most commonly find these days is that my notebook contains what I want to use in my article. I'm normally glad I have a recording of the interview, but it's chiefly there in reserve, something to fall back on—but most times I don't require such a gymnastics mat. Maybe I don't rely on tapes because by now I'm a fairly experienced note-taker. No doubt the less accustomed one is to conducting interviews, the more desirable it becomes to have a recording device at hand.

There's another problem with recorders. Once—and only once—when I was recording an interview, my batteries died on me. I had spare batteries, good Boy Scout that I am. But the fumbling process of changing the batteries was quite disruptive to the interview, and before I knew it the man I was interviewing me was asking all sorts of questions about my recording device—consuming much of our allotted interview time. And worse: Ever since that single instance when my batteries croaked, I've invariably found myself in subsequent interviews anxiously monitoring the little red LED light on my recorder. The interviewee takes the cue from me and does the same. It soon becomes distracting for the both of us, and faintly ridiculous: two grown adults sitting across a desk, mesmerized by a little red lamp.

Bear in mind one more important fact about using a recorder: Its presence often inhibits interviewees. Indeed, sitting across from a subject with just a notebook on your knee can make an interviewee nervous ("My God, this kid's actually taking down my every word—I really have to be careful with what I say!"). All the more inhibiting is the recorder ("My God, this kid's actually preserving my every word—this could be entered in court as evidence!"). Now some people, like maybe your university president, are quite comfortable with being interviewed, and for such folks neither the notebook nor the recorder will be a source of anxiety. But most people are not used to being solicited for their views. They may be flattered when you seek them out for their expertise, but the interview process may turn out to be a surprisingly nerve-racking experience for them. But more about interviewing below.

Meanwhile, I can already hear some of you saying, Cool, I'll just conceal the recorder in my pocket and therefore the interviewee won't feel nervous at all during our chat. To which I say you'd better check the law in your state, because secretly recording a conversation (in movie parlance, wearing a wire) is quite likely illegal, and it's hard to conduct an interview if you're being frog-marched off to jail.

All these problems aside, the bottom line is, if you feel you need a recorder, then by all means use one. Again, your newspaper office should supply your recording devices. But hold on, let's let Sam Freedman have the last word on the subject: "These matters of mechanics, like notebook versus tape, make no difference whatsoever to the quality of a journalist. You can etch your notes with a stick onto a clay tablet in cuneiform and succeed extravagantly if you have intelligence and tenacity, empathy for human experience, and appreciation of complexity. Those are the things that matter."

Put that in your notebooks. I did.

The Little Black Book

Another essential tool every reporter has—mentioned here last but far from least—is a source list. This is a compilation of names, addresses, phone numbers, e-mail addresses, and Web sites of people and institutions you may have to consult for information, both those you contact on a regular basis and those you might need to reach on the odd but important occasion. The source list, which often includes notations, is among a reporter's most prized possessions. When you need to reach anyone on your regular news beats, when you need to contact again that professor you interviewed last year about electoral reform, when you want to locate that representative on the education committee in the state capital, when you want to phone the public relations office at your university or the archivist at your town's newspaper or whoever it might be, you don't want to waste time Googling or combing through telephone directories or pestering your colleagues. No, you want to have those names and numbers at your fingertips—either in a little notebook or in your Rolodex or on your cell phone or in your computer or in a combination thereof.

Such a source list is not only an invaluable reporter's aid, it is also an organic tool, one that you edit and update constantly. As soon as you are assigned to a beat, the first thing you should do is to ask whomever you're replacing for his or her list of sources. If that predecessor is conscientious and is concerned about seeing the beat covered properly, he or she should accommodate you gladly. If the person you are replacing declines for whatever reason to share that list of sources, beat it of out of him, or her. By the same token, when you leave a beat, you should be helpful to your replacement and turn over your list of sources. Otherwise, your replacement, who may have read this book, might well wrestle you to the newsroom floor and stand on your throat until you yield.

Other tools a reporter should have at hand include some basic books like a good dictionary, a grammar book, and whatever stylebook your newspaper uses (see the Bibliography for specific suggestions). As indicated in chapter 3, such books should be in every newsroom—but reporters would do well to have their own personal copies. And for heaven's sake, there is no shame in displaying a dictionary or grammar book on your desk; only the most insecure of writers hide their dictionaries in the drawer or are embarrassed to look something up when someone is looking over their shoulders. The nature of the English language is such that nobody has all the answers in his head. (Quick, is *dominancy* a word? What's the difference between *affect* and *effect*? Have I spelled *liaison* correctly here?) So keep those reference books at hand and use them. And don't rely solely on computerized spell-checkers and grammar-checkers; I haven't found one yet that isn't flawed. (Who rights those things?) Then again, the Internet offers vast numbers of excellent reference sites—dictionaries, almanacs, city directories, and specialized sites for finding things like how many miles between two cities. Compile site lists, keep adding to them, and make such lists available to all staffers.

MS. MANNERS

In addition to acquiring the basic tools of the trade a reporter should also observe some basic rules of journalistic etiquette. The first of these says that when you're speaking to someone in your role as a journalist, you must identify yourself up front as a journalist. This is not merely a matter of courtesy. In the old rough-and-tumble and less professional days of journalism, it was customary for reporters simply to sidle up to people—say, at the scene of an accident or in a bar or over the telephone (can you sidle over the phone?)—and ask questions without revealing themselves as reporters. The idea was to catch people off guard and hence to get candid information. Such a practice might well have been efficacious. But it is now viewed as unethical. You don't want your sources claiming after you've spoken to them that they didn't know they were talking on the record. They will feel misused and duped. Think about it: Would you like to engage in what you believe is a casual conversation, only to discover later that your comments are appearing in a newspaper article? No, I didn't think so. Now in truth reporters occasionally still resort to questioning people without telling them that they're speaking to the press. The journalists will justify this by stating that there was no other way they could get reluctant or inhibited sources to talk ("See, I had to work undercover!"). But such an argument is usually hard to sustain, and the tactic remains tacky—if not downright sleazy. Overall, you're better off losing a source—having someone decline to speak to a reporter—than tricking someone into speaking and then having that person later complain about your trickery.

So identify yourself immediately by name and by your role ("reporter for *The Slavering Newshound*"). Even better if you can hand your sources your card. This way, there can be no misunderstanding later that your sources didn't know who you were or why you were speaking to them.

Doing this has an additional practical effect: When your sources are aware that they are speaking to a reporter, then it is established that the sources are speaking for the record. That is to say, in the midst of a chat, sources cannot legitimately interrupt themselves, or after an interview backtrack, to say: "Oh, wait, I don't want you to quote that." In truth, they can request this, but they can't insist on it. (Whether or not you grant such a request remains a matter of your discretion.)

The next element of etiquette to consider is to be considerate of the person to whom you are speaking. This means, first, don't waste that person's time. Your source—the firefighter on the job or the dean across his desk—is doing you a favor: He or she has granted you time and opportunity to gather information and views. But you shouldn't waste your interviewee's time by gathering information you should have gathered before the interview. This means, for example, in a formal interview, you shouldn't be asking a professor how to spell her name, what her rank is, how long she has been at the university, and so on. This is information you should have collected before the interview. Similarly, if you're interviewing an expert on, say, Norway, you shouldn't be asking that person to name the capital of Norway. That's a discourtesy, because it's wasting the professor's time—and it's not reflecting very well on you.

Now of course in the event of spontaneous news—a fire in the dormitory—you're not going to have the opportunity to Google the fire chief before you race to the fire. That's understandable; but consideration for the source's valuable time still holds. Get the chief's name, sure, but you can always check the spelling later in the phone book or get background on the chief's career later with a phone call. Right now you want to concentrate on the action at hand: likely cause of fire, estimate of damage, things like that.

Etiquette also dictates that in speaking with your sources you focus on your topic of interest. Presumably that topic is in your source's area of expertise. It is perfectly appropriate to ask a fire chief about the code inspection schedule of a building; it sounds out of order to ask the chief his opinion on the upcoming presidential election. Likewise, if you're speaking to the dean of the School of Liberal Arts, presumably you want to speak about the School of Liberal Arts, and not, for instance, to inquire about the university's admissions policies, which is more appropriately addressed to the Admissions Office.

To this end it is proper etiquette when you contact a source to request an interview to give that source a heads-up as to what you wish to inquire about. Naturally, you won't have the opportunity to do this when you're catching someone on the fly in the midst of a spot news event—the cop at the scene of a traffic accident, the firefighter at the fire. But you certainly will have the chance when, say, you phone up a professor to arrange an interview. Telling the source that you want to elicit his or her views on the latest developments in U.S. policy vis-à-vis Latin America allows the source to be prepared for the interview. And for heaven's sake, once you've established what you want to speak to a source about, stay with it. Sure, conversations can take unexpected turns—that's to be expected. But it's hardly sportsmanlike to arrange, say, a meeting with the head football coach to discuss the new equipment the team is adopting, only to arrive at the interview and ambush the coach with questions about why season after season the team has had such a piss-poor offense.

Some additional courtesies I've found sensible to practice when gathering information from people:

1. Let people speak. You are there, after all, to get information and views from your source. So don't interrupt or otherwise cut them short. (Of course, some loquacious bores really need cutting off; in such cases, I usually sigh and mutter something like, "Gee, this is all fascinating, but you've already given me much more than I can use in my article. Perhaps on another occasion I'll be able to follow this up with you.")
2. Don't challenge, argue, or interrogate in an aggressive manner. I've actually seen reporters do this, and it is counterproductive. Withhold your disdain even when someone is obviously feeding you baloney. You can get more by gentle nudging. ("Gee, you really mean to say little men are living on the moon? I never heard that before. Could you please tell me more about that?")
3. When something your source says is unclear, say so—but of course blame yourself. Don't say, "Man, you physicists always seem to be talking pure gibberish." Better to say, "Sorry, but I'm really having trouble getting my head around that concept of string theory. Could you please expand on that?"
4. Dress appropriately, especially for a prearranged interview. No, this isn't a job interview, and no one is suggesting you should "dress up" when you're doing journalism. Heaven knows, journalists traditionally are a scruffy lot. ("Gentlemen of the press" is obviously an ironic locution.) Still, your appearance suggests something about your attitude to the work at hand. If your interviewee could easily mistake you for a coal miner, a combat veteran, a hooker, an aspiring gangsta rapper, or something that flapped its way out of a Gothic novel, this could start things off on the wrong footing. Why should the source take you seriously when you don't appear to do so yourself? In addition, when you're out on the job you're not representing

just yourself; whether you want to or not, you're representing your news organization and maybe even your college as well.
5. Thanking a person at the end of an interview is one of those common courtesies that even professional journalists commonly overlook. You should, however, indeed thank your source as you would thank anyone who gives you something. In an interview, what you're granted is the source's time, assistance, information, insight, and maybe even wisdom and guidance.

In addition, I customarily fold two more elements into my expressions of gratitude at the end of an interview. The first is to ask: "If I find I need to get back to you for further information or clarification, when is the best time to call?" The second is: "You've been extremely helpful. I'm just wondering if you think there's anyone else I should speak to about this subject?" Such questions display courtesy—and more. On the one hand, they subtly reacknowledge the interviewee's expertise, and a little flattery can go a long way; on the other hand, such questions just might yield you an additional worthwhile source (who knows—maybe even a better source).

CONDUCTING THE INTERVIEW

If my previous point seems to smack somewhat of game playing, let me say right up front that conducting an interview does involve a certain amount of game playing. That's because interviewing can be a dicey game, and let me say even in front of what I just said right up front—getting a good interview isn't always easy. In fact, at the risk of scaring off my reader, I'm going to say it's very easy to have a bad interview. A bad interview is one in which you don't get much of what you're after. A bad interview is a waste of everybody's time. All that's something you want to avoid.

There is no way to guarantee a good interview, just as there is no way to guarantee good reception on your TV or radio: You can't control the weather or sunspot activity or the power of the broadcaster's transmitter. But you can at least see to it that things on your end are at the optimum—like having a good TV receiver, adjusting the sound and picture, and making sure the antenna is working. That's also what you have to do in an interview.

The first and the supremely important task to undertake in regard to experiencing a worthwhile interview is preparation, and what your preparation largely consists of is creating, shaping, and arranging your questions. Now obviously if you've just jumped out of your car with your notebook in hand to investigate an accident at your intersection or the smoke pouring out of a second-story window you don't have time to prepare questions; no, you simply go with the standard "hey-what's-happening-anybody-hurt-who-called-the-ambulance?" But for a prearranged interview you should carefully prearrange your inquiry.

For such an interview you want to have an abundance—and even an overabundance—of good questions to ask before you sit down for your chat. It's far better to have too many questions than to have too few. One of the most embarrassing things that can occur in an interview is running out of questions, which leaves you sitting there with your thumb in your mouth and looking like . . . well, looking like a jerk with his thumb in his mouth. Much better is having way more questions than you can ever get to in your allotted time; if there's something you really needed to ask but couldn't get to, you can always get back to your source later.

So how do you develop good questions prior to an interview? Well, this will sound paradoxical, but the more you know, the more you will have to ask about. Which means that if, say, you're going to interview that physics prof about the latest theories on the origin of the universe, the more you know about the subject the better you'll be able to ask pertinent questions. So, yeah, the bad news is you just may have to do some reading up on the topic before the interview. And be grateful you have the opportunity and the time to do so. (Many years ago I had the unhappy experience of having to interview Sierra Leone's ambassador to the United Nations. It was an unhappy experience because I had about fifteen minutes in which to prepare for the interview. The only thing I knew about Sierra Leone was the continent in which the country is located; beyond that I was in Zip City. To make matters worse, this was going to be a live television interview. What happened was I had arrived as a guest journalist prepared to interview a diplomat from an entirely different country and I got the gentleman from Sierra Leone as a substitute. Guess what? I faked my way through the interview. Guess further what? The interview looked an obvious fake.)

Anyway, you should rarely find yourself in the position of interviewing someone you don't know on a subject you know nothing about. So you take the opportunity to start learning about the subject—Big Bangs or African exports, whatever. And from these your questions should arise. Write 'em down, as many as arise and as quickly as they come.

After you've accumulated a solid bundle of questions, step back and examine your bundle. See if there are logical groupings for the questions. Within those groups or clusters look for verbal or conceptual clues that will allow you to gracefully segue from one question to the next. In other words, try to impose some coherence in the pattern of your questions. (For example, had I but world and time enough to research and prepare questions about Sierra Leone, I might have found logical categories of inquiry—the country's political structure, economy, history, relations with its neighbors; I'm just guessing here, because I still don't know anything about Sierra Leone. But you should have an idea of what I'm talking about.)

Anyway, you've created questions and made some effort to impose order on them. Bear in mind that it's quite possible your interviewee will take your discussion into areas you haven't asked about—or haven't asked about yet—to the extent that your neat interview structure crumbles. But that's all right. The fact that battles never go according to plan doesn't mean generals abandon making battle plans; no, they plan the best they can—and hope for the best. You do the same for your interview.

Beyond creating and arranging your queries, one of the most important things you can build into your battle plan is examining the character of your questions. Questions can be classified in a variety of tones. One category is texture: soft and hard. A soft question is a friendly, cheerful inquiry, like, "Well, coach, the squad looks pretty good for the upcoming season, wouldn't you say?" A hard question is edgy or aggressive: "Well, coach, are those jerks you call a basketball team going to have yet another losing season?" Another example of the soft: "Well, Dean of Admissions, how does the incoming crop of freshmen look to you?" Hard: "Well, Dean of Admissions, the figures released on SAT scores suggest standards have fallen for the incoming crop of freshmen. What do you say about that, huh, huh?"

The above questions vary by tone—and they are likely to set the tone for the rest of the interview. People don't like to be attacked, so they'll react to your aggressive questions by being defensive or close-mouthed. But this doesn't mean you should ask only mushball questions. Ask mushy questions and you'll get a mushy interview. Use your head. Obviously if you charge into your interview asking probing, stinging questions your interviewee is going to get his back up. Much better to soften up the source with a soft question or two, thereby establishing a friendly relationship, then probe for something deeper, then maybe pull back to the softer side, then probe again and eventually go in for the kill. ("Students are circulating a petition calling for your dismissal—care to comment, coach?")

Another way of categorizing questions is by what we call close-ended and open-ended inquiries. Close-ended questions are formulated in such a way as to yield a short and possibly even monosyllabic reply. Example: "What is the library's budget this year for acquiring new books?" Answer: "Fifty thousand dollars." Another example: "Do you think the library budget is adequate?" Answer: "No."

The advantage of the close-ended question is that it elicits a specific answer to a specific and focused question. That's all to the good. But you should recognize that if you ask only close-ended questions, you're likely to receive only short, pointed answers that may well add up to a mighty short interview. That's why you should be sure to follow up basic fact gathering with open-ended questions, which means questions that allow or even require your interviewee to give you expansive replies—ones that are likely to reveal fuller information. That's why it's good to follow up that close-ended question on the size of the budget with something open-ended like this: "What kinds of things might the library be doing if it had a larger budget?"

Let's go back to the coach for another set of examples. Close-ended question: "So, would you say the athletic department achieved its recruiting goals this year?" Open-ended question: "Would you describe how recruiting went this year, and if you encountered any problems?"

Note how that first question will most likely yield you a mere yes, a no, or a grunt. Note how the second question maneuvers the coach into giving you an extensive answer.

Not incidentally, note also how my last question to the librarian taps into his aspirations and how my last question to the coach lets the coach air his problems. People love to discuss their dream projects, and they likewise love to bitch and moan about their limited budgets, lack of support, institutional obstacles, bureaucracy, indifference to and misunderstanding of their needs and desires, and so on. Open-ended questions aimed at these areas give people the chance to air their grievances, to show how well they're doing despite all the stumbling blocks in their way, to make a public relations pitch for their pet projects and, oh boy, if you just tap the right roots you'll be gathering more good quotes than you can use.

That's why I say giving your questions a good close think before your interview will put you on your way to a fruitful encounter.

YOU CAN QUOTE ME

Since the focus of an interview should be the person you are interviewing, his or her words should make up a large portion, if not the majority, of your story. Quotes come in two varieties: direct and indirect. A direct quote, which is enclosed in quotation marks, should be an accurate and exact transcription of what a person said. That's why reporters say that quotes are sacred—we don't alter them or otherwise mess them up. Having said that, journalists usually allow for a little wiggle room here. For example, if a source stumbles or stammers, it's not necessary—and in fact it seems unsportsmanlike—to include every repetition, each incomplete sentence, every *ah, er, well,* and like in his or her discourse. Certainly you don't want to clean up the grammatical and syntactical slips of some skateboard-riding slacker to the point where he comes off sounding like Winston Churchill; that just wouldn't be believable. At the same time, if you faithfully re-create the inarticulateness and scatology of, say, some inner-city resident, you might well be accused of racism for doing so. There's no universal agreement on how much scrubbing you may apply to quotes; it's a judgment call on your part. But there is universal agreement on this: *Whatever you do or don't do to a quote, you must not distort its meaning.*

The above rule applies, first, to direct quotes, especially if you are shortening the quote, eliminating some phrases, or otherwise lifting the quote out of a larger stretch of discourse. You are permitted to do such editing, as long as you make it clear to the reader you are doing so, usually by using ellipses—otherwise known to you as the three spaced dots (...), or by inserting a clarifying letter, word, or phrase in brackets.

Example of a distortion by ellipses: When the film professor says, "*King Kong Meets King Lear* is nothing short of a great big waste of time," it is a gross distortion to write: "Professor Phlyx declared, '*King Kong Meets King Lear* is nothing short of ... great.'" Granted, that's a crude example (although movie ads regularly engage in such crudity), but you readily recognize that my editing of the quote yielded an overtly dishonest representation of what the good professor said.

Example of fair trimming and bracketed insertion: When the professor says, with typically professorial prolixity, "In my considered opinion, and I want to stress that I really considered this, I made no snap judgment, because this wasn't a case where I'd made up my mind before going to the theater, the film was a big waste of time," you might condense the quote like this: "In my considered opinion . . . [*King Kong Meets King Lear*] was a big waste of time." Note three things: (1) I shortened the quote by cutting three redundant clauses; (2) I inserted the name of the film in brackets, so the reader would have no doubt about which movie is being discussed; and (3) I did not distort the professor's sentiment.

Being vigilant about distortion equally applies to indirect quotes, where you recast a source's words into your own words—and where you don't use quotation marks. You are allowed to summarize like this, essentially to express the source's ideas more succinctly than the source did. But again, be careful here; when condensing the source's words, be careful about altering the person's views.

Here's an example of a full quote: "Turning to the recent box-office hit *King Kong Meets King Lear*, Professor Phlyx said, 'In terms of style, cinematography, acting, pacing, scripting, direction, and in all technical senses—dialogue, lighting, special effects, set design, and production values—I thought this film not only highly unsatisfactory in execution, but in its very conception a doomed attempt by a film studio to create a blockbuster out of a muddle-headed conjunction of figures from low and high culture.'"

Here's how that quote might accurately be changed to an indirect quote: "Professor Phlyx judged *King Kong Meets King Lear* a failure in every respect." The direct quote contains nearly sixty words. The indirect version conveys the teacher's views accurately and at around ten words has the virtue of brevity.

Now of course you might be tempted to paraphrase the prof even more succinctly, to wit: "Professor Phlyx said *King Kong Meets King Lear* stinks." This would not be an inaccurate representation of the professor's judgment. But the rather crude word "stinks" certainly doesn't reflect the teacher's level of vocabulary, so I wouldn't go that route.

Be aware that all sorts of distortions can unintentionally creep into your writing even when you think you are making every effort to quote or to summarize sources accurately. Good practice is to read back every quote to yourself against your notes and your memory and ask if you are properly reflecting the speaker's intention. It should be noted that some, although not many, journalists customarily go back to their interviewees and show them their articles before they are printed. This certainly can assure that the interviewee is being quoted correctly. But there's a real danger here, which is why most journalists frown on this practice. The danger is that interviewees invariably want to edit the article. The interviewee on second thought wants this cut, that phrased better, the other thing added. Well, you already have one editor; you don't need another editor, and a self-interested one at that, working over your text. Of course, if there is something particularly complex, controversial, or questionable, you may well choose to read the pertinent paragraphs back to the source to see how it flies. In general, however, showing an article to an interviewee is not a good idea, and if the person demands to see it, tell the person to take it up with your editor.

All in all, the matter of quoting sources requires care and consideration, so take your time over them.

Q&A?

With so many opportunities for error in quoting your interviewees, students will often say, "Look, why don't I just record the interview and present the whole thing in Q&A form? I've seen that plenty of times in magazines." It's a reasonable question, but I have to reply that my view of Q&A is N&O. An interview should be the basis of an article, not the basis of a raw document. Your reader wants a news story or a profile, not something that could be entered into evidence as Exhibit A. Being a reporter is not the same thing as being a stenographer or the student government's recording secretary. In truth, the question-and-answer format is readable, but it's lacking—and what it's lacking is your writerly input. By that I mean all the interpretive observations and details that might help bring your interview—and your interviewee—alive for the reader. Q&A does not permit you to tell the reader how the subject behaved in the interview ("nervously bending paper clips, then tossing them angrily into the waste basket"). Q&A does not allow for describing how the interviewee answered your questions ("candidly," "enthusiastically," "guardedly," "thoughtfully," "hesitantly"). Q&A has no place for you to create a picture of the interview setting ("across a desk stacked with back issues of *Maxim* and *GQ*"; "in an office crammed with scholarly books and populated with *Star Wars* action figures"; "speaking while a mildly pornographic screen saver flickered on his university-supplied computer monitor"). Q&A does not let you describe the interviewee ("wearing a rumpled corduroy jacket and a Bugs Bunny necktie"; "nervously pacing the office in her scuffed Dr. Martens and avoiding the reporter's eyes"). You don't want to overdo such descriptions and interpretations, and obviously you'll have more in a profile of an individual than you would in an interview whose purpose is just to elicit news, but having a touch here and there helps the reader visualize and even "hear" your interviewee. In other words, Q&A is too limiting. It's transcription, it's not writing.

And writing is what you have to do. Following on the preparation and the conducting of the interview, your third and final step is writing an article. Your first task in this regard is finding and crafting a lead. Let's say that among a variety of interesting things that the director of the campus health center said in your interview, she revealed she has just filed a sex discrimination suit against the university. She let this slip after some twenty-five minutes into the interview, but you decide that this is hot news and want to make it the lead. Fine. (In your Q&A format, this important development would be buried twenty-five minutes into your transcript.) So you create your lead concerning the suit, and you proceed to fill in the background about her complaint. As for the other interesting matters concerning the health center, you either get into them later in the article or you hold them for another story on another occasion. To do all this you choose and most likely rearrange quotes, being careful not to wrench things out of context or otherwise to distort what the lady said. You trim quotes and summarize some statements into your own words, again being vigilant about accuracy. You describe and interpret where useful or necessary. And before you know it, you've written your interview. If you've carefully placed all your ducks in their proper rows, the interview should practically be writing itself.

Which is not to say you're done with your day's work. Because you're not.

For one thing, you've just been gathering and writing up information from a source. He or she may have been a good source—but it's just a single source, and you should bear in mind the principle that the more sources you have the better your story is likely to be. Even a personality profile is strengthened when you can bring in additional sources.

TAKE SIDES

How many sides are there to a story? All together, class: "Two sides to every story." Oh, yeah? Well, there are often three. Or four. Or more. And if you have only one, you haven't got the story.

Obvious example: Health center lady makes claims of sex discrimination against the university administration. Sounds like a good story. But it can hardly be a fair, balanced, or complete story if you don't attempt to get a response from an authoritative administration source. And to be thorough, you'd also be wise to research the sex discrimination statutes, maybe get some expert opinion on these laws, and then explain all this to the reader.

Less obvious example: You speak to the fire chief after he's overseen the extinguishing of a blaze in a student apartment. The chief is a good, knowledgeable source, and what he tells you will be the basis for a good story. But you'll have a much better story if you also speak to the kid who rents the apartment, his girlfriend who started the fire by heating up the Chinese takeout in their cardboard cartons, the neighbors, other witnesses, and anyone else who might have any pertinent information or observations about the incident. You might want to speak to the student's landlord to learn about the insurance situation for the building and to ask about the last time that ancient gas oven was checked or repaired. You also might want to scroll through your newspaper archives to find out when the last campus fire occurred, how common such incidents are, and what the cooking regulations are in on- and off-campus student housing. You might want to order Chinese for your own dinner. You might want to do a lot of things, but the one thing you don't want to do is rely on a single source for your story. Because regardless of how authoritative and helpful your single source, that's unlikely to provide the complete story.

VERILY, I VERIFY

Now, after all the pleasant experiences I've described about gathering information from people and from other sources, I have some shocking news for you: Not everything people tell you will be accurate or true. Even more shocking news: Not everything that appears in books or in journals or on Web sites will be accurate or true. Oh my, what's a reporter to do?

Well, what reporters are supposed to do is verify—which means check—the information they collect. What exactly are reporters supposed to verify? Answer: everything. Do reporters in fact verify everything? Answer: no. Why don't reporters verify everything? Answer: because they're rushing to meet deadlines, because they trust their sources too much, because the info they've gathered "sounds" reliable, because they're relying on editors to do the checking, because they're lazy buggers. The excuses, and that is what they are, of course, go on and on. Still, it's a reporter's responsibility to check everything he or she sees into print.

Does this mean you have to worry not only about your own reporting being accurate but also about the accuracy of what people and other sources tell you? In a word, you betcha.

Of course, journalists customarily maintain that they need not verify matters of fact that are common knowledge or that are readily found in general references (e.g., Sacramento is the capital of California; John F. Kennedy was assassinated on November 22, 1963). But "common knowledge" is an uncommonly slippery term, and a reporter is better off checking more rather than less of what he or she is putting in an article. Okay, you won't have the time or the inclination to check everything. But remember, there really is no excuse for not verifying the spellings of names, addresses, full titles, or job descriptions of individuals, as well as the correct designations of the school board or the zoning commission or all those other things that are readily verifiable in the telephone directory, in the city directory, in the government handbook, and on infinite handy Web sites.

Same goes with statements supplied by your interviewee or by other sources. When Professor X tells you that 150 million Asians currently live in New York City, you might think, "Gee, that sounds like an awful lot, but hey, I don't have to verify it; after all, Professor X told me, so it's attributed to him. If it's wrong, it's his mistake, not mine." Wrong—it's his mistake *and* it's your mistake for allowing that mistake into print. Why would you want to permit misinformation to get into your newspaper? So check it out. Check the obviously dubious or debatable or disputable statements for sure. Then, time permitting, check out even the innocuous stuff. And keep in mind the old journalistic axiom: Listen to your mother—but verify even what Mom tells you.

WHO SEZ?

The last paragraph contains the word "attributed," so let's make sure we understand the concept therein. Attribution tells the reader who said what. It doesn't make what was said true or accurate, and in fact if what was said is defamatory, attributing the statement to a source won't protect you from a charge of libel if you print it. All attribution does is answer the reader's question "Who said so?" But that's a reasonable question, so you should attribute the statements, assertions, and facts in your story.

Let's say, for example, Officer Dooley tells you the accident occurred because the red Camaro was speeding wildly down Main Street. Well, when you include that statement in your story you must attribute it to Officer Dooley. Not to do so leaves the impression that *you* are the source of the information, and if you were not an eyewitness to the accident you would be misleading the reader in regard to the source of the allegation. Similarly, if you write that Tom Cruise is coming to campus next month to open the college's film festival, you'd better indicate a source for that information; not to do so suggests that you are the authority for the assertion, and when Tom fails to show up it will be your person the student body is going to beat up on. Note again—naming the cop as the source for the accident information or the head of the film festival for the Cruise announcement doesn't make either statement true; it simply tells the reader who said these things. But that is no small point.

Anything unattributed in a news story is assumed either to come from the reporter's personal knowledge (e.g., the reporter witnessed the accident) or is a well-established and easily verifiable fact (e.g., Saudi Arabia is the world's largest exporter of petroleum). But as with verification, if you're unsure whether or not a statement or fact is common knowledge or readily researchable, then supply attribution in your story. It is better to err on the side of caution and to overdo attribution rather than to underdo it.

OBJECTIVITY

Making clear to your reader who said what and verifying what they said serve not only to give the reader an accurate report, but these actions are related to providing an objective report. So let's talk for a moment about objectivity.

Now everybody out there is saying, "Yeah, sure, we already know, news writers are supposed to be objective." Well, things are rarely as simple as they seem. First of all, in the journalistic community there is no unanimity on the necessity or even on the intrinsic virtue of objectivity. Some journalists argue that maintaining total objectivity is not even possible, that your very word choice is bound to skew your reporting. Other reporters maintain that even if you could achieve total objectivity, such reporting might not be serving the readers. This last view suggests that it's not enough to supply the facts, you have to tell the reader what the facts mean—even if such interpretation might be a matter of debate. Let's consider a few examples:

Say a member of your state House of Representatives holds a press conference to announce that she's promoting a bill that guarantees free speech on the state's college campuses and provides for penalties against anyone inhibiting such free expression. Interesting, and of course worth reporting. But simply reporting what the state congresswoman is promoting doesn't seem to be adequate. Too many questions remain unanswered. First of all, the readers think, Hey, don't we already have free speech on campus? Second, they wonder, Why is this woman pushing this issue? Third, they ask, Is there some threat to freedom of speech that we don't know about? Answering those questions is the kind of thing that might take the reporter beyond the purely objective reporting of the representative's bill. Looking into who this lawmaker is, how she got on to this issue, what her political orientation is, and what she's really aiming for might lead to a whole new light on the story—for example, that she's a staunch right-winger who believes colleges are hotbeds of liberalism that stifle conservative points of view among both students and faculty. Presumably the reporter would determine these things by consulting several reliable outside sources and expert opinions. Now it might be argued that, even if the reporter stifles his personal opinion on the issue, just bringing in such background material to the story is in and of itself interpretive and therefore beyond the bounds of pure objective reporting. One journalistic view therefore might be: Just report what the legislator is proposing and leave it at that; you've delivered the news, you've done your job. But another journalistic view might be: Just reporting the news doesn't properly inform the reader—you have to explain the context, the motivation, the agenda behind this proposition.

Another example: Say the company that provides the food services to your campus releases a report on the nutritional values, caloric counts, fat contents, and so on about the garbage served in the college cafeterias. You could present all these facts and figures, complete with charts and graphs, in a straightforward and objective manner. But are all these numbers and percentages, these grams per serving and recommended daily intakes and so on, going to make sense to the readers? More important, are the readers going to get an idea of how healthful the offerings are in the caf? The answer is, probably not, unless the reporter subjects the facts and figures supplied by the (nonobjective) company to some good critical analysis and maybe brings in some expert outside opinions.

See what I mean? Simply reporting what the legislator is proposing or what the food service has published may be objective journalism. But many will argue that that isn't sufficient journalism. And guess what? Even if you make every effort to present all aspects of the issues at hand in a fair and balanced manner—comment on the proposed legislation from both liberals and conservatives, Democrats and Republicans, on the views of the cafeteria food from nutritionists and physicians, students and chefs—still, some readers are going to complain that your stories are unbalanced and unfair—too much of this, not enough of that, why did you go into this and ignore that, and on and on.

So what's a reporter to do? You do the best you can. You consult with editors and with others, you work carefully and conscientiously, you take your time. You make judgment calls and you make mistakes. And you keep going and you keep striving to do better.

I said it would be interesting. I didn't say it would be easy.

WORDS WORDS WORDS

Last but hardly least, a few words about words. Right, you plan your story, you line up good sources, you carefully craft questions for an interview, you conduct the interview intelligently, you gather supplementary information, you verify and attribute, you strive for accuracy and fairness and balance—you do all those good things and more. Well, there's one more thing to do: Master the language.

Oh, thanks.

You're welcome.

Since entire libraries have been written about the art and craft of writing, there is little I care to add to all that fine instruction. But here's my small contribution:

The first thing I usually tell student journalists is this: Writing can't be taught—although writing can be learned. (I cribbed this Zen-like observation from the essayist Joseph Epstein, but I think I recall reading it elsewhere as well.) Can't be taught . . . can be learned? What can this mean? It means that no one can really teach you how to write. You learn to write the same way you learn to ride a skateboard—by doing it. Practice will not make you perfect, but it will at least make you . . . practiced. So if you want to write, you should write—preferably every day.

Unlike mastering the skateboard, however, writers also learn to write by . . . reading. I suspect you knew that was coming, and I know the very thought makes you shudder, but there it is. Read everything—newspapers, magazines, books, Web sites—and a process of osmosis takes place. Read your eyes out and you'll absorb to some degree a feel for language, a sense of how to describe and explain things. Alternately, don't and you won't. In other words, neglect reading at your own peril. I'm always staggered by the students who aspire to careers in journalism, yet who confess they don't regularly read. It makes no sense to me. It's like the would-be filmmaker who never goes to the movies. Oh sure, you can paint a picture without ever looking at other paintings—but why would you want to reinvent the wheel each time you pick up a paintbrush? To maintain some notion of influence-free "artistic purity"? Why would you want to ignore seeing how other artists have achieved their effects, or tackled problems and resolved them, or found innovative ways to use color and form, or made hideous mistakes and miscalculations? We get the same sort of craft instruction from reading—observing how it's done so that we can do it in our own sweet way. But okay, let's not get too lofty here. Plain language: Two students apply for a writing job; give me the one who reads the cereal box in the morning, not the one who stares into space as he shovels in the Froot Loops.

Which brings me to words. The second thing I tell student journalists—after telling them that I can't tell them how to write—is that, unless they are TV reporters or photojournalists, the only device they have for conveying their stories is words. So the more tools in your toolbox, the better. The English language contains upwards of a half-million words; most Americans limp along with vocabularies of well under 10 percent of that number. So how many words have you got at your command? When you've finished counting, get back to me.

But size of vocabulary is not an end in itself, and in fact an oversized toolbox can easily trip you up. (What's the point of using words that only baffle the average reader?) More important than just accumulating words is developing a sensitivity to exactitude and nuance. Listen to this: Eight girls are somewhat under average weight. One is thin, one is trim, one is lean, one is willowy, one is slim, one is slender, one is svelte, one is skinny. All eight are perceived differently depending on which adjective we apply to which, and if you're a writer you had better be attuned to those differences. Similarly, there's a difference in writing "The provost refused to answer the question" and "The provost declined to answer the question." Being alert to these and a few thousand other distinctions in the language will be no end of help to your success as a writer.

To put it another way: Use the right word, and not the word that's almost right. It's like the difference between, oh, say, being sighted in a display of public nudity and being cited for a display of public nudity. In the first instance you were simply observed. In the second, you got busted.

So how do you achieve this mastery of subtlety and nuance? Ask me how you get to Carnegie Hall. (If you don't happen to know the punch line to that hoary old joke, it's "Practice.") Practice won't make you perfect. But it will make you professional.

WHO WROTE THIS MESS?

A few words about bylines. Bylines are earned, they're not given as a given. This means that if reporters haven't done some original reporting—like maybe they just rewrote a press release—their stories should simply be credited as "By *Slaverhound* Reporter" or "By *Slaverhound* Staff." By the same token, if a reporter turns in a story that requires massive rewriting or additional reporting, that reporter doesn't deserve his or her name in print. And for the reporter who added some bits to a story but didn't do the majority of the reporting, keep the option of adding at the end of the article, in italics, *Skippy Scribe contributed to this story.* Bottom line: Awarding bylines too readily cheapens their value.

FINALLY

Finally, as mentioned in chapter 1, the more reporting info, guidelines, and so forth that editors can put down on paper to hand to novice reporters, the more smoothly the reporting should go.

6

Investigative Journalism

Thanks mainly to movies and TV, the term *investigative journalism*, also called *enterprise* or *in-depth reporting*, conjures up romantic images of fearless journalists uncovering low morals in high places, of heroic news hawks revealing deeply buried scandals and secrets, of the reporter-as-detective if not savior-of-Western-civilization. In short, Butch Cassidy and the Sundance Kid Bring Down President Nixon.

Well, it's not exactly quite like that. True, the investigative journalist attempts to get the story behind the story. In doing so, this journalist often seeks to uncover information that someone, for a variety of reasons, justifiable or not, may prefer not be made public. But this does not mean that the investigative journalist is driven by a desire to provoke scandal. Nor does it mean that the investigative journalist aims at seeing some malefactor carted off in chains. Investigative journalism, moreover, does not mean reporters functioning as self-appointed law enforcement agents, vigilantes, or adjuncts to the district attorney's office. No, investigative journalism simply involves reporting deeply and thoroughly on a subject so that readers will have a fuller understanding of a matter than they would likely get from a standard news story.

For this reason, an investigative journalist more accurately resembles less some rootin' tootin' hero and more a drone beavering away in a dusty archive or a graduate student hacking away at computer databases. (Virtually every Pulitzer Prize awarded for investigative journalism in the past decade or more has gone to reporters who most likely could not have done their stories without the resources available on the Internet or via databases.) To be sure, it's the reporter who does the story—not Google or Yahoo—but the fact remains that, more often than not, when we talk about investigative journalism, we're talking about computer-assisted reporting.

THE COMPUTER ASSIST
Computers, for example, are playing an ever-growing role in one of the most common of investigatory pursuits: compiling the personal profile. Let's say your college announces the appointment of a new member of the institution's board of trustees. (What exactly does a board of trustees do? I must look that up some day.) Accordingly, the campus PR office issues a press release extolling the new board member's bio—his educational background, his accomplishments in the local business community, his public service, his kindness to dumb animals, the usual guff. But let's say the student newspaper wants to know more about this dude. What more might one find? These days, just about anything. Traditionally, an investigative reporter might start a profile by accessing public records, usually at the county courthouse (or at other municipal, county, or state offices) and increasingly these records are available online, so a trip to the dusty stacks may not even be necessary. What might an investigator find? The assessed value of the man's home, the tax record of his property, outstanding liens and mortgages on the property, all this information, and more, is available to the public. Has your new trustee served in the armed forces? Has he registered to vote? Has he made campaign contributions? Is the man married? Has he ever been divorced? What are the details of his divorce settlement? Does he own a dog? Does he own a car? What kind? Does he own a business? Has he ever applied for a business loan from a government agency? Has he ever declared bankruptcy? You find that he runs a restaurant. What ratings has the board of health given that restaurant? You note that the restaurant has no liquor license. Has he ever applied for one? You find that he has but he was turned down. Why? Has the man a police record? Hey, he was convicted of felonious assault with a deadly weapon. Why is this guy on your college's board of trustees?

Yep, you can amass a great deal of information on an individual, much of it from your office computer workstation, some of it by visiting the appropriate offices in your local or county records offices. The same is true about many other aspects of your campus. Let's say, for example, your university announces a long-overdue major renovation and upgrading of your outmoded natural sciences building. Cool. Once again, the PR office puts out a news release boasting about the multi-million-dollar rebuilding plan. Fine, but you're also curious about the story behind the story. How was the upgrading decided upon and designed? What problems if any had to be overcome in the project? What environmental issues (asbestos, lead paint, etc.) obtain in the current building, which is so old it is the object of campus jokes? In fact, were the elevators, wiring, and other aspects of the physical plant up to code? Had the building been inspected regularly? And what did those inspections reveal? How was the contract for the renovation awarded? Where is the money coming from? What local, state, and federal agencies, if any, are involved in the project, and in what manner?

Most of this information should be readily available, either from the university's budgetary and other financial reports, or from the relevant government agencies. Public universities are normally required to provide more open access to their records than are private institutions, but even the latter will make a remarkable amount of information available, at the least to avoid the charge of excessive secrecy, and because increasingly, private institutions receive some public money and are therefore likely to be more forthcoming about their affairs than they were in the past. Moreover, what the college doesn't make public, your public agencies often will.

PUBLIC RECORDS AND THE PUBLIC

Ah, but you say, how am I supposed to find all this stuff? You say you don't know the difference between the county clerk and the county auditor, the Bureau of Licenses and the Department of Motor Vehicles, a zoning board and a skateboard. To which I respond, this is where you thank your parents for spending all that money on your orthodontics. To which you demand, Hah?

Be patient, I'll explain. Look, one of the most marked differences between you and your professors is that while your profs all have brown and crooked teeth, your generation has nothing but perfect and dazzling smiles. So this is where you put those smiles to good use. Of course, visiting the labyrinthine archives of government bureaucracy for the first time is intimidating and bewildering. That's why you go to the borough hall, county clerk of courts, or whatever and you beam your smile, tug your forelock, act deferential, and plead your case. More often than not, the folks who staff these offices are going to be helpful to you. In fact, they have to be; that's their job. And the second time you visit, you'll know some of the drill, so that helps; and in each subsequent visit you'll know how to focus your searches better and the job gets easier. But keep that gorgeous smile at the ready.

I do not, however, wish to paint too sunny a picture regarding public records. Journalists and others attempting to access public records often encounter problems, and these usually fall into two categories. The first situation runs something like this: The reporter comes into a public records office with a clear notion of what records should be public (this information usually can be found easily enough by accessing the public records legislation and guidelines on your state's government Web site). However, the clerk behind the counter—or the cop behind the desk—is ignorant of the law regarding open records and stonewalls the reporter. Or sometimes the clerks simply don't approve of the open records law (maybe because it means more work for them), or they feel proprietary and overly protective of their records. None of these reasons is valid for denying you access to records, but you may have to patiently explain the law, or cajole, or pound a desk, or demand to see a supervisor, or write letters to get what you want. Again, this stonewalling doesn't happen very often, but it happens often enough. And sometimes just trying to see the arrest reports at a local police station can earn you a threat of arrest for harassing a police officer.

The other large category of problems in accessing public records involves records not being made public, for whatever reason. In these instances you may have to formally request the data you need. If you're dealing with a federal agency, you'll likely have to request your information via an application as outlined in the Freedom of Information Act (full information on FOIA is available from the U.S. Justice Department Web site, www.usdoj.gov/04foia). The Freedom of Information Act, first passed in 1966 and enhanced in 1974 in the wake of the Watergate scandal, mandates federal documents being made available to the public, every federal agency having an officer who will respond promptly to requests from the public for documents, and so on. Similarly, each state has a law, called Freedom of Information or Public Records Access or something like that, covering its government records. Be aware, however, that these laws are not comprehensive. The federal FOIA, for example, allows for no fewer than nine exceptions to public access to records, including things like criminal cases still under investigation, matters of national security, commercial trade secrets, and certain information regarding gas and oil exploration. State laws are usually similarly circumscribed. In addition, reporters have often found to their dismay that some documents they do manage to pry out of government file cabinets are heavily redacted; the CIA, FBI, and Justice Department, for example, often have names and other pertinent information blacked out on their documents. Appeal mechanisms are built into FOIA laws, and often appeals will yield better results. But the process can be frustrating and time-consuming.

To be sure, in most of the investigations conducted by student journalists whether preparing a personal profile or looking into a campus building project—the obstacles described above won't arise; I just thought you should be forewarned. At worst the most common sort of problem the student investigative reporter will encounter is the odd grumpy records clerk who, like the supercilious reference librarian, will resent being disturbed from his routine by your inquiries. But in my experience and in that of my students, most individuals are more than happy to help expedite your requests. So polish your smile and go for it.

DIG (INTO) THIS

Beyond the realm of the public records paper chase, the student newspaper reporter has plenty of opportunity for practicing investigative journalism. This is especially true if your newspaper is not a daily. Publishing on a weekly or even twice-weekly schedule often means you're going to be late with breaking news. One good way to compensate for that deficiency is to supply your readers an abundance of in-depth, behind-the-news articles.

We've already suggested some investigatory work in the previous chapter. That chapter focused on getting the basic story, but when I discussed the fire in the student apartment I moved into the story-behind-the-story. Indeed, it might be said that any time a reporter goes beyond reporting spot news, such as describing a car accident or summarizing a speech by a university administrator, and seeks out additional sources, then the reporter is engaging in investigative journalism.

Still, many a student journalist might think, Heck, I write just for a college newspaper. What kind of investigative journalism could I possibly do? My response: You'd be surprised. And if you're not doing it you're not serving your readers as well as you could.

Viewed as an entire society in miniature, the college campus is a rich and ripe venue for investigative journalism. What merits such in-depth reporting? Just about everything.

Let's take a couple of examples. My examples won't be original, because I don't think any original ideas remain in journalism: Most of the things to be done in journalism were done by 1800. But that doesn't mean they're not worthy of doing again and again. The two-headed chicken story and the corrupt sheriff scandal made for good articles two hundred years ago and still do today. (Of course, if you find me a corrupt two-headed sheriff story I'll ... where was I?) Oh, yes. So, if my examples are of investigations that have already been carried out on numerous campuses, that hardly means they shouldn't be done on yours. To the contrary, if they were worthwhile doing once, they're most likely worthwhile doing again.

The first example goes like this: Faced with the increasingly common problem of too many cars on campus, the university administration authorizes the introduction of parking meters in the lots adjacent to several college buildings. The installation of the meters is the basis of a news story, amplified by the standard disapproving noises from students. Then after the grumbling dies down, let's say a reporter decides to dig into the subject of parking meters. Like virtually all investigative stories, this one begins with questions. So perhaps he wonders: Just how accurate are these new infernal machines?

An investigation into this matter might take the form of a simple test. The parking meters supposedly allow ten minutes of parking for ten cents. So the reporter sticks dimes into ten meters and times them. If he finds the meters function accurately, well, that's a testament to American technology. But if he finds some meters yield only eight and a half minutes for a dime, others allow nine minutes, another eleven minutes, and so on (as has been found to be the case with some meters) well, that might make for an interesting story. Go further. The meters promise thirty minutes for a quarter? Get out your stopwatch and engage in some capital expenditure once more. Interesting results? The reporter now may have not only a bigger story, but who knows, maybe the basis for a class-action lawsuit as well.

What that reporter has just done in answering that single question—are the meters accurate?—is investigative journalism. It's a fairly limited form of investigative journalism, but it might still be enough to yield an interesting follow-up to the original story announcing the adoption of campus parking meters. At the very least, the meter test could make for an amusing news feature that depicts the intrepid reporter racing among parking meters, coins in one hand and stopwatch in the other and notebook between his teeth.

But wait, our reporter asked and answered only one question about the parking meters—how trustworthy are they? Now, as the breathless reporter contemplates all the hard cash he's devoted to these no-armed bandits (presumably his newspaper will compensate him—upon presentation of receipts, heh-heh), new questions are arising. How many meters have been installed, and how was the number determined? How much money do these meters collect in a day? Where does the revenue go? Does the university make money off of these meters? Are the meters purchased or rented, and who paid for their installation? Since these meters have proved to be inaccurate, why were they selected? Were meters of other manufacture available? Are more accurate meters indeed on the market, or are they all about the same? How was the contract for these meters awarded? And considering that the university now has to pay meter attendants to check the meters and write tickets for violators, just how cost-effective are parking meters? And ultimately, do they really have the desired impact on overcrowded parking lots?

That's a dozen questions about the economics of parking meters, and it's quite likely that as the reporter starts seeking their answers even more questions will arise.

VOICES FROM THE BACK ROW

Okay, now I'll field some of your objections to the parking meter story.

The first complaint I hear is, "Hey, all those questions! It would take me weeks to track down the answers." To which I say, Okay, take weeks. Just get a good story.

The second cry I hear (am I guided by voices?) is, "But heck, it's just parking meters. Is this worth all that investigating?" To which I reply: Well, deciding on stories is always a judgment call. But I don't think this story is just about parking meters. I think it's about, among other things, students' money, and since students, like real people, are concerned about their money, isn't that worth investigating?

Next complaint: "But hey, some of those questions sound mighty hard to research. Can I really find answers to those questions?" To which I have several responses. First, if investigative journalism is to be worthy of the name, why should it be easy? Second, my view is that 999 times out of 1,000 the information you want is out there—it's just a matter of finding it. And third, why don't you quit whining and start investigating already?

"But how can I do that?" complains crybaby number four. To which I respond, This is not like analyzing the intricacies of the Pentagon's selling an advanced weapons system to a foreign nation—we're talking parking meters, for heaven's sake. Does the college administration have the info on the parking meter decision and the contract? Does it have a reason for keeping such information secret? Has it the facts and figures on the parking meter revenue? Can you get in touch with the meter manufacturer, whose name is probably right there on those diabolical devices? Is there such a thing as a trade journal for the parking meter industry? Have studies been done on the efficacy of parking meters? Do you know how to use a library—and do you know how to Google?

Do the job right and your problem won't be finding enough interesting stuff; your problem will be the same one most other investigative journalists have to contend with: uncovering more good stuff than can be used. (And hey, if along the way you just happen to discover that the parking meter franchise is controlled by the university president's brother-in-law, all the better.)

Okay, time's run out on that example. You've turned in your thirteen-part series on parking meters and your editor has sent you off to the college counseling services for psychiatric evaluation. Now let's look at another investigative campus topic. This one is more frequently done than parking meter studies. But according to the stories I've seen, it's not frequently done well.

TEXT MESSAGES

It's the beginning of the semester and students are grumbling about the high cost of textbooks at the campus bookstore. Or it's the end of the semester and students are grumbling about the cheesy buy-back policies at the campus bookstore. Yes, the perennial question of campus bookstore economics.

It's an excellent question, or series of questions. This again is an issue concerning your readership's hard-pressed wallets. You can never investigate such matters enough. You certainly can never inquire into the campus bookstore enough.

The thinnest article I ever read on this subject ran to the order of a reporter quoting some students bitching and moaning about the cost of textbooks and then quoting at length a self-congratulatory, self-serving interview with the campus bookstore manager who stoutly maintained, "While we are subject to costs established by the publishers, our sole purpose is and always has been supplying books to students at the lowest possible price."

End of story. Value of story to readers: zip.

But here's an entirely different approach to the subject: Using funds provided by her newspaper, a reporter enters the campus bookstore and buys new copies of six of the college's most widely used textbooks. She does the same at a privately owned off-campus bookstore in town. She then compiles prices for these books from several online textbook sales sites. She contacts the publishers and determines the wholesale prices of the books and then calculates the mark-up of the stores she has visited. She visits the Web site of the National Association of College Auxiliary Services (a campus bookstore association) for its sales guidelines. Then after some time she visits the stores again and purchases used copies of the same books at the two bookstores and checks out their prices on the Web. Eventually she sells back the books she's purchased to determine the buy-back rates of the various vendors. She does some research to determine what methods of textbook sales exist on other campuses and discovers student-run cooperative stores, textbook swap fairs, and other innovative book programs. She also looks into the financial structure of the campus bookstore; is this a university-run entity or is it simply a private entrepreneur's enterprise for which the university provides space in the student union building? Whatever the case, what kind of overhead does this campus bookstore have? Does it pay rent and utility costs to the university? What about business and property taxes, and how does all this compare to the overhead of the privately owned bookshop in town?

Next the reporter analyzes all her data, which she has carefully organized and filed. Then—and only after she is well informed on her subject—she embarks on a series of interviews with the bookstore managers, with the appropriate university officials, with professors who assign textbooks, with student shoppers, and so on. Now she has more information to analyze. But she's on her way to a comprehensive story that will truly inform her readers on the economics of textbooks.

"But wait," you say, "isn't that an awful lot of work? After all, I have a biology midterm to worry about!" To which I reply, okay, it's a fair amount of work. And maybe that's why investigative reporters often work in teams.

Sigh of relief.

Sure, make it a team effort. Wise news editors will assign their best computer nerd to the Web-based part of the investigation, their best graphics person to work up some comparative price charts, their best interviewers to the interviews, and the reporter with the strongest arms to do the book-buying and schlepping part of the story. In any event, whether it's a lone reporter or a team of two or more, I don't really think doing this story is all that demanding; it should be a matter of days or weeks at the most. And your biology exam can't compare in any way with what your investigation might find out.

So what might you find out? After all your fact gathering and analysis, you might unmask your campus bookstore as such a hotbed of rip-off artists that a grassroots campaign gets under way to develop an alternative method of marketing and reselling texts. Cool. Conversely, your facts might indicate that, hey, your campus bookstore manager was right, it really is providing the best service and the best prices to the students. Does that mean your investigation was a failure? Not in the least. There's no shame in presenting good news to your readers. Remember—investigative journalism is propelled by questions, not by predetermined agendas. In an investigation you don't set out to "nail" anybody; you set out to find the truth. So either way—scandal, accolade, or perhaps some third way in between—you've performed valuable public service. You've thoroughly informed your community on a situation. You've done your job.

MONEY MONEY MONEY

Both of the examples above—parking meters and textbooks—involve money, and following the money, as Deep Throat advised Bob Woodward and Carl Bernstein (if only in the film version of *All the President's Men*), is more often than not a fruitful pursuit for the investigative journalist. Just think of all the money issues on your campus that might be worth looking into:

1. Tuition. How is the cost determined and where does the money actually go?
2. Activity fees. Same questions as above.
3. Scholarships, athletic and otherwise. Who's getting money, for what, and how much?

4. Meal programs. How are these determined, and are alternatives available?
5. Housing. On campus and off campus, how does the price of shelter compare with that at other colleges in the area?
6. Financial aid. How much is available, who gets it, and why? What's the trend in aid over the years—getting better or worse? And why?
7. Student employment. How many students work at the university, how are the wage rates set, are the students really serfs?
8. Salaries. Administrators, faculty, staff. Who's overpaid, who's underpaid?
9. Maintenance. How much does it cost to keep this campus up and running?
10. Fund-raising. Gifts, grants, endowments, the alumni association—how are we doing?

That's another of my quick ten topics, and you should be able to think of many more. Any of these is likely worthy of investigating, for the simple reason that they all have some degree of impact on your readership. And of course any of the topics listed above can be broken down into subtopics, meaning that you might get more than one story from this area of inquiry—or perhaps a whole series. Take, for example, number 3, athletic scholarships. Which sports get the most money, and why? How is this decided? How are the scholarship awards prioritized? Are any sports being neglected or otherwise treated unfairly in regard to scholarships available? How much latitude does the college have in designing its scholarship program, and how much is determined by athletic associations or other agencies? Are male and female athletes being treated fairly in regard to scholarships? How does the scholarship program affect athletic recruitment? How does your college's athletic scholarship program compare to that of similar colleges? Where does your college's scholarship money come from? Does your athletic department feel it has enough scholarship funds? What would it do if it had more funding? Is the department planning to increase its scholarship program? What are the overall prospects for the future of athletic scholarships?

Any one of these questions might yield a story that your readers will relish. So—follow the money.

But be aware, too, that some topics are going to be more difficult to investigate than others. For example, access to financial information will vary from campus to campus. This may result from the particular culture of a campus—its tradition of informational openness. Access will also depend on whether or not your college is a public or private institution. In short, sometimes all you'll have to do is request the information and you'll get it. But sometimes you'll have to pry it out. In other instances you may have to file suit to get what you want. In addition, while state and federal laws may require certain information be made available to the public, laws also protect the privacy of other information. Therefore, one of the first things student journalists should do when launching investigations is to familiarize themselves with laws regulating what kind of information may or may not be made available. I'll discuss legal issues more in chapter 17, but for the moment I'll just mention that such organizations as the Student Press Law Center (www.splc.org) and Investigative Reporters and Editors, Inc. (www.ire.org) can be very helpful in this arena. And for heaven's sake, don't overlook the many good resources right there on your campus, like law professors and other persons with relevant expertise.

THE SENSITIVE AND THE SECRETIVE
Beyond money, a lot of other sensitive topics exist on campus that might prove fruitful for enterprising reporters. One such topic is campus crime. Another is affirmative action and minority issues. Another is sex and sexual abuse. Another is drinking and drugs. Another is hazing. Another is grades and class ranking. Yet another is compliance with regulations—whether it's the American with Disabilities Act or the National Collegiate Athletic Association rules on recruitment and eligibility. Gays, women's issues, religious groups, speech codes, political action committees—gee, what a controversial campus you have.

You betcha, and student journalists should not shy away from any topic just because it is controversial, or because rules and regulations might make accessing pertinent information difficult. There probably are legal limitations on the dozen or so topics I've just listed—but that doesn't mean you can't write stories on these topics. What it does mean is that you inform yourself on your rights and limitations and you proceed accordingly—and with care.

Sensitive topics, however, come with their own baggage, and a common piece of that baggage involves people who don't want to be quoted on the record. This is a phenomenon in lots of reporting, but especially in investigative stories dealing with hot, or potentially hot, topics. You may find a student, for example, who alleges that during an office conference her professor made lewd suggestions to her. You may run across an athlete who claims that on a recent road trip the coach slipped off to a casino and blew thousands of dollars. You may hear from a student government officer that members of the student government have been using the organization's credit cards to pay for phone sex. All very juicy stuff. Trouble is, each source fears retribution or at least embarrassment and will not allow his or her name to be used in connection with these charges in print.

The anonymous source is one of the most nettlesome issues journalists face. You may have an informant whom you believe is eminently credible and who is making very serious charges and who has an understandable desire for anonymity. But if you can't put a name to the allegation, why should the reader put any credence in the story? Indeed, is it fair to publicize an allegation against someone without revealing the name of the accuser? Not in our democratic tradition it isn't.

This is why mainstream news organizations acknowledge that using anonymous sources is undesirable. Yet these same news organizations frequently do the undesirable thing, because in their judgment the anonymous source's information is both believable and important to get before the public. Often the news story will attempt to explain why the source demanded anonymity ("The source spoke on condition that his name not be used for fear of jeopardizing his job or of getting the crap beat out of him"). This may go a step toward reassuring the reader the source is trustworthy, but it's a small step. And why should someone accused of malfeasance even bother to answer an anonymous allegation?

Nevertheless, even as journalists acknowledge the messiness of using anonymous sources, they maintain that the option for anonymity should remain. Too often, they say, we simply can't get important inside information if we can't promise anonymity to a source. Indeed, some journalists—Bob Woodward, for one—believe the press doesn't use anonymous sources enough. Without his Deep Throat, for example, Woodward says he and his partner Bernstein wouldn't have had, among many other things, that important money trail to follow.

Then of course there are other ramifications of using anonymous sources. You may promise a source confidentiality, but if a criminal matter is involved, the cops or the district attorney might get a court order that requires a reporter, professional or student, to reveal a source. Noncompliance with this demand could mean being fined and/or jailed for contempt of court. Now you're caught between the rock of your promise and the hard place of being ordered to break that promise. This is precisely the situation in which former *New York Times* reporter Judith Miller found herself in the 2005 investigation into the leaking of a CIA agent's name; when Miller insisted on keeping her promise to protect her source, she wound up spending eighty-five days in jail, an experience she did not much enjoy.

It gets even messier. Most states have so-called shield laws to protect journalists from such legal pressures, but these laws are far from comprehensive. Shield laws normally have enough exceptions that reporters may still be compelled by law to reveal sources. Knowing this, sources understandably may clam up when talking to reporters—even when those reporters promise not to reveal their names. This clamming up is known as the chilling effect—a cutting off of often vital information to the press. Thus around and around it goes.

So what's a poor student investigative reporter to do? First of all, some perspective: Most colleges and universities are not cesspools of high crimes and misdemeanors. Yet while we may agree on that, some people on your green and pleasant campus still may know about things they wish kept from the public eye, and if they are willing to talk about them they may do so only off the record. Thus you should be prepared for the eventuality of a source suddenly demanding anonymity in return for information. If such a request comes your way, think two and three times before making a promise to that effect. Do everything you can to get your source to speak on the record. (It's surprising how many times, after some judicious cajoling, sources will finally give in and agree to having their names attached to their information.) Failing that effort, make every attempt to get this information elsewhere. (In any event, you'd want confirmation—that is, multiple sources—of serious allegations.) Failing that, ask yourself if it is justifiable from an ethical and moral standpoint to run a story with unnamed sources accusing someone of malfeasance of misbehavior. Failing that test, tell yourself you just may have failed to get the story. That happens to reporters. We don't like it when it happens, but sometimes, because we couldn't properly wrap it up or nail it down, we just have to let a story go.

TATTOO YOU

But let's not get too melodramatic here. Again, most of the investigative stories you might pursue are not going to involve meeting shadowy, anonymous informants in underground parking garages in the dead of night. Most investigations involve much more conventional kinds of fact gathering. Let's look at such a story.

Tattoos are a tried, true, and even trite topic that has been written about in countless student newspapers—yet you still might do a good story on the subject. Tattoos would most likely be considered a trend story, and since virtually all stories begin with questions, you might inquire into the state of the trend: Are tats rising or falling in popularity? What percentage of students on your campus have tattoos? What are the most popular designs? Who has 'em, where do they wear 'em, where did they get 'em, at what age did they get 'em, how do they feel about 'em now that they've got 'em, and how common are removals? The areas of inquiry are manifold. The question here is how to gather such information.

Probably the most reasonable route to determine the state of tattoos on your student body (groan!) is to conduct a poll. Now polling is a science, and to understand it fully you'd be wise to consult some texts on psychology, sociology, maybe political science and math. For our purposes I'm just going to make some general observations about conducting polls.

First of all, it is very easy to conduct a useless poll. A reporter can stand outside the cafeteria and try to buttonhole students as they head into and out of lunch. He may ask ten students about tattoos. He has conducted a poll. But in terms of valid information, his poll results are virtually meaningless. One reason is obvious. If you have ten thousand students on campus and you poll only ten, how meaningful is that? Yes, polling thirty or fifty or a hundred students sounds better—but it's really not. Why? It's a random sampling, isn't that fair and objective? Again, not really. It can be argued that the students who actually stop and take the time to answer your questions, as opposed to blowing you off, are those nerds who either are (a) temperamentally disposed to answer poll questions or (b) students who are interested enough in tattoos to reply to your questions. In other words, your poll respondents sound not random at all but rather a self-selected group. Beyond that, a pollster doesn't want a *random* sampling, he wants a *representative* sampling. This means if you want to gather stats on the tats covering the student body, you should examine that body properly. You must poll a representative sampling of both men and women students, as well as freshmen, sophomores, juniors, seniors, and graduate students, kids from a variety of majors, commuters and those who live on campus, and so on. And of course you shouldn't interview just ten or thirty or a hundred but a large and proportionate number in each of your categories of respondents. Moreover, to avoid getting responses from only those who for whatever reason are eager to answer your questions, you would do well to conduct your poll in some sort of controlled situation; in other words, instead of just standing outside the caf and waving a questionnaire at the passing crowd, you might do well to arrange with some profs to take ten minutes of their class time to have students fill out your tattoo forms.

Most important, you want to have the right questions formulated in the right manner. As Jack Rosenthal, a veteran *New York Times* executive, pointed out in a column in that newspaper in 2006, it is widely believed among pollsters that men are reluctant to admit they are "worried" about something. So instead of asking, for instance, if men are "worried about terrorism," pollsters consider it more meaningful to ask men if they are "concerned about terrorism." In addition, as important as word choice in poll questions is clarity. As an example, Rosenthal quoted the notorious "double negative" that figured in a July 1992 Roper poll question: "Does it seem possible or does it seem impossible to you that the Nazi extermination of the Jews never happened?" The finding: One of every five Americans seemed to doubt there had ever been a Holocaust. To many observers, however, that finding didn't seem to make any more sense than the original question. Roper subsequently asked a clearer question, and in the new poll the number of doubters dropped from the original 22 percent to 1 percent.

Likewise, asking "What do you think of tattoos?" is obviously general in the extreme. And asking "What is your view of permanently disfiguring the body with the so-called artwork of a tattoo?" is obviously leading and biased. In short, the worthiness of your polling results is going to be directly related to the worthiness of your questions.

To repeat: What's needed in polling is (a) weighing and crafting your questions very carefully; (b) seeking the same information from several directions; (c) not inundating the respondent with too many questions; (d) phrasing your questions so as to elicit hard and specific data; and (e) formatting your poll in an easy-to-respond manner.

As an example of this last, consider a multiple-choice question: (a) I am very happy with my tattoo; (b) I am fairly happy with my tattoo; (c) I don't think much about my tattoo; (d) I could do without my tattoo; (e) I'm really sorry I ever got the tattoo. Something like that. In addition, you'll want questions that elicit some information about the respondent (sex, age, major, etc.). You'll also want a substantial number of respondents—the more the better, but probably in the hundreds. It would also be useful to have some in-depth interviews to supplement, illuminate, and humanize your statistics; a few dozen such interviews would be good, from which you may then choose a number of representative and interesting voices. And you're still not finished. Interview some experts about tattoos—maybe a sociologist, an art historian, someone from the health center, operators of tattoo parlors. Still not done. Get on the Internet and see what studies of the subject have been conducted, find out how the trend looks on other campuses, learn about the history of tattooing and other "body modifications" (piercing, branding). I could go on and on.

Here come your objections. "Oh, man," I hear you moan, "that sounds like a lot of work." Well, guess what? This is why we call it investigative journalism.

"But," you continue complaining, undaunted, "there's so much info out there we could write a book about tattoos." Yes, and many have. But I'm not suggesting you write a book. I'm simply suggesting you write an article that tells the readers something interesting and illuminating about tattoos on their campus. Do the article properly and you'll have done the definitive piece on the subject. Do the article in a quick and haphazard manner and you'll have a mildly entertaining piece that has little or no true informational value.

There. Tattoo that on your skull.

7

Opinions

Let's get the key point up front and fast. You've all heard the old saw "Everyone is entitled to his (or her) opinion." I hope you recognize this adage for its unusual character, for it is at once true and meaningless. What do I mean by that? Well, consider this: "Everyone is entitled to belt out 'My Way' in a karaoke bar."

Got that? The First Amendment to the U.S. Constitution clearly guarantees every citizen the right to sing karaoke. But that doesn't mean all citizens should exercise that right. Or if they do, that we have to listen. Or that we all wouldn't be infinitely better off if we simply took up a collection and sent the wannabe warbler home in a taxi.

It is generally agreed that opinion has a place in the news media, but that place is not in the news pages or in the main segment of the news broadcast. Some news weeklies, radio talk shows, and *Fox News* have gone a long way to undermine this venerable view, but the general agreement on keeping opinion out of news remains.

Fact is, readers and viewers like to read and hear opinions. Op-Ed, which stands for either "opinions and editorials" or "opposite the editorial page" or an individual article appearing on such a page, is among the most widely read offerings in a newspaper, and very much so in student newspapers. We like to learn how the experts interpret things, even if we disagree with them, or maybe even because we like to disagree with them. (A writer has really arrived when the writer becomes someone the readers love to hate.) Among the most popular items in the opinion pages are readers' letters, about which I will have more to say below, but for now let's focus on one phrase that appeared a moment ago and that might have rushed past you: "how the *experts* interpret things."

Possessing expertise, or at least possessing an informed foundation, is what makes an opinion worth sharing. This is the equivalent in karaoke of having a good set of pipes, a sense of rhythm and pitch, and maybe a winning personality to boot. Everyone is entitled to take up the microphone, yeah, sure, but that is not at all the issue. What makes a writer's opinion worth heeding is how knowledgeable that writer is—in other words, the writer's command of the facts. Not coincidentally, this is the very same thing that makes a news writer credible.

Let's put it another way. Every person on the newspaper staff—and very likely every reader—has an opinion on abortion. Or on the death penalty. Or on tuition costs. Or on any number of other hot-button issues. In addition, if pressed, everybody probably could pump out a seven-hundred-word opinion piece on any one of those topics. But guess what? Some of those pieces are going to be a lot more worthwhile than others. Why? Because while everybody has "feelings" about issues, feelings don't amount to much in terms of convincing discourse. Everybody has a right to feelings, but there just isn't much value in espousing those feelings to everybody else. Ah, but the informed individual—yes, that person qualifies to share his or her views. And the more informed such writers are, the more legitimate is their claim to our attention.

I'm beating this horse (no animals were actually harmed in the writing of this chapter) because familiarity with the facts is the crucial criterion for determining whether or not an opinion piece deserves to be published. I've heard far too many editors defend the publication of an opinion piece on that "everyone's right to an opinion" argument. Well, take that "right to an opinion" and toss it out the window. (Well, no, but put it in the back of a lower desk drawer.) You don't want my article on the game of cricket (I'm not British and have never seen a cricket match, not that it would help). You shouldn't publish my piece on what it means to be an Asian woman in America (two big strikes against me). And you sure as hell don't want to hear my version of "My Way."

Now it would be very nice if the opinion pieces in your newspaper could be written by experts. But unless you've opened your columns to syndicated columnists—or maybe to your professors—you're probably relying on students to express their opinions. That in fact happens to be how I think it should be. Trouble is, most students don't have much expertise in foreign affairs, economics, law, and all those other heavy-duty, industrial-strength subjects (it's something else if we're talking Dungeons and Dragons or beer pong or the NBA or accessorizing). Still, expertise aside, student writers can be informed. And when they do inform themselves—by reading up on the death penalty, by researching the history of tuition costs at your college—then they are validated to pontificate in your opinion pages.

Indeed, it is commonly held in journalistic circles that the best opinion columns and essays are those based on reporting. That almost sounds paradoxical, but you should see the point. Sure, some opinionistas can perch in their lofty offices high above the gritty streets and conjure up interesting columns out of the clouds—the think pieces we call thumbsuckers. But such philosopher-kings are rare. The best purveyors of opinion, it seems to me, are those who get out in the world, collect the data, then analyze and interpret the facts for the rest of us in their columns or editorials.

I suggest that student editors should keep all that in mind when they're assigning a piece for the editorial page, or when they're evaluating a submission. And if the reporting-based column sounds like more work than the piece merely based on feelings and attitudinizing and philosophizing, then so be it. Worthwhile writing *is* hard work. Dirty little secret, but there it is.

WHAT'S THE (EDITORIAL) MATTER?

The stuff we stuff into the editorial and opinion pages comes in about five varieties. Since students often confuse or misuse their designations, let's take them one at a time.

The Newspaper Speaks

An *editorial* generally refers to an unsigned article that represents the view of the newspaper as a whole. The piece is unsigned because it ostensibly speaks for the entire editorial board; this presupposes the editors have discussed and reached a consensus on an issue (e.g., the campus food service contractor sucks and should be replaced). The editorial may be written by any member of the staff, although often the staff has one or more designated editorial writers. Editorials alternatively may be written on a rotation basis by editors, or they may be written solely by the editor in chief. Editorials may appear in every issue, or only now and again, or only when special occasions seem to demand them, or never. I've seen newspapers with all sorts of authoring and editorial scheduling; it's all up to you. (In any event, it's good policy to disclose the names of your editorial writers in your masthead.) As for content, editorials can cover everything from campus developments to world events to the first robin spotted this spring—but probably the best ones will deal with issues that affect your readers (military service sounds more germane than Medicare drug plans). There's an argument for not running editorials. But I think there's a stronger argument for having them. ("Okay, your news story described the new campus meal plan, but it's confusing; now tell us, is this really a good deal?") In line with this latter view, newspapers usually see the editorial as an opportunity—as a service to their readers—to express the opinion and judgment the reporters have rightly kept out of their news stories. There's another interesting view that says editorials should not tell readers what to think—but rather what to think about. Many editorialists see that as wishy-washy, but I rather like that attitude; if nothing else, it's a fence against editorial arrogance.

A few final points on editorials. First, as with all opinion pieces, the best will be those that are supported by a full and fair assessment of facts. Second, the best will shorter rather than longer; only the most extraordinary of circumstances, it seems to me, should require an editorial to rattle on for paragraph after paragraph; length will likely only dull your point, just as the swordsman with the longest saber doesn't always win (but no, I don't really want to go there). Third, editorials should always be readily identified as editorials, either by a logo or by distinct headline style and font or by regular placement on the editorial page; whatever the identifying device, a reader shouldn't mistake an editorial for a news story.

Roamin' Columns

The column normally refers to an opinion piece written by a member of the newspaper's editorial staff. This could be a reporter, an editor, or a pundit who does nothing but write opinion pieces. The column expresses a personal view of a topic, and it seems to me the best columns also have a distinct personality or voice. That is to say, a column by *The New York Times*'s Maureen Dowd sounds inimitably like Maureen Dowd, and the same is true of Jimmy Breslin,

Mike Royko, Red Smith, and H. L. Mencken. (You mean they all sound like Maureen Dowd?) Now one might argue many student journalists don't yet have their own unique styles or voices but in fact they do, and if these things haven't yet revealed themselves, they eventually will, especially if the writers write columns and especially if they write them on a regular basis. Writers can produce columns on a one-time basis, or only on those rare occasions when the spirit moves them, but usually the most enjoyable columns will be those that appear with some regularity, because it's in this fashion the writers get to exercise and develop the muscles of their individual voices, and it's here that the readers greet those familiar voices with anticipation (or loathing). Whatever the reaction, columnists have an opportunity to build a personal relationship with readers, and that can be a very gratifying experience—a reward that reporters rarely receive.

Now it's no easy thing to produce a column on a regular basis, but we're never interested in the easy thing anyway. (I once asked the Israeli writer Ephraim Kishon how he could produce a humorous newspaper column year after year six days a week. He simply shrugged and said it was his job; he added that he could produce humor even when he was feeling suicidal. Now that's what I call professionalism.) Yes, writing on a fixed schedule is a challenge, which is one reason why in the world of professional journalism being assigned a regular column is usually considered the highest of accolades. The writer should be deeply flattered, because the editor has implied that the writer is up to that challenge. Anyway, when student editors discover writers who seem to have a gift for the personal essay, the editors should cajole, bribe, stroke, and in any other way encourage those writers to produce. Whether the writer eventually pens a column once or twice a week or once or twice a month, it's great from the standpoint of both columnist and reader to establish and maintain that special relationship the regular column generates.

Columnists of course are free to write about anything. Some may specialize—world affairs, environmental issues—but columnists are probably better off if they don't set limits for themselves. Concentrate week after week on your own personal obsessions and you may find yourself with a readership of one (well, two if we count Mom). A personal column suggests your personal take on an issue, not your personal take on your personal navel. Note too that readers can tolerate and even enjoy some bitching and moaning, but overdo it and the readers will have something to bitch and moan about themselves.

As with all other Op-Ed writers, columnists should be information gathering rather than wool gathering. Indeed, when regular columnists moan that they have "nothing to write about" this week, that probably means they haven't been paying enough attention to the world around them.

When Outsiders Want In

Outside contributions should be welcomed. There was a time in journalism—and not that long ago—when "outside contributor" was an oxymoron; newspapers jealously reserved their pages for "professionals" and disdained anyone trying to muscle in on the act. Today for a variety of reasons editors view that as unnecessarily exclusionary and arrogant. You therefore would probably do well to have the little box on your Op-Ed page that encourages submissions to the opinions editor. You would also do well to have a set of guidelines for outside contributors available upon request and issued to anyone who does contribute. These guidelines can cover such things as style (referring the writer to the Associated Press style book or your own peculiarities), format (submit hard copy, electronically, on disk, keep a backup copy), and editing (informing the writer that all pieces can and will be edited for style, clarity, length, and taste) and perhaps even warning the writer about libel and other legal concerns.

Even as you welcome outside contributors, however, you should avoid making promises of acceptance, and you should always be wary about promising a date on which the piece will run. At best, you can tell a contributor that the submission looks good and you hope to use it soon. The reason for this constructive ambiguity is that a staff member might produce a better piece on the same subject, and the staff member, by virtue of his or her regular work for the newspaper, should have priority. Or another outside contributor might submit a superior piece on the same topic. Or you may have so many good pieces to run that the first piece you got simply keeps getting put back on the pile and before you know it the piece is no longer timely. Anyway, the idea is, if you don't make promises you won't have to break them.

About length: There's an axiom regarding opinion pieces that if the writers can't say what they need to say in seven hundred to nine hundred words, then they probably don't know what they want to say. There shouldn't be a hard and fast limit on length, but remember, most people these days have the attention span of garden gnomes. More seriously, the longer the piece, the more readers you're going to lose. Brevity is not only the soul of wit, it's also likely the soul of wisdom. And the longer the sword, the more unwieldy . . . but no, I vowed I'm not going that route.

Penultimately, Op-Ed columnists should be identified to the readers so as to give an indication of the writer's credibility and authority. Examples: If a columnist is complaining about conditions in the residence halls, the credit line might read: "Ivana Smith is a senior marketing major and a resident of Trump Hall." The dude who writes about water pollution might be identified this way: "Trey Hugger is a president of the Ecology Club." The political columnist might be identified thus: "Candy Cain chairs the campus Young Republicans."

Finally, absent staff writers who will take on the challenge of producing a regular column, editors should always keep an eye out for the one-offer who might be cultivated as a regular.

Take a Letter

Letters to the editor repeatedly rank in readers' polls up there with comic strips as among the most popular of all features in newspapers. This popularity disconcerts journalists; knowing that readers apparently enjoy what other readers (that is, amateurs) have to say more than what the professionals are publishing is hardly good for journalists' easily wounded egos, but there it is.

Keep in mind that the newspaper must treat readers' letters as editorial matter, which is to say the letters should be subjected to the same editorial principles of rigorous editing for style, taste, content, and legal concerns. On this last point, need I reiterate (yes, I need) that a letter containing a libel makes the newspaper liable (libel consists of *publishing* defamatory material), so just as you must be careful what you wish for, be careful what you publish. In other words, if Rosalie Reader writes a letter claiming that the captain of the equestrian team beats her horse, the newspaper publishing that letter is potentially as guilty of defamation as is Rosalie herself. (Provable truth would be a defense in a libel suit, but you can't bank on testimony in court from the horse to help your case.)

You would do well to have a notice box on the Op-Ed pages that at once welcomes letters to the editor and points out that letters should be concise, are subject to editing, and so forth and so on. You needn't lecture readers in the box on the legal and ethical aspects of publishing letters, but you should keep those matters in mind yourself when you're selecting and preparing letters for print.

On the subject of selecting letters to print, bear in mind you are under no obligation to print every letter you receive. Some letters are so poorly written that they may be beyond editorial repair. Others may be worthless in terms of their argumentation or logic. Others may be repetitive—there's little point in publishing a raft of letters making the same point. In this regard, since mainstream newspapers normally receive far more letters than they can print, they try to choose letters that fairly represent readers' opinions. There is also a view, but by no means a universal one, that letters published should reflect opinion on issues proportionate to the opinions expressed in letters received. That is, if 80 percent of correspondents write in to denounce a new tax proposal, it would be misleading, according to this view, simply to publish one letter for the proposal and one against. But not all editors agree with that; some argue that just allowing a range of views to appear in the letters column is sufficient, and that striving to suggest proportionality might also suggest endorsing the majority view. This matter of balance and proportionality remains a murky issue.

A few other important points remain about publishing letters. First, it is standard practice before publishing letters to verify that the signatories are actually who they say they are. It is all too common for pranksters or provocateurs to write letters—especially those of a critical or accusatory nature—and to sign false names or other people's names. Some of the nation's largest newspapers have been stung in the past by this ploy, which is why newspapers have safeguards in place now against such embarrassments. These safeguards generally run to phoning letter writers to confirm their identities. For this reason your invitational box should ask that correspondents include their full name, address, phone number, e-mail address, or whatever in their epistles.

Following up on this, when the letter is published, it is desirable to include after the writer's name a phrase or two identifying the correspondent: "Bill Overdew, senior business major," "George W. Bridge, class of '09," "Purple Hayes, Gay and Lesbian Alliance."

What do you do if a letter writer wishes to remain anonymous? Glad you asked. As a general principle the media endorse the view that readers have a right to know who's saying what, whether the person is a source quoted in a news story or the author of a letter. But just as the press accepts that a source's anonymity sometimes should be preserved, so there are sometimes compelling reasons to publish a letter signed "Name withheld upon request." You most likely would not withhold the name of a letter writer making a serious accusation ("My gym coach keeps watching me in the shower"), but you might well allow anonymity for a writer who is revealing something sensitive or possibly embarrassing ("I found it easy to cheat on an exam"; "I'm a virgin"). Consider requests for withholding names on a case-by-case basis, but consider carefully.

Also be wary of the temptation to print a letter (or anything else) simply because it's outrageous or especially foolish or otherwise likely "to really stir things up and piss people off." No, mere provocation is rarely if ever a good enough reason to see something into print. It's too easy to "stir things up" with the shameful or the shocking. Rather than publishing something controversial merely for controversy's sake, it's far more honorable—and challenging—to stimulate your readers with something that demands thinking about.

Finally, there's a charming adage in journalism that says: "Never argue with anyone who buys ink by the barrel." What this curious maxim means is that newspapers always hold the advantage over the reader in regard to having the last word. When a reader sends in a letter to the editor, it is often very tempting for the editor—or for some other staffer—to publish a reply to that letter. The temptation is especially hard to resist when the correspondent is griping about something. Examples: "I think your editorial on the death penalty really sucked." Or: "Your coverage of the fight at last Saturday's hockey game was incomplete and biased." Or: "Your review of the new DMB album was way off base—clean your ears!" My suggestion is to resist replying to such criticism—even if you deem such criticism as totally unfounded. The idea of publishing letters is to permit the readers a forum for sounding off. If you're going to shoot them down at every opportunity, readers will conclude there's not much point in sending you letters. Beyond that, replying is taking easy advantage from your vantage point atop all those barrels of ink. It's terribly tempting, not to mention satisfying, to have the last word, but it's not necessarily the gentlemanly thing to do. Chivalry is why I always allow my wife the final word (that and the fact that I can never think of an appropriate riposte until the following day). Certainly you may use the reply option to correct a misstatement of fact. That is, when a letter states, "This university has been proudly teaching Darwinism longer than Los Angeles has been the capital of California," you might gently point out the error. But you also might well ask yourself why you would publish such an error in the first place.

In sum, when it comes to letters, do the necessary weeding and pruning, but let a hundred flowers bloom. And if you get jabbed by a rose thorn or two, just lick your wounds and go your way. (And since I'm not doing much better with my garden metaphor than with my swordsman simile, enough said on the subject.)

Name That 'Toon

Editorial cartoons are in my opinion among the most delightful and terrifying of any material that appears in newsprint. They're delightful because some of the sharpest wits in the nation express themselves via the peculiar expedient of the editorial cartoon. Cartoons can also be terrifying in their power to impress an idea so forcefully into the mind; one editorial cartoon can sometimes convey a viewpoint more effectively than a score of analytical and interpretive articles. Despite the millions of words published about him in his lifetime, nothing is said to have affected Richard Nixon more profoundly than Herblock's cartoon on the editorial page of *The Washington Post* depicting the president climbing up out of a sewer. And need we mention that worldwide uproar over the Prophet Muhammad cartoons? It is just for such reasons *The New York Times* declines to publish any editorial cartoons. It views such drawings as blunt instruments, too reductive, too crude, too incapable of the kind of nuance and subtlety that newsworthy issues demand and that presumably the *Times* writers can deliver. Well, what does *The New York Times* know? Actually, a lot. If words can be devastating, so too can caricatures. Editorial graphics can be hilarious, but they can just as readily be wrenchingly cruel and unfair. It's not incidental that the term "graphic" has become a synonym for "violent" and "stomach-churning."

So keep that in mind. You needn't follow the lofty justification of the *Times* for eschewing editorial cartoons—hardly any other publication does—but you should be exquisitely sensitive to the capacity of cartoons to hurt. That said, here's hoping three hopes. The first is that you use editorial cartoons, the second is that you use good ones, and the third is that your cartoons are students' work. I hope this last hope because I know there are so many good professional editorial cartoons available to you at little or no cost, either via syndications or Web sites or whatever. But if you can fill your cartoon space with something ripped from an editorial service or Web site, why not fill the entire paper with such ready-made canned text, save yourself a lot of time and grief in the newsroom, and spend the night playing Texas Hold 'em instead?

In short, I think a student newspaper should be student reported, student written, student edited, student designed, student photographed, student financed, and student cartooned. For some reason, finding student cartoonists is usually difficult, but you should try. Start by badgering campus art professors and art students; with luck, you just may uncover the next Garry Trudeau.

8

Features

Feature material is essentially anything that appears in your pages other than news reports, Op-Eds, sports, and advertising. While your newspaper may have a clearly designated section called Features (or Living or Forum or Inside or Lifestyle or Hear and Now or any of the other unimaginative and overused rubrics that appear in newspapers throughout the nation), feature stories can slop over into some of the other parts of your paper. Several of the stories I referred to in the chapters on news and investigative reporting, for example, might well be categorized as feature stories. An interview with a student whose fiancée is serving in Iraq would be considered a news feature, as would the profiles or the parking meter investigation. None of our story classifications are official in any sense, and their parameters and boundaries are quite loose. No journalism term is looser than "feature material," for this may encompass anything from a well-researched piece of reporting to a lighthearted sketch, a weather graphic, or a crossword puzzle. In this chapter I'll focus on the kinds of features that normally wouldn't fit in specific sections of the paper. That is to say, concert reviews could be classed as feature stories, but I'll discuss those in the chapter on arts and entertainment; a preview of the upcoming basketball season may well be more feature than news, but I'll cover such stories in our sports chapter. In this chapter I'll also skip the news feature, backgrounder, and analysis-type articles and concentrate on . . . well, for want of a better term, the feature features.

A BAD RAP

Features have long had something of a bumpy reputation among many editors and reporters. To serious journalists—or perhaps to overly serious journalists—*feature* was just another word for *fluff* or *filler*. History supports this view. In the earliest days of daily newspapers—those days being roughly two hundred years ago—the techniques of news gathering and reporting were crude, tardy, and haphazard to say the least, and newspapers were quick to pad their empty columns with anything and everything: poems, stories, diaries, how-to advice, travel essays, observations on nature, recipes, medicine (or what passed for medicine), and the most fanciful of pseudo-news reportage. Small wonder that dedicated reporters grew accustomed to looking down on features—and on feature writers. To illustrate just how enduring this prejudice was, while the Pulitzer Prizes were established in 1917, it wasn't until 1979 that the prize committee recognized feature stories as worthy of awards. (Even editorial cartoons were getting Pulitzers as early as 1922.)

Many journalists today still think of feature material as "soft" material, as opposed to the "hard" realm of news. Some troglodytic reporters and editors likewise consider feature writing something "creative" types churn out for the arts or "women's pages," while maintaining that only the manliest of men can properly patrol such fearsome beats as Wall Street or Foggy Bottom. This attitude also relates to the perennial question of which is more difficult to write: news or features? Well, frankly, Scarlett, I don't give a damn. Some writers by talent and temperament are probably more suited to one desk than the other, but that's got nothing to do with the work being hard or easy. Doing any kind of story well shouldn't be easy, it should simply require the appropriate effort, end of argument. I will add, however, that when certain reporters find themselves chafing under what feels like the straitjacket of news gathering and news writing, such free spirits may flourish on the features beat. Editors therefore might encourage these reporters to try their hands at stories that allow for more structural latitude and creative flair. Indeed, a nice feature of feature stories is that they don't follow any formula; they can be crafted in any format, from straight exposition to dramatic narrative. Features are where your creative-type reporters can write articles that begin: "It was a dark and stormy night..." (and then where you can edit the hell out of them).

Meanwhile, a funny thing happened to newspapers on their way to the bankruptcy courts: Editors discovered not only that readers liked features, but in staggering numbers it was features and not news that were attracting readers in the first place. After all, and as we have observed elsewhere, by the latter half of the twentieth century news was so damn ubiquitous you could hardly avoid it. News was available 24/7 on your TV, in your computer, in your headset, via your iPod, in your car radio, in your shower radio, over your cell phone, from your toaster. So the revelation was that those shrinking numbers of people who still liked newsprint weren't buying the paper to discover what's new; they already knew all that. No, they were buying the paper for all the other stuff the paper provided.

The irony is that features in the main are never the kinds of stories that newspapers are obliged to run. By this I mean a newspaper must cover the news or it isn't worthy of the name "newspaper." But features are strictly frosting on the cake. You must run the story on the appointment of a new university president. You are under no compulsion to run a story on the history of football mascots. Yet readers, who are obligated to read nothing, will likely read both of those stories—and they'll smack their lips over that frosting. Why not? Features provide the color and the vitality often lacking in straight news.

It is therefore to be hoped that, along with an abundance of worthy news, your newspaper will be stuffed with all that other sort of stuff I've been talking about. Let's consider some varieties of stuffing.

It's Only Human

The human interest story is a feature that focuses on people as people. Now people aren't always news, but people nonetheless are always interesting. If you don't believe me, just ask David Johnson of *The Lewiston Morning Tribune* in Lewiston, Idaho. For some twenty years Johnson has been writing fascinating profiles of average citizens of his community. How average? Each week he actually picks their names at random out of the telephone directory, that's how average. And guess what? While occasionally an individual declines to be interviewed, Johnson maintains that of those he does interview, he has never failed to get an interesting story. Not once.

And guess again. Johnson isn't the only practitioner of this kind of feature writing. I've seen several student newspapers that do exactly the same thing. Under such headings as "Random Shot" and "Student Body," they pluck a student out of the crowd for each issue to be the subject of a profile. And guess what else? Readers relish these stories. Sure, people love to read about Tom and Brad and J-Lo and Ben. But as I pointed out back in chapter 4 in discussing localizing, readers also love to read about themselves and their peers.

Despite apparent evidence to the contrary, your campus is full of human beings and therefore it runneth over with human interest, so there are endless stories there. And don't think you can't do the random profile just because some other newspapers are already doing it. That a number of papers employ the same story idea proves only that it works. In truth, no original story ideas are left, so don't waste time searching for something totally novel. It's perfectly legitimate to tackle a tried and true journalistic concept; just do it better than it's ever been done before. By the same token I'm almost tempted to say don't waste time seeking out interesting or special human subjects. Just get out there and encounter people and you'll meet stories.

At the lowest and laziest end of the random person kind of human interest feature is the sort of man-in-the-street (or kid-on-the-campus) mini interview. This sort of feature, which I've seen in numerous campus papers, runs to the order of regularly buttonholing people at random and asking them a single question. On one level the value of this feature lies in direct proportion to the quality of the question. Ask something like, "What do you think of the new 8 percent hike in tuition fees?" and don't be surprised if you get some pretty uninspired (and unanimous) replies. Pretty much the same holds true for, "What did you do over spring break?" which to my mind smacks of the old tedious high school essay assignment on "How I Spent My Summer Vacation." A more challenging question might be something like, "If you could change one thing on our campus, what would it be?" But again, don't be surprised if these sound bite replies don't make for terribly good reading. Still, at least this sort of over-easy feature gets some student names and, if accompanied by photos, faces in the paper, and readers always seem to appreciate that. Then again, one student newspaper I know and which will remain nameless has been running this sort of feature for years, taking up an entire half-page each week with the mug shots and sound bites of a measly four or five students. I don't consider that a good use of space, and I keep advising the editors that if they insist on publishing this sort of space filler, they should at least justify it by having ten or twelve students participating each time.

An abundance of other kinds of human interest series have proved successful. How about a series on students with unusual jobs? (Any students spending their weekends capping burning oil rigs?) Or students with unusual backgrounds or lifestyles? (I once read a great story on a student who couldn't afford dorm fees and was therefore cheerfully spending his undergraduate years living out of his Honda Civic.) Or students with unusual means of transportation? (Anyone commuting by unicycle or Segwaying between classes?) Who is your oldest undergraduate? The youngest? The one carrying the most credits or majors?

Your campus community of course doesn't consist solely of students, so don't neglect the other folks on campus. Professors, for example, can be a good source of human interest—paradoxical as that may sound. I personally am leery of profs writing for the student newspaper, but I'm very much for their having an opportunity to sound off in interviews. Students are usually curious about their teachers, and good interviews and profiles feed into that appetite. I like the sort of prof interview that allows faculty to reflect on their chosen fields. (What moved a professor to profess philosophy for a living? Who was the most influential figure in that biology teacher's education? Can the lit professor really justify the study of all those logorrheic dead white males?) Also interesting are the nonacademic sides of these sterling intellectuals. (One of the most entertaining stories along this line that I read was one revealing a certain math instructor's obsession for collecting Coca-Cola memorabilia. I always knew the guy was nuts, but this was a revelation.)

What about other staff? Profiling a cleaning woman sounds like the worst of journalistic clichés—until you discover that the woman is also accumulating credits toward a degree in theology. And many a campus groundskeeper I've talked to has impressed me with both his horticultural knowledge and his commitment to beautifying the college.

By now you should get the point. Whether as source material for a series or on a hit-and-miss basis, the people on your campus are often underexploited. And if you've suspected your newspaper has been a little colorless lately, you might want to ask if it's been sufficiently humanized.

With Trends Like This . . .

Trends invariably make for trendy stories. Collegians are always eager to know what's hot and what's not, and a newspaper should tap into that appetite as well. Trends might refer simply to what's in fashion (such as the tattoos mentioned back in chapter 6), and that's cool, but trends can also refer to weightier matters. For example, not long ago a campus reporter stumbled on the fact that a certain department at his university had only three students majoring in that department's subject. In good journalistic fashion, that got the reporter wondering: How many other departments have a small number of majors? Which has the least, and how few are permitted before a major—or a department—might be pruned from the academic tree? Which departments have the most majors? How have students' choices of majors shifted over the years? How does the reporter's university compare with other campuses in terms of major popularity or lack thereof of? What are the factors influencing the popularity of majors? Before you knew it, the reporter had enough questions to pursue not just an article but a series of articles. And a solid series it was.

An interesting aspect of trends is that some may be highly visible, like goatskin boots, or virtually invisible, like the kind of exams professors are inflicting on their students. Sure, write about a visible trend, like the sudden popularity of rutabaga martinis, and your readers will be entertained, which is fine. But write about a less noticeable trend, like that of students taking more than four years to complete their bachelor degrees, and your readers will be enlightened.

If some trends are hard to spot, that only means you and your staff should be all the more devoted to trend spotting. Reporters should be reminded and encouraged regularly to sniff out trends. (A useful practice at editorial meetings is to throw on the table this question: "So—what's happening on campus? Any new trends? Any seismic shifts in the order of things? What, in short, is new?") Prod people to find trends and they just might find them, and if they find them in a timely fashion, that's all to the good. (But "timely fashion" is important. One of the lamest things you can do is run a big story on the discovery of a trend that all your readers already know about. "Video cell phones? Oh, really? I already gave my old one to my kid brother. . . .")

Don't Know Much About . . .

History can be a fruitful source of feature material, especially your local history. Not everyone agrees on this—some think this takes us immediately into cornball country—but I suspect more people than care to admit it enjoy the venerable "looking backwards" feature. Otherwise why would the Associated Press and countless other news organizations compile a daily box reporting "This Day in History" or "From Our Pages 5, 25 and 50 Years Ago"? And it is of no small significance that you're most likely sitting right on the necessary source material. You've got those cupboards stuffed with back issues (or at least I hope you have). Why not put them—and your electronic archives—to some good use? I think most people on campus are delighted to read about what was happening at the college five, twenty-five, or fifty years back. What were the burning issues of yesterday? What were the controversies, the tuition costs, the academic work, the fashions, the scoreboards, the Greek activities? How have things changed or not changed? Can anything be learned from the past?

The history feature can be handled in a number of ways. The easiest, but quite possibly the least satisfying, is simply to rip an article out of the dusty files and reprint it. A better option to my mind is to reprint the article, or part of it, but also to accompany it with some commentary. This gives a writer an opportunity for an exercise in tone—humorous, nostalgic, sarcastic. The history feature, moreover, is an excellent assignment for novices, perhaps new staffers who are unsure of their reporting and interviewing skills but who are still keen to write. Why not let them loose in your yellowing stacks of newsprint and see what they come up with? And for heaven's sake, don't overlook those old photos—like the ones showing the long skirts on the coeds and the long hair on the now-bald-pated professors.

Beyond raiding your archive, there are plenty of other interesting stories about your campus waiting to be discovered. For example, how many of your readers know for whom the campus buildings are named? Who gets honored or memorialized and who doesn't? Who decides on the names? This could be the makings of a solid series of feature stories. And if you discover your newspaper has run such a series in the past—guess what? Every four years you have an entirely new crop of readers to whom such stories will be new.

Another example: Your campus boasts a library of over half a million volumes. Cool. But how did the library achieve that? What is the origin of the collection, where did the money come from, what does it cost to maintain and to update the collection, how has the cyber revolution affected the library's budget, policies, and services, and how have all these things been transformed over the years? (How on earth did students do research papers in the pre-Google age?) Libraries are stuffed with boring old books, yes, but they also contain tons of potential for fascinating feature stories. Seems to me you have another series in the making, this one built around a facility that all of your readers should be using at least at some point in what passes for their academic careers.

History features also arise out of anniversaries, so keep your eyes open for those. The one-hundredth anniversary of the college's founding, the fiftieth anniversary of the construction of the stadium, the twenty-fifth anniversary of the college president's tenure—all of these can be the inspiration of an informative feature. Sources for such anniversaries include the public relations office, the alumni association, the local historical society, and the old geezer who tends the shrubbery around Old Main. Reporters should check in with such sources (okay, not the gardener) periodically to learn what's new about what's old.

The glance back feature certainly doesn't have to run daily or even weekly. But if you never run it, I think you're overlooking something that will both entertain and enlighten your readers. (Gee, if only your professors could do that. . . .)

A parallel story to the history feature is the local geography story. By this I mean the things to do and places to visit in your area. The student body too often doesn't know what lies beyond the quad, so features on local nature reserves, hiking trails, rock-climbing centers, caves, museums, battlefields, butterfly farms (butterfly farms?), and the like are much appreciated. Bear in mind that each fall you have a crop of new customers on campus who will benefit from such informative recreation stories.

That's Funny?

Humor—oh, Lord, must I? I must. I'll say just a few things on this very heavy subject. First, everybody enjoys a joke, and no one will ever admit to not having a sense of humor. That said, humorous writing is a lot more difficult to produce than most people think, and if you've ever tried your hand at it you might well know what I mean. What's funny? Well, wiser men than I, such as Sigmund Freud and Carl Jung and Theodore Reik and George Carlin, haven't had much success in defining it. Comedy is very much in the ear of the beholder, and something you consider hilarious will leave the guy on your right groaning—or worse. Does that mean you shouldn't attempt humor? Of course not. But when you do, tread very, very carefully.

Why carefully? Not just because a lot of what you think is funny may well fall flat with the reader, but because much humor, parody, satire, and the like make their funnies by making fun of some target or other. Even if we weren't living in an age of heightened sensitivities to sexism, racism, faithism, ageism, sizeism, and so on it would still be very, very easy to offend someone's sensibilities. Does this mean you should never joke about anything controversial? Of course not. But it does mean there's a fine line between poking fun and pissing off the readers. Where is that fine line? Next question. Should you never piss off the reader? Well, maybe sometimes some readers deserve it. But again, tread carefully. I think it's wise to look beyond what simply tickles your funny bone as a standard for publishing humor. I'd say test it out on a number of other staffers. See what flies, see what flops—and try to determine why. Perhaps a humor piece can be salvaged; perhaps not.

It also works in the other direction. I've never forgotten a lesson I learned in my very first year as a working journalist. The editor of this small suburban newspaper had bunged onto a page a boilerplate cartoon, the sort of generic space filler supplied by a low-cost features syndicate that pumped out amiable rubbish like "Thought for the Day" and "Great Quotations." I objected to the editor, asking why we should fill space with such a lame, innocuous cartoon, which if I remember correctly involved a very large dog or a very small child, or perhaps both. "Who the heck could possibly find that amusing?" I demanded. "You'd be surprised," the editor replied sagely. "I don't think it's funny. You don't think it's funny. But certain readers will clip it out and stick it on their refrigerators. Others will mail it to their daughters in Des Moines and Tuscaloosa. Others will phone us for reprints. Sure, in most situations you have to trust your own judgment. But you shouldn't let your personal sense of what's entertaining be the sole standard."

Point taken, O sage editor. Here's another take on the subject: Many readers will see my above toss-away idiom, "piss off," and not give it a second thought. Others will be mildly amused by it. Others will snort with delight. Still others will react by asking: "Jeesh, why did he have to use such a crude term? What's the purpose? Does he think using toilet terminology is witty? Or cool? If so, he's a jerk. Gimme a break." There you go. What you consider riotously funny will translate that way to some but may well be cause for a riot among others. Sometimes you can't help upsetting readers—by their nature certain news stories will do this—but do you want to alienate readers unnecessarily? I certainly don't, which is why I would never use a phrase like "piss off" in a book.

Cartoons, as mentioned above, are very often the worst offenders in the category of offensive humor, and I think I've seen it all in college newspapers: racial stereotypes, misogyny, excretory excess, and just plain artless drawing.

Look, I like comic strips. And I much prefer a half-baked comic drawn by a student in *The Slavering Newshound* to a full-baked reprint of some 'toon found in the local *Daily Bugle* and in five hundred other mainstream papers. But just as photos can engender more revulsion than words, so too campus cartoons seem even more apt to affront than witless campus articles. Not for nothing is immature, tasteless humor labeled "sophomoric." (Can't you at least assign the laffs to the juniors and seniors?)

But I know I'm preaching to the wind here. So yeah, run your funnies and your funny essays, and of course your devilish April Fool's issue, as you must. Just take care and don't take the fun out of it. Bear in mind, too, that the April Fool's issue or a satire piece should not be an opportunity for venting personal vendettas or vindictiveness. Publishing humor should be for the purpose of entertaining readers, not scoring off of some target who can't score back. And while satire and parody might be constitutionally protected speech, they might also be enormously wounding and unfair.

Final point: Be wary of in-house humor. Many times I've seen student newspapers that include in-jokes, something whose point is based on, say, the way the features editor scarfs up pizza. The newspaper staff no doubt finds these things hilarious. The hapless reader is out of the loop. That means for your readers the in-joking is nothing but a waste of space. Remember: You don't publish the newspaper for yourselves.

Take My Advice

Advice columns have been an enduring feature in the media going back to Mrs. Beeton's household hints in Victorian England and Ben Franklin's almanacs in colonial America. Advice columns are popular in the collegiate press as well. One of the best I've ever seen dealt with holistic healing, homemade cosmetics, organic food, and the like; I was interested in none of those topics but invariably found the columns both informative and entertaining. By contrast, one of the worst series of columns I ever read was a lonely hearts advisory played strictly for what the Agony Aunt mistakenly thought was laughs.

I'll offer just two pieces of advice concerning advice columns. The first is that, whatever the topic—love, sex, health, personal grooming, fashion, technology, cars, academics, finances, gardening—the columnist ought to know what he or she is talking about. That may seem axiomatic, but little in journalism is axiomatic. What I mean is that it's all too easy for staffers to take on any old advice topic as a lark, blithely figuring they can make up for what they lack in expertise with clever turns of phrases and punch lines and other literary sleight of hand. Well, no. If a columnist professes to dispense guidance about dating or computers or careers or whatever, the writer should have something of substance to deliver. Sure, we read advice columns voyeuristically for entertainment. But such columns can also be of clip-and-save utility—and why shouldn't they be? Above all, what you don't want to provide is misinformation, and if that's true in regard to tweaking a Web browser, it's all the more pertinent when it comes to dispensing psychological or medical information. Be cool. The "advice" a frivolous columnist dispenses can do real damage. That's why it's crucial for columnists to know what they're talking about—and if they don't, they should seek out expert opinion before replying to readers' inquiries. There's certainly no embarrassment in a columnist—or any journalist—consulting a law professor or someone over at the health center for information and insight.

Which leads me to the second piece of my mind. Unless there is clear evidence to the contrary, the columnist should assume that the reader appealing to a newspaper for advice, whether it's about fixing a wonky hard drive or fixing a broken heart, is a real person with a real problem. This is especially pertinent in the realm of sex-advice columns, which have been growing in popularity on campuses in recent years. Very often the Q&A in these columns is played for laughs (why not, sex is such a hilarious topic). Sure, sometimes the readers are being cute or coy or purposely provocative with their questions. But not always, and many times I've seen the "sexperts" denouncing their correspondents in print for their supposed ignorance or wrongheaded attitudes or whatever. In writing their advice columns, the writers too often play to the crowd ... forgetting that out there is a reader genuinely seeking advice. So my advice is: Remember not to forget.

Game Time

Crossword puzzles, anagrams, Suduko games, and the like? Sure, and why not columns on bridge, backgammon, Texas Hold 'em, and whatever else is the pastime flavor of the month? I'm not kidding—such goodies are among the chief explanations for newspaper subscriptions. I'm all in favor of such frivolities—with only two caveats. First, like all features, they should be a supplement, and not a substitute, for news coverage, and second, they will be best appreciated if they are home grown. You can all too easily fill in your games section with inexpensive boilerplate from features syndicates or by ripping stuff off the Internet—but why replicate what your readers' home dailies are supplying? Much better if your puzzles and teasers or whatever are handcrafted by your staff members and tuned to the local knowledge and interests of your readers. Personally I think a Trivial Pursuit–type of affair relating to your campus goes down a lot better than a general knowledge quiz. And how about a crossword puzzle built around the names of popular professors (if that isn't an oxymoron)?

Oh, yes, and if you want a challenge, go ahead and try to construct a serious crossword puzzle. You'll discover mighty quick that it ain't that easy. But as I've observed before, us folks in the newspaper business aren't interested in the easy, are we?

Don't Be Starry-Eyed

Astrology charts are about as popular as any of the pastime features mentioned above, both in the mainstream and in the college press. Yet open as I am to crosswords and anagrams, I am very closed to astrology. Here's why: Although most people probably read the charts for amusement, some put too much faith in this pseudoscience. How many is some? One is too many, and I'd hate to think of anyone making decisions or altering behavior because some stargazer says the moon is in the seventh house. Beyond that, I think astrology is firmly lodged in the house of superstition, and I don't fancy perpetuating superstition. Unless you are attending something like Guru U., your university presumably doesn't offer courses in astrology—and presumably for the reasons I've outlined here. Beyond all that, I dislike astrological journalism because it's too easy to write: Astrologers can unload any bull on a Taurus and take no end of liberties in advising Libras and who's to know the difference? In short, if the task is too easy, I'm suspicious.

I acknowledge, of course, that my views on star charts and the like appear to be in the minority, based on the incredible number of newspapers that insist on publishing astrology columns. Add to this the fact that, based on polls I've conducted over the years, far more of my students know their astrological signs than they do their blood types (big help when you're hit by a bus). Still, if only on this matter, I believe I'm right and the majority is wrong.

The Weather

The weather? Yes, the weather—people apparently can't get enough weather info. (I mean, think of it, a whole TV channel and heaven knows how many Web sites devoted to the advisability of toting umbrellas.) So yeah, why not give your readers a forecast? And here's an even better idea: As with everything else in a student newspaper, it's best if you could have a student weather reporter. How can you do that? Comb your campus for a weather nerd. Might such a creature exist? You'll never know unless you search, and you just might be surprised. People have all sorts of hobbies and interests, and yes, we even have avid amateur meteorologists. Check with profs who teach climatology, earth science, geography; run an ad in your paper and, who knows, you just might wind up with your own exclusive weather column.

QUOTH THE RAVEN, "NEVER WORN"

A final thought on feature stories, this one growing out of a classified ad that allegedly appeared in a newspaper some years back:

> For sale: Wedding gown, size 5, never worn. Box 237

The advertisement may be apocryphal, but it's nevertheless been used over the years to point up an important journalistic lesson. A typical reader notes the ad, chuckles or shakes his head, then resumes reading the classifieds. The reporter sees that ad and says, "Ah, there's a story there."

My point is this: A news organization may experience a slow news day or even a slow news week, but it can never claim even a slow features hour. Feature stories are out there waiting to be discovered. They are in the people on your campus, in the issues that concern them, in the matters that entertain them, in the very sidewalks on which they bike and skateboard, in the very grass they trample. Go get 'em. (And by the way, despite what I wrote at the beginning of this chapter on features as filler, a good savings bank of features is important to have on those slow news days. So deposit features regularly in that bank.)

9

Arts and Entertainment

It's a bit of a paradox, but I've come to believe that in many campus newspapers the arts and entertainment pages are the best read and worst written. Readers care more about movie reviews, college concert previews, news about the latest video games, and everything else pertaining to the wide world of entertainment than they care about their final exams or their latest test for STDs. Yet far too often the A&E writers fail to deliver—or at least fail to deliver in anything approaching a professional fashion. The reason for this disconnect arguably lies in training. Very likely, members of your newspaper staff have taken some news writing and editing courses. Very likely, your sports reporters memorize the stats and play sports themselves and have been scrutinizing the sports pages from the time when they read by moving their lips. But when it comes to A&E, and specifically when it comes to writing reviews, few students get any specific instruction in this regard ("arts journalism" is a relatively new and still fairly rare area of study). As a result, sure, the arts beat gets covered; it just doesn't get covered very well.

This state of affairs has its counterpart in the mainstream press, where not enough arts reporters and reviewers have the requisite combination of journalistic and arts training. Indeed, when it came to appointing a reviewer for the paper, the classic scenario used to run something like this: The old music critic died at his workstation (it is hoped he was thoughtful enough to finish his review of last night's production of *Madama Butterfly*), and after his carcass was hauled out of the newsroom and after thirty seconds for silent reflection, the managing editor bellowed across the office: "Anybody here take music appreciation in college?" Someone—let's say general assignment reporter Sam Saperstein, vaguely remembered having had such a course and timidly raised his hand. "Okay, Saperstein," snapped the managing editor. "You're the new music critic." "But—but what do I do?" sputtered Saperstein. "Consult the clip file," said the managing editor, turning on his heel. "Read what the last guy—what was his name?—did. Do the same."

Do I exaggerate? Well, perhaps a tad. Certainly the *Los Angeles Times* and *The Village Voice* don't choose their critics in quite that fashion today. A&E in general has become more professionalized in recent years—largely in response to the explosive growth in entertainment as an industry and as a component of American life. Yet a surprising number of newspapers (and TV shows and Internet sites and so on) still have arts reporters and critics who pretty much learned their jobs, well, on the job. (Hey, it's worth the effort; those free CDs and theater tickets are no small supplement to those meager salaries.)

College students of course are not exactly at ground zero when it comes to covering A&E. They're practically born with earbuds, they've grown up immersed in popular culture, and they should have had at least some exposure to classroom critical thinking and writing. Most of your staffers will be English or journalism majors, most will have taken at least an introduction to literature course, many have taken a music course, and everybody at one time or another has had to download (I mean, to write) a book review. So, yes, you probably could choose someone virtually at random from your corps of reporters ("Yo, Saperstein!") and get at least a half-decent reviewer/arts reporter.

You should, however, never be satisfied with the half decent, because that implies the accompanying baggage of the half incompetent. So let's consider a few guidelines and ponderables concerning the A&E beat. And let's consider them in terms of the two broad categories of articles that appear in the A&E pages: (1) reviews and (2) other stuff.

TIME FOR REVIEW

Reviews are widely and eagerly read. People like to be told if they were justified in liking this play or in disliking that CD. Readers peruse reviews for news about the latest artistic offerings, and they're even willing to take guidance from reviews ("Whoa, that movie certainly sounds deserving a skip. Glad I didn't waste any money on that one"). Because many readers are passionate about movies and music and books and video games, they also love to argue with reviewers and they love to hate certain critics. So, Mr. and Ms. Reviewer, be aware that you have a hungry readership out there.

We'll use the terms *review* and *criticism* more or less interchangeably, although it's generally accepted that a reviewer is someone who knocks out a report on an artistic offering like a reporter, on deadline, while a critic is on a somewhat loftier plane, usually writing longer, more thoughtful essays on the arts and on a looser schedule. In addition, reviewers are often called upon to cover a variety of things (music, plays, films), both reviewing and reporting arts news, while critics tend to specialize and normally don't get their hands dirty with mere reporting. But no matter. Reviewers and critics basically perform the same three functions in their articles: They analyze, interpret, and evaluate.

It's not my purpose here to offer a short course in criticism, but I'll just remind you of some basics and indicate how they apply in your A&E pages. So a review incorporates analysis, which means taking a subject apart and examining how the creative offering was done and what makes it work. A film review considers the elements of movies (acting, directing, script, cinematography, etc.), an art review does the same (medium, draftsmanship, use of color), a restaurant review likewise (the menu, the food, the presentation, the ambience, the service), and so on. Interpretation seeks out the creator's intention (point of the story, what the sculpture is supposed to evoke in the viewer, why the osso buco was served in coconut sauce). Evaluation judges how well the artist achieved his or her intentions, whether those intentions were worthwhile pursuits, and what degree of satisfaction the artwork engenders. The three functions may be done in any order (although the listing here is probably the most logical) or mixed together and in any proportion, but if a review is done properly, analysis, interpretation, and evaluation will all be in there to some degree or other.

The interesting thing is that these critical functions apply in all kinds of reviews, whether written about an art exhibition, a concert, a book, a new library building, a circus, even a meal in a restaurant. A second point is that a good reviewer will perform these functions without being aware of it. A third is that reviews, unlike news coverage, are expected to convey an opinion.

Opinion is justified because the reviewer has examined and interpreted what's going on in the book or the CD. Of course, the validity of a reviewer's analysis and interpretation is going to depend on how thoughtful, knowledgeable, and sensitive the reviewer is. Critics need not be creative artists themselves. Being a musician would likely be an asset to a music critic, but being an appreciative and experienced listener is sufficient. At the same time, a restaurant review written by someone who has never dined outside of McDonald's is more than a bit suspect. In addition, not every reviewer will respond to an artistic offering the same way (differing viewpoints are why we have horse races). But if you're an A&E editor and you see the reviewer has passed judgment based on a reasonable examination of the work under discussion, you can conclude that the reviewer has done the job. And done it in a fair matter.

A few other points about reviews. The first is a caution against extremes. Student reviewers are prone both to overenthusiasm and to hatchet jobs, and rarely are these things justified. Virtually all artistic offerings, like virtually all people, are a mixture of good and bad, weak and strong. To declare a work of art execrable in every aspect ("the worst movie ever made") is over the top and hard to believe. (Are you certain it's the worst ever? Have you indeed seen every movie ever made?) Likewise, it can be embarrassing in the extreme to overpraise. When you declare a CD "the best album of the year!" and it's only February, what are you going to say about the even more brilliant set of tracks released in March? And who knows what work of genius is coming in November? So, yes, express your opinion, just don't overexpress it; don't lose your balance—or you'll lose your credibility.

(And while we're on the subject of volume—save your exclamation point for falling off a cliff.)

Another caution is to avoid promotion. A review serves to a large extent as a shopper's guide, and that's cool. But that's not the same thing as huckstering. Your job is not to sell tickets ("So come on out, gang, and support this production!") or to hustle CDs ("Grab your copy today!"). It's one thing to inform readers of what's worthwhile; that's reviewing. It's crossing quite a line to push sales; that's public relations.

Pushing sales, public relations, and publicity—those are all the jobs of concert promoters, record companies, publishers, and the like, and if you're not taking advantage of their services you should be. Background arts articles and reviews provide precious publicity, even if that is not their purpose, and why should artists and their representatives get all this free coverage instead of pur-

ARTS AND ENTERTAINMENT

chasing advertising space in your paper? Well, we hope they do buy ads. But at the very least they should be providing reviewers with samples of their products. In this regard it is perfectly legitimate for the A&E editor to contact record companies, book publishers, concert promoters, and such to request CDs, books, and tickets. (A good place to start is Web sites, which often have publicity sections.) More often than not these outfits will comply and even put you on their lists of regulars receiving their largesse. This is not just because they're nice guys. College students are a highly desirable demographic—a major market for the arts—and the record companies and publishers and their ilk always budget for publicity. Before you know it they'll be flooding you with press kits and promotional DVDs, inviting you to press conferences with lunch thrown in and so on. All that is cool, but be wary. Reviewers must not allow themselves to feel obligated or indebted in any way to providers of publicity materials and sample goodies. The PR people are doing their job, and you do yours. A&E editors would do well to make all this clear to reviewers and maybe even have guidelines ready on dealing with those seductive publicity people.

Finally, a word about local versus national, and amateur versus professional, both of which are related to a reviewer's standards. First of all, while your readers are eager for news of the latest big-name bands and books and movies, your A&E pages should not supply these exclusively, and certainly not at the expense of reviewing local talent. As we suggested back in chapter 4, your readers are going to get those reviews of professional artists elsewhere anyway, but the national press won't be covering your campus theater productions and your battles of the bands. (Bear in mind, too, that artists live for reviews, so if you don't cover your creative peers, you're really depriving them of much needed and desired commentary.) Second, if your theater department's production of *Sweeney Todd* isn't as slick as the Broadway version, or if a campus coffee house guitar plucker isn't exactly another Springsteen—well, is that a surprise? No, it means you're applying the wrong standard in your evaluation. So keep your critical expectations and demands in proportion.

OTHER STUFF

A&E pages feature lots of stuff in addition to reviews that readers appreciate:

1. *The interview* is a staple of A&E reporting. For general news interviewing see chapter 5, but for A&E interviewing stick around. Readers relish

reading interviews with creative folk, so when a well-known poet (if that isn't an oxymoron) comes to campus or when a student is directing a theater department play, interviews can supply valuable background and insight. Celebrity interviews, however, offer a special challenge. They are often unsatisfying because (a) the celebrity has more experience with interviewing than does a student reporter and therefore tends to take control of the discussion, and (b) celebrities have been subjected to so much questioning that they're often bored giving interviews. The only remedy I know for the flat celebrity interview is for the reporter to craft fresh, original questions before the sit-down. Instead of asking a film star, for example, "What was your favorite role?" you might ask, "Can you talk about what makes a good or bad director, and discuss some of your experiences with each?" Such a question might get you thrown out of the VIP suite—but I think it's worth a shot. Creative interrogation, meanwhile, also applies on the local level. A senior pre-med major plays heavy metal gigs at a local bar three nights a week. The guy is really wild—makes Eddie Vedder seem like Harry Connick, Jr. Good opening question: "How can you play your guts out like this with your band on a regular basis and yet keep up with your studies?"

2. *The advance* is another common element in A&E pages. This story previews an upcoming event—a campus concert, a theatrical production, whatever. Your sources of information range from press handouts to interviews to background stuff you find online. Cool. Just be careful in a preview story not to prejudge. It's perfectly fine to report that *The Los Angeles Times* has declared this comedy troupe "fresh and funny." It is unfine to write, "These comics are great, so let's have a huge turn-out and really show our appreciation for their choosing our campus to showcase their phenomenal talents!" The objective of an advance is to inform, not to persuade or to provide puffery. Keep your eye on the objective.

3. *Industry news*, for want of a better term, is yet another popular feature on A&E pages, although for the life of me I don't know why readers have such an appetite to know about Michael Jackson's financial woes (a subject that seems pertinent only to Mr. Jackson's creditors), which movie blockbuster failed to bust the block (something that seems of significance only to the studio's shareholders), and which country album is topping the charts (which seems relevant only to those insecure readers who buy whatever everyone else is buying). But these, like everything else here, are just my cranky views. Read-

ers evidently can't get enough info on the entertainment industry, so better to feed the beast. My only advice is, yet again and unsurprisingly, to localize. Sure, you can rip a best-seller list off the Internet and bung it into your A&E pages. But it's a lot more enterprising—and interesting to your readers—if you can list the top ten downloads of the week on your campus, what TV shows your readers are watching, the hot movies among your readers, and so on. May take more effort—but the effort should be worth it.

LEGAL CONCERNS? ETHICS?
Chapter 19 deals with journalism's legal and ethical matters, but it's worth pointing out right now that A&E has its own particular set of concerns in this area.

A primary and not unreasonable worry that a reviewer, and particularly a novice reviewer, might have runs something like this: "Hey, I'm supposed to write a review of this guy who did a stand-up performance last night. I thought his show was really lousy. But if I write a review to that effect, can't he, um, like sue me for defamation?"

The short answer is no. Or more precisely, wounded artists might be moved to sue, but they aren't going to have a case—as long as the reviewer's criticism is directed at the *work* and not at the *individual* presenting it. Big legal difference. Courts provide protection to critics from defamation suits under the principle of Fair Comment and Criticism. This means artists, performers, and the like, who put their work out there in the marketplace must be prepared to have that work evaluated—and to take it on the chin when the work gets trashed.

Most artists accept those rules of the game. But the significant point here is that the *work* is the object of the trashing, not the *artist.* Some years back a book reviewer for *The New York Times* learned this distinction after he wrote not just that a particular *book* was full of erroneous and inadequate information, but that the *author* was a careless writer, a poor researcher, and in general not up to the task he had undertaken. The author sued, claiming the newspaper had defamed him, stained his reputation in the literary community, hurt his book sales, and harmed his chances for getting another contract for a book. He won a settlement. So reviewers want to be careful here. You may criticize, sure, but know what you're criticizing.

A host of ethical problems also attends the wonderful world of arts and entertainment. In most cases the law will not tell you what's right or wrong;

that's for you to decide. I won't tell you either. Let's frame them like a midterm exam and see how you would handle the following situations:

1. As a reviewer for your student newspaper, you are assigned to review a major Theater Department production. The play is directed by your significant other. Do you have a problem? Maybe a couple of problems? What do you do?
2. A local community opera group mounts a lavish production for a two-week run, with all proceeds going to the local children's hospital. You cover opening night. The opera is a disaster: terrible singing, ugly sets, cast members bumping into scenery and waving to their friends in the audience, the works. Do you have a problem?
3. Touchstone Pictures invites you and other film critics to a press screening of the new Sylvester Stallone movie. They offer to fly you to Hollywood, put you up at the Beverly Hilton for the weekend, supply you a press kit with photos, and arrange a thirty-minute interview with the star. Any problems accepting such an invitation?
4. You are interviewing a visiting rock star in his hotel room the day before he and his band open a three-night gig at the local stadium. While visiting the performer's bathroom, you notice a number of tightly rolled $100 bills, some cute little silver spoons, and some suspicious white powder. Do you have an interesting new angle to your story?
5. Only it's not a rock star, but a prominent TV evangelist.
6. You edit the arts section of your campus paper. The advertising manager of the paper tells you she can get a badly needed $1,000 in ads from the touring company of *Phantom of the Opera*—but only if you present a big promo preview and a review with a positive spin. Are you having a bad day?
7. The editor of your newspaper is a board member of the university chamber orchestra. She would like you to write a big feature previewing the group's upcoming concert, and a review. She lets it be known that it will be personally embarrassing to her if the review is not extremely favorable. Have a problem?
8. A record company sends you its entire back catalog of CDs, promotional material, and latest releases for review. The company simply requests that whenever you review its titles, you mention the label. Any problem? What if among the packing materials in the carton of CDs are several hundred-dollar bills?

9. The Hispanic Students Organization has long accused your newspaper of insensitivity to its interests and needs, and your editor is unhappy about the accusation. Now the HSO is sponsoring an exhibition of two dozen young Hispanic artists. You cover the fine arts beat, but the HSO has demanded a Hispanic be assigned to review the show. Your editor thinks that might be a good idea. What do you think? Incidentally, you've had a peek at the show and in your view it has little artistic merit. Una problema?
10. As music critic for your student paper, you are assigned to review a concert on campus by a visiting alternative band. Turns out the band's lead guitarist once judged you when you played in a battle of the bands at a community college—and he saw to it that your group placed last. Any difficulty here?

And you thought arts and entertainment was all fun and games, eh?

10

Sports

I rarely even look at the sports pages. There. I said it. The only time I read sports is when I'm paid to do so, like when I'm critiquing a student newspaper. Even then I'm bored rigid reading about sports and have to prop up my eyelids with toothpicks while combing through all that play by play. This is because I have never had any interest whatsoever in matters athletic. I realize this is a major flaw in my character, is downright un-American, and, if you had any doubt up until now, this clearly confirms my weirditude. But there it is.

Given my lack of interest in sports, I don't have a great deal to say about sports writing. Therefore, this threatens to be the shortest chapter in this book. Still, I do have a few things to share—not least because I acknowledge that the sports pages are vitally important in a newspaper. People are fanatical about sports. It's not by chance we call them fans.

So let's look at what this sports ignoramus can possibly have to say about the sports pages.

BRIGHT WRITING

Sports writers are an enviable lot. Unlike, say, reporters writing on municipal matters or education, sports writers always have a sizeable and eager readership. In addition, because sports are never out of season, sports writers always have something to write about. Not only that, but sports writers—most if not all of whom are fans at heart—get to meet their heroes, travel with the teams, visit the dugouts, and enjoy the comforts of sideline seats and press boxes. But perhaps most enviable is that sports writers have great latitude in how they address their audience. Sports writers share a bond with their readers that allows for a companionable and fairly freewheeling journalism. Sports writers have their own jargon, they get to use all those exciting verbs and colorful adjectives, and, since they're usually writing about competitions, sports writers can daily describe contests and trials in a dramatic manner. To top it all off, sports writers seem free of the restraints under which other reporters must operate. For some reason we allow sports writers to libel athletes ("This guy doesn't belong in the major leagues!"), to defame coaches ("She simply doesn't know anything about coaching"), to be sarcastic ("The ump needs a seeing-eye dog—let's take up a collection!"), and even to incite to violence ("The quarterback should be tarred and feathered and hung from the goal post!"). Sports writers even get to use exclamation points! (Yuck—maybe that's why I don't follow sports.)

But gee, sports writing sounds like so much fun—how did I miss it?

Oh, yes, I'm not interested in sports. Which is part of my point. On the one hand, given all of what I just said in the preceding paragraph, it would seem that there's no excuse for dull sports writing. Yet I've read many a dull sports story. So the first thing I would advise sports editors is to look over their pages and ask themselves if the writing and reporting are as bright as they can and should be. Not that the prose should be purple or that the tone should be exclamatory; that's not bright writing, that's insurrectionary pamphleteering. But if "hit" is the only verb the baseball reporter has at his command to describe a bat propelling the ball over the fence, then I think some brightening is in order.

EXCLUSIONARY REPORTING

Here's an additional test editors can apply to their pages: Do you have sports articles that would appeal even to a non–sports fan, say a nerd like me?

I'm not being facetious with this last question. I have no interest in business or finance, for example, yet many times I'll read articles on those subjects because the writing is so good. I truly admire a journalist who can capture and hold my attention on a subject in which I have no interest. Similarly, I deeply respect a writer who can make an arcane topic clear and comprehensible to me. Certain business writers have done just that with pieces on the stock market and corporate takeovers and the like. Not many sports stories have commanded my interest that often, but some have, and I view that as a considerable accomplishment.

Now I'm not suggesting the sports pages should be written for the nonfan. It's reasonable to write baseball stories or to present basketball coverage with the assumption that such stories will be read by aficionados. The same would be true of, say, an opera review and its readers. But it seems to me both a good baseball article and a good opera review should be comprehensible and even enjoyable by nonspecialist readers who just happen to wander onto the respective pages. I know as much about opera as I do about lacrosse, but there have been occasions when I've read an opera review and I've said to myself, That really sounds interesting, I ought to check out that production. How did the writer of that opera review manage to pique my interest? Because she wrote it well, made the subject understandable, and conveyed both the achievement of the production and the reviewer's enthusiasm.

On the other hand, I've read lacrosse stories that left me baffled by the whole point of the contest. Even worse—*I've read sports stories in which I was not even certain what sport was being discussed.* Think I'm exaggerating? Such a story ran like this:

> The Golden Warriors looked sharp when they took the field last Saturday afternoon, but by the last quarter the visiting Jefferson U. Blue Devils had just as sharply whittled the warriors down to size.
>
> Blue Devil Doug Hanson led a fabulous defense that left the Golden Warriors scoreless for the entire first half of the much-anticipated contest. Meanwhile, the Devils steadily racked up its successes, much to the dismay of the home team, whose handling of the ball all afternoon ...

And on for six or eight more paragraphs. All the while I was scratching my head. Soccer? Rugby? Field hockey? Volleyball? Touch football? Jai-alai?

When I complained about this "mystery ball" article to the sports editor, he just shrugged (while his eyes condemned me as beyond hope). And while this example may be extreme, I think the point is still valid. Nowhere else in a newspaper would stories be incomprehensible to nonspecialists. So sports editors, be careful; don't be so insular in your reporting and writing that you exclude everyone but the most devoted fans. That just doesn't sound like good journalism.

PARTISANSHIP?

The fact that sports writers tend to write for their own readership about their own world reflects that bond of enthusiasm the writers share with their readers, which is cool. But what about partisanship? It's natural for locals—in your case, the student body—to support the home team. But how much boosterism should sports writers indulge in? I'm not sure I can answer that question, but I think it's one worth considering—considering that journalism is supposed to value objectivity. Is it then appropriate to describe every loss suffered by the home team as a "heartbreaker" and to exult in every defeat of the competition? When the home team takes a title, is it proper journalism to run a screamer of a headline like "WE WIN!"? Is it the sports pages' duty to publish articles, such as I have seen countless times, urging an apathetic student body to "get out there and support the varsity team—they count on it!"?

I doubt if many object to this sort of nonobjective sports coverage—and I'm sure the players, the athletic department, the university administration, and the alumni association are all perfectly happy with it. But you're really not writing for them. Just as the campus newspaper as a whole does not exist to "raise school spirit," I think it's a dubious proposition for the sports pages to be expected to do so. Sports may be a special case, but I still have my doubts. Journalists fiercely believe in maintaining a firewall between reporting and promotion in all other parts of the newspaper; should sports be an exception? If it is, it could well come at the expense of solid and respectable journalism. Interestingly, war correspondents have to struggle with this very same question. When American reporters cover U.S. military activity abroad, for example, should those correspondents report objectively? Should they emphasize "home team" successes and minimize failures? Is maintaining our side's morale more important than reporting something that, say, may reflect badly on our side's performance on the field? Such questions have bedeviled journalism since war reporting began. I don't know that they have bedeviled sports writers and sportscasters—but perhaps they should. At the very least this seems a subject the sports staff should discuss thoroughly.

One side note in regard to boosterism: Many times sports editors can't get anyone to cover minor campus sports—the rifle team, intramural Wiffle ball, the tiddledywinks competition—other than actual participants in those sports. To avoid charges of conflict of interest, such writers should be identified as such—such as by an italicized note at the end of the article.

ALL SPORTS ALL THE TIME

What should the sports pages cover? If I say, first of all, the campus, you won't be surprised. But there's more to campus sports than the varsity teams. Of course you must cover the major team sports—football, basketball, and the like. Yet I've seen many a campus newspaper that largely neglects other official sports. I've even talked to sports editors who were only vaguely aware that their colleges had a rifle squad, an equestrian team, a golf team, and so on. Sure, the majority of readers may have little interest in these less glamorous sports—but what would you expect if your readers never hear about them? Those golfers and sharpshooters and archers are competitive athletes. Like your swimmers and wrestlers and footballers, they're out there giving their all to their sport. The college evidently values them; it supports the minor sports, recruits its athletes, probably gives them athletic scholarships. And there are good stories there that deserve exposure. Cover these minor sports in proportion to your overall campus sports reporting—but cover them. And remember, the more student names and faces you have in the paper, the more you're serving the readers.

Same holds true for club and intramural sports. The players here are not Big Men (or Women) on Campus. But they are something more important: They and their supporters are your Big Readers on Campus, and their activities are a vital part of your campus life. Again, I've seen student newspapers that leave the impression that the college has no club sports. Seems wrong to me. Just as the news pages should seek out news from every corner of the campus, so too should the sports pages.

What about off campus, in the wide world of sports? This is a judgment call on your part, so use good judgment. You may decide it's important to report regularly on the NFL and the major league baseball team in the city closest to your campus—but will you be giving your readers anything they won't already be getting from TV, city newspapers, and the Internet? Certainly you don't want to neglect major sporting events like the World Series or the Olympics. But unless you're publishing daily you can't supply the news the way the mainstream media do, and even if you could, do you simply want to repeat what the mainstream is reporting?

I'm asking a lot of questions here and not supplying many answers. These are matters your sports staff should hash out, and perhaps your decisions are going to depend on your frequency of publication, your resources, your geographic location, and the kind of sports coverage being provided by your competing media. But you should be able to work out policies that suit your needs. I'll share one opinion; what I appreciate in campus sports pages is less the blow-by-blow coverage of national sports and more the commentary on those sports written by a bright and knowledgeable student sports editor or writer. As noted, sports pages allow for a lot of journalistic freedom, so why not use it? When readers get a student sports column evaluating, say, the Yankees' strengths and weaknesses, or critically examining the telecasting of a major track and field event, those readers are getting something beyond the scoreboards—and they're getting something fresh and original in their student newspaper.

BEYOND THE SCOREBOARDS

Somebody mention beyond the scoreboards? Oh, yeah, I did. What I mean by this is all the rich opportunities sports writers have for doing stories beyond simply reporting who played who last week and how the contests turned out.

Of course you want to report who played who last week and how the contests turned out. But good sports pages will deliver a lot more than that. First of all, bear in mind that by the time you appear in print your readers probably already know who played who last week and how the contests turned out. This is definitely true if you publish only once or twice a week, but it's true even if you're a daily. Now, of course you want to report who played who last week and how the contests turned out, because that's part of the record, and one of a newspaper's roles is, well, to record the record. But there's so much more you can do with sports reporting. The things you can do run to this order:

1. *Looking forward.* This means that even as you tell your readers what happened in the world of sports last week, or at the beginning of this week, or even yesterday, you'll freshen your stories if your leads speak to the future rather than to the past. Here's an example of a lead weighted with ancient history:

> The Slaverhundt Mongrels took a licking last Thursday as the hoopsters dropped a hard-fought basketball game against the Dixie U. Doppelgangers, 97–80, thus all but ending the home team's chances in the regional playoffs. Plagued by injuries, the Mongrels lacked two top-ranked starters, forward Jim

Smith and guard Sam Jones, which led to the Dopps dominating the game from the first whistle. . . .

Now here's a lead that favors the future over reporting the past:

Next Saturday's regional playoffs has the Slaverhundt Mongrels fighting for a berth, but only if they can pick up a division win against Mason and Dixon tomorrow night—and if powerhouse Podunk U. happens to lose its home game tomorrow.

Following a heartbreaking 97–80 loss to Dixie University's Doppelgangers last Thursday, the injury-plagued Mongrels are looking to salvage what remains of their reputation by . . .

Not being a sports writer, I may not be making much sense regarding the "fighting for a berth" and all that, but the point should be clear. The first lead is simply a recap of last Thursday's game: appropriate for the record, but since it's yesterday's news it's rather stale. The second story will report last week's game, but the story is freshened by a lead that looks forward; it places the play-by-play of the last game in a perspective that makes the old news relevant to what's coming up next. You may not be able to add a forward thrust to every sports news report, but more often than not you can if you try. The result will be newsier sporting news. Not only that, you'll be revealing to the reader the significance of what's happening with the team—not merely what happened last week. Big difference.

Beyond freshening game coverage in this way, you also have the opportunity to keep your pages fresh by writing advances. Keep the readers current on what's coming up: a new season for this sport is about to get under way, a new coaching staff for that sport is about to take over, new NCAA rules to take effect next semester, divisional trials here, training sessions there—I don't know what I'm talking about but you should get the idea. Look forward. Your job as sports reporter is not simply to be varsity historian or scoreboard accountant. Stress the new.

2. *Profiles and interviews.* The athletes and perhaps even the coaches on your campus are often viewed as gods. They are usually admired and respected by the student body and yet are often quite unknown. One of the things the campus newspaper sports pages can do is bring these gods down from Mt. Olympus via profiles and interviews. Interestingly, gaining access to

varsity athletes may not be all that easy. Colleges with sizeable athletic programs, and certainly the major colleges, customarily issue guidelines to their varsity athletes about granting interviews. Usually those guidelines will run to the order of advising the reporter to clear requests for interviews with the sports information office.

A sports information officer explained this policy to me this way: "While we have no intention of limiting an individual's freedom of speech, it's felt that for purposes of team solidarity, for the overall objectives of the athletic program and so on, individual players shouldn't as a rule speak to the press on their own. We don't want misinformation to be put abroad. Individual players might not have the proper perspective or access to information that would keep them from disseminating misinformation. A player's slips or mistakes in an interview might actually do some damage to a team, or to a coach, to an individual's career, to an entire program. Beyond that, the overall idea is to protect the athlete from being badgered for interviews at every turn."

The sports PR guy added that, in reality, with student reporters and student athletes living in close proximity (sharing dorms, sharing classrooms), they often get to know each other, and so it isn't all that uncommon for athletes to share their thoughts with the student press. Still, if a hard and fast guideline is in place, my source said, athletes may face some penalty if they speak out of turn. "We take it on a case-by-case basis," he said. "It may well depend on what the athlete said. You know, if he dissed the coach or his teammates, he might be reprimanded. Or even benched. It all depends what he says and how he says it."

The sports spokesman concluded by noting that on many campuses, access is often controlled even in terms of photographing athletes. "If a photographer is accredited, then yes, the photographer can shoot at a practice or a workout. Otherwise, again, we don't want every kid with a camera popping flashbulbs in a player's face all day."

Having said all that, you can get interviews and readers will appreciate them. And having said that, let me issue a caution against the cliché questions that we see so often in sports interviews. One of those classic questions is the how-did it-feel inquiry. How did it feel to win the game? How did it feel to lose today? How did it feel to fumble the ball and see the other team recover it and score the winning touchdown? Most often the reader can predict the replies to such questions, so why even ask them? I think my all-time favorite dumb sports reporter question—one that I hear at least once a week on the nightly newscast—is when the reporter asks a player: "Why do you think the other team beat you tonight?" I'm always waiting for this answer: "Because the other team scored more points." None of the interviewees has ever quite said that—but what they do have to say invariably doesn't add up to much more than that.

As I suggested in the previous chapter when discussing the celebrity interviews, the value of an interviewee's responses seems to be in direct proportion to the originality and freshness of the reporter's questions. Thus, before you go into a sports interview, and before you prepare to assemble a sports profile, ask yourself if your questions are intriguing enough to elicit interesting answers.

I probably don't know enough about sports myself to suggest "questions [that] are intriguing enough," but I think I can at least think of some questions that should get your interviewee talking. Some of these might be: What professional athlete do you most admire and why? What mentor or model did you have who was most beneficial to your career? If you could change anything about the athletic program at the college, what would it be? Why do you think there is so little fan interest in track and field? People often stereotype jocks. Comment?

Again, these might not be the most brilliant questions, but at least they are all open-ended and designed to get your athlete talking.

A final point about interviewing and profiling athletes, and by extension coaches and anyone else involved with the athletic program at your campus. Rather than just chatting with your subject across a desk (and for heaven's sake don't do it over the phone), get your subject in action. Get the coach on the field, go for a run with the track star, get in the pool with that butterfly champ, get into the weight room with that wrestler. Sound silly? Maybe, but your story will read a lot better.

3. *Physical education.* Sports pages too often focus solely on competitive varsity sports at the expense of the side of sport that is compulsory for the entire student body. What are the options available in P.E. classes and how are they determined? Is the department adequately funded? How does the phys ed program at your campus compare with that of other colleges? How do the students feel about the P.E. requirement? When did archery drop off the list of course offerings and why did tap dancing take its place?

I recently discovered that what used to be called gym class at my university is now under the aegis of the Department of Human Kinetics. What is that all about? Readers are always asking, "What is that all about?" Reporters—including sports reporters—should be answering that question.

4. *Investigative stories.* There's a lot of profitable digging to be done behind the scoreboard. Examples: steroid use and drug testing; enforcement of rules; practices and problems in recruitment; athletes and academics; sports gambling; perks for players; athletic program funding; team hazing; team traditions; athletes' superstitions; alumni support; ticket sales; coaching strategies and tactics; safety on the field and the court; sex equality in sports.

That's another dozen or more of my quick topics—all of which could lead to good stories or even good series of stories. Like any other area of society, sports are a source not only of good stories but also good stories-behind-stories. If your sports reporters aren't engaged in some investigative work (see chapter 6) at least some of the time, the beat isn't being covered.

5. *Season previews.* Readers love 'em, especially when you do a nice big spread with lots of photos, stats, schedules, and the like. Sports fans will often save these special pages or sections and tape them to their walls. Previews also provide editors with opportunities to get creative with layout and photography. So go for it.

OH, SHOOT!

A word about photography. Just as sports gives writers exciting opportunities that the news pages normally don't offer, so it is with photography. Athletes are involved in action, contests, conflict, triumph, and heartbreak. In other words, you've got nothing but great photo ops here, so sports pictures should reflect all this drama and more. More often than not the best photos I see in newspapers are sports photos (that I don't read the sports pages doesn't mean I don't look at the pictures). Sports photographers should therefore be instructed to get in on the action and to get in close. Editors laying out the pages accordingly should budget plenty of space for those pix—show 'em often and show 'em big. There is no excuse for sports pages to be full of nothing but posed pictures of teams or mug shots of individual athletes.

By the same token, when you have a really dynamite photo, why not share it with all the readers, not just the fans who read the sports pages? There is no rule that says a fine sports picture can't go on the front page—just as there is no rule barring a sports story from being your lead story ("Hounds take state title," "Saperstein vaults over dorm"). In other words, if you've got it, flaunt it.

Photographers should be instructed, by the way, that they are obligated to stay for the entire event to which they are assigned. Too often, photographers will pop in for the opening minutes of a game, snap some snaps, then pop off for a be— I mean, for a Coke someplace, thinking they've covered sports for the day. Yeah, and miss that winning touchdown, or that wrestler getting his arm wrenched off? Uh-uh. Just as it is with reporters, if you're supposed to cover an event, then cover it. Arrive early and leave late—that doesn't apply just to your keg parties.

Dig it—cover your sports well enough and maybe even I will read your sports pages.

11

Photos and Graphics

Journalists are often categorized as either "pencils," meaning they write, or as "cameras," meaning they snap photos or shoot videotape. I've always been a pencil, which I suppose is why I've long believed that a well-chosen word can be worth a thousand pictures. Nevertheless, I deeply esteem photojournalism. You should, too.

The photography I've seen in student newspapers ranges from the spectacular to the stale. I don't know why this range is so wide. The quality of student press photography may derive from the newsroom culture at each individual campus. Some student newspapers perhaps never developed a tradition of solid photojournalism, and they're just doggedly continuing in that tradition. Some campuses may not have classes in photography or graphics or even photo clubs. Some editors (and advisers) may not think in visual terms—although in this media day and age, *The Wall Street Journal* excepted, that seems unlikely. Some student newspapers simply may not have the budget or the printing facilities to permit anything beyond minimal publication of pictures. Nor does photojournalism seem at all related to the size or prestige of the campus at which a newspaper is published. For example, I've seen first-class photos in student newspapers like *The Monroe Doctrine* (Monroe Community College, Rochester, New York), to name just one institution that may not have a high national profile, and I've seen wretched photos in dailies published in Ivy League student newspapers.

Anyway, I don't care what the excuse is, it's still an excuse and it doesn't wash with me. I don't see any legitimate reason why student newspapers shouldn't feature pictures that are as outstanding as the writing. Whether you've got big bucks or small, great equipment and facilities or not, you're still obligated to publish respectable pictures.

But just what are good news and feature photos? This book, you will recall from the Introduction, is not a how-to but a what-should-and-why, so I'm not going to go all technical on you and present a primer on how to take and make good photos. But I can discuss some principles that should suggest the differences between good pictures and bad.

GO ORGANIC

Good news photos are organic, meaning they've been raised without artificial fertilizers or pesti— . . . no, that's not what it means at all. (Just wanted to see if you were paying attention.) An organic illustration is one that incorporates some life. Usually this means the photo will depict people. Example: A student apartment was burgled the other night. Now unless he or she was part of the burglary team, your photographer will not get a photo of the crime in action. Understood. But you want a photo to go with your story, so what does the photographer supply? What I've seen over and over again is . . . a picture of a doorway to the apartment house where the burglary occurred. So what's wrong with that? What's wrong is the doorway to one apartment house looks very much like the doorway to any other apartment house, and apartment house doorways are pretty boring. The student newspaper I advise once published doorway photos in five or six consecutive issues, with some issues boldly flaunting more than one doorway. I hit the roof. What is this publication? I demanded. A watered-down version of *Architectural Digest*? *Student Screen Door Review*?

The doorway shot not only conveys minimal information (the site of the burglary had a doorway) but is so lifeless that readers will give it barely a glance. That's just a waste of precious space. Granted, a photo after a burglary is a photo after the fact, but this story could still be illustrated better. After all, your story is also after the fact, but how do you get an interesting story? Right, by talking to people (burglary victims, neighbors, landlord, cops). By now you should be getting the idea. A good illustration for such a story might be the burglary victims staring wistfully at the space where their stolen stereo system and CD collection used to be. Or the housemates picking through the rubble of their trashed apartment. Or the cops taking down statements from the residents. Some picture that has people in it. And if the photographer can't gain access to the apartment and its residents and has to settle for an outdoor shot, well, at least shoot that doorway with someone entering or emerging. Human figures humanize a photo, give the surroundings perspective, and overall make for pictures that will earn more than just the briefest glance from the reader.

Let's consider some examples less dramatic than an apartment break-in. If the main residence hall on campus has a newly furnished lounge, for heaven's sake don't run a photo of the lounge without students lounging in it. Just show the sofas and chair and your photo would look like a home furnishings ad. If the library has a new computer lab, show the lab with students enthusiastically playing their video games—I mean, doing their research. If the athletic department inaugurates a new rugby pitch, never run a picture of an empty field; get some players out there loosening each other's teeth. If you're publishing a season celebration picture—spring in blossom, autumn leaves carpeting the campus—get some people in the shot fondling each other under the dogwoods or hurling Frisbees amid the fall foliage. Animate those photos. If not with people, then with cocker spaniels. If not dogs, then squirrels. If not squirrels, then Japanese beetles. All, right, I'm getting carried away. But the point should be clear. Lively photos will have some breathing going on.

Every time I see a photo in a student newspaper of a snowy campus scene sans human beings, of a swimming pool with no swimmers, of a hiking trail with no hikers, of a health clinic with no nurses or patients, of a job fair that shows simply tables and placards, then I'm seeing the handiwork of photographers and photo editors who don't know their jobs. I'm seeing pictures raised with chemical fertilizers and pesticides. Inorganic.

LET'S FACE IT

With my tendency to repeat myself, I've stated several times in this text that newspapers should contain lots of faces. But there are faces and there are faces. It's appropriate to illustrate an article with pictures of the people featured prominently in the story. That's cool. But that's no excuse for publishing the equivalent of police mug books or line-up group shots. I've seen too many head shots that appear to be lacking only the prisoner's number across his chest, too many rows of grinning Environmental Club members or field hockey team members arrayed like so many duck pins on the grass. Boring. Junior high school journalism. Ouch.

Now, of course sometimes you have little choice in the matter. A guest lecturer is coming to campus and his PR people have supplied only a head shot. The Environmental Club posed in a row and wouldn't sit still for anything else. Okay, so now and again you have to go with what you have. But at least be sure such photos are doing the job. Does the head shot convey the image of a living person? Can you get in tight enough on the group picture so faces can be seen clearly and the line-up won't be mistaken for that of some other student group? If the pictures are lifeless, if they're waxwork dummies, if they're static, if they don't work, if they can't be read easily, then why use them? You're better off running that photo of the groping couple under the dogwoods. Or the squirrel.

Two additional points, one on head shots, one on group photos:

If you're using a head shot, or even a half- or full-body portrait, you don't necessarily have to have the subject looking straight at the reader. It's certainly all right if it does, but some argue that a photo is more lifelike if the subject is looking off to a side, as if to suggest the person in the picture is engaged in something rather than just posing for the camera. That said, if the person in the picture is looking to a side—or if it's a profile shot—the conventional wisdom is the photo subject should not be "looking off the page." That is, the face should be turned toward the interior of the page rather than beyond the border of the newspaper. This especially holds if the photo is appearing on the first or last column—the border columns—of the page. No law says you must keep the face from gazing off the page; the reason is psychological, nothing more. It's felt that readers are somehow disconcerted when confronted with an image that gazes off the page. The idea is that readers somehow follow that gaze and lose the page. All of this may be nonsense, but it's nevertheless a principle most page designers observe. You would probably do well to observe it, too, by reversing the picture and keeping faces within borders. (Some editors believe that flipping or reversing pictures falsifies the reality of the shot and therefore is unethical, but some think that's taking ethics too far. You decide.)

On group photos: As noted, these pictures are essentially a waste of space unless the mugs in the group can be clearly discerned. Otherwise, one herd of students looks quite like another. To me, one of the most irritating photos of multiple individuals is the sports picture snapped from the bleachers—you know, the sort of image that shows a dozen players whose faces are not only indistinguishable but even whose shirt numbers can't be made out. Captions are often no help—I still can't tell from the photo who is doing what to whom. That said, all photos should have captions (also called cutlines), and photo captions should include the names of the people in the group. We'll have more to say about captioning in chapter 14, but for now just let it be noted that photo editors should make it a rule for photographers that pictures are incomplete without caption information. Photographers, you're not just shutterbugs, you're photojournalists. Along with your cameras, pack a pen and notebook in your camera bags.

THE LOWDOWN ON DOWNLOADS
Far too common among student newspaper editors is the practice of ripping photos from the World Wide Web. I fully understand the temptation. Why send a photographer out to shoot a person or a scene when you might just as well find an appropriate photo just waiting to be appropriated on the Internet? This sort of thing is especially common on the A&E pages where, say, you have a review of a new CD and you'd like to illustrate it with an action shot of the band. But photo-ripping might and does occur anywhere. Colin Powell is coming to speak on campus and the general's lecture agency hasn't yet come up with a photo? Rip Powell off the Web. Your photographer failed to get that good shot of the geese flying south for the winter that you scheduled for page 1? Download those downy geese.

Well, not a good idea, and for two reasons. First, many if not most images accessible on the Web, just like much of the text, are copyrighted. This means that to reprint the image you should first seek permission and pay any fees required. You are not protected from copyright infringement simply by including a credit line under the photo. (I've seen credit lines in student newspapers that read like this: "Photo courtesy of beatles.com." Exactly what kind of courtesy has beatles.com extended when the newspaper never asked beatles.com for use of the picture?)

In actual practice you won't normally have lawyers threatening infringement suits. Film stills are usually fair game to accompany movie reviews and previews. Many individuals and outfits—say, rock performers or nonprofit organizations—are likewise happy for the publicity you're providing them and won't seek payment for their photos. But none of this is universally true, and certainly individual photographers who make their living selling their work aren't sanguine about seeing it reproduced without their knowledge or permission. So you should seek before you rip.

Lawsuits and payments aside, however, I always think it a sign of failure when a newspaper, student or not, publishes an Internet photo rather than an original of its own. It's the same principle with news or feature stories. Readers understand that a local paper must rely on international agencies or other outside sources to provide news and pix of that tsunami in Japan. But a nature photo? A shot of a band performing in town? A book jacket photo when the author is reading right on your campus? A photo of a state trooper, or city hall, or anything else in your area? You rip and I'll say ouch.

GIVE CREDIT WHERE

Since I mentioned photo credits I'll say a few words about photo credits. No picture should run without one. Just as stories (other than press handouts) should have bylines, so pix should have picture credits. Many readers don't give a tinker's about either, but readers do have the right to know who's responsible for what, and you should include bylines and photo credits if only for the record. At the very least, your photographers are building portfolios of their published work, so a picture printed without a credit is of no use to them.

To indicate how seriously this matter is regarded, I will mention that I once worked for a newspaper that had a policy of compensating freelance photographers five times their normal rate if the page editor neglected to include a credit for a picture . . . and twenty-five times their normal fee for a second such omission. (There were not, as I recall, ever any third offenses; editors were mighty careful after a second slipup, since the photographer's compensation was coming out of the responsible editor's salary.) Other news organizations often have similar policies. I'm not suggesting that student editors should hurl themselves on their swords if they forget to credit pictures—but a correction in the next issue goes a long way to assuaging a neglected photographer, and with the correction the picture can now be added to the cameraperson's portfolio. In any event, give credit for all images—even those you are lazy enough to take from the Internet.

QUANTITY AND QUALITY

What percentage of your pages should be devoted to photography? My feeling: a lot. I know that's a rather vague response, but it's the best I can do. All I know is I've seen student newspapers in which photography is wildly neglected, and I've seen student newspapers that seem to have more pictures than anything else. First principle, of course, should be quality rather than quantity, just as it is with text (a well-written and well-produced eight-page paper is superior to twenty-four pages of rubbish any day). If you shouldn't run stories just to fill space, the same holds true for photos. So certainly assign a lot of photos each week, and publish as many good ones as space permits.

There are two reasons for my suggesting you publish "a lot" of pictures. One is that readers like them and expect them; we are, after all, living in a visual age, and any publication that doesn't feature good photography doesn't look like it belongs to the twenty-first century. The second reason is that since the ascendancy of this visual age (movies, TV, the Internet) newspapers, and this includes the venerable *New York Times*, have steadily become more like magazines in both content and appearance. *USA Today*, a highly influential pioneer of newspaper design and production from its founding in 1982, has even been referred to as "television on paper." I'm not suggesting student newspapers need strive to become TV in print (being labeled "television on paper" is not entirely a compliment anyway). But you do want to be part of the visual age—just as your readers are. Especially if you're not publishing on a daily basis, your newspaper is more magaziney than you might recognize. So yes, recognize that and honor those photos.

MORE ON QUANTITY

Photographers should not come back from an assignment with only one or two shots to offer their editors. In this era of digital pix and pixels, there's no reason not to fill those memory cards. The more options editors have for using pictures, the better the paper will look.

SIZE MATTERS

How big should photos be? I do wish you would quit asking these nettlesome questions. I can't really answer this question definitively except to observe that over the years newspaper photos have steadily grown. This no doubt reflects our visual culture mentioned above, but it also underscores the simple fact that sizeable photos have sizeable impact. I can't imagine too many instances when a head shot deserves to occupy half a page—although I have seen this and I must admit it does have its effect. You be the judge. But what is clear is that there is little point—or excuse—for running postage stamp head shots and Brownie snapshot-sized group or scene pictures. Such pix are old-fashioned, dull, and, small as they are, still a waste of space.

COLOR?

We not only live in a visual age, we live in a color visual age, and newspapers that don't print in color look so yesterday. *The New York Times*, once affectionately known as the Gray Lady, was among the last major American dailies to introduce color printing. Many devoted *Times* readers were outraged by this development; they just didn't want their newspaper to change in any respect. But the editors had what I thought was a sturdy defense of its introduction of color photos: The world, they noted, was in color, and to cover the world, they said, the *Times* should be in color, too.

Color printing, of course, costs a lot more than noncolor, and if you have the budget and the facilities for it, then good on you. (You can make up some of the extra costs of a color print run, of course, by charging more for color advertising.) If you cannot print in color, however, don't despair. I know that people under twenty-five years of age have an aversion to watching black and white movies, but there's still a lot of art to be had in the world of black and white. Just because you can't print in color doesn't mean you can't print excellent photos. Even a subject that ostensibly cries out for color—a nature shot, for example—can be striking in rich black and white. If you don't believe me, check out any Ansel Adams calendar—or more to the point, any of the fine student newspapers that run fine b&w photos.

By the same token, if you are printing in color, don't waste your color opportunities. I've seen many dull color photos—pictures in which the added expense of color added nothing to the image. Example: a dean shaking hands with a top student at a graduation exercise. Two guys shaking hands? Dull in color or black and white. Much better to shoot a wide overview of the graduation ceremony, showing the graduates in their variously colored robes, the grass and trees in the background.

So—photographers, when you're shooting color, make sure every shot is colorful. And editors of color photo pages—when you're thinking of images for your pages, dream in color.

OUT AND ABOUT

A piece of advice from an old pencil stub to student press photographers: Much of your work will be the result of assignments, but as with any good reporter the totality of your work should not be based on instruction from your bosses. I like to think of student reporters at all times between waking and sleeping, between classes and down at the neighborhood tavern—I mean, Starbucks—always having with them pens, notebooks, and inquiring minds. Same principle for photographers.

Case in point: Once I saw two wonderful photo ops on the very same day that no photographers saw. The first was in a small shopping mall where an Amish horse and buggy were tied up against a funky music store's colorfully decorated wall (psychedelic portraits of Jimi Hendrix, John Lennon, etc). I immediately called the student newspaper office and left a voice message alerting the photo editor of this cool picture possibility. By the time anyone from the newspaper arrived—if they ever did—the horse had long moseyed on.

Later that afternoon I saw a fairly spectacular collision of two vehicles, just a half-block from the student union building. Couple of serious injuries. Again I called the office and left a message. This time the newspaper did get a picture, which it ran on the front page of the next edition. But the picture it ran was taken hours after the accident, long after the wrecked sedan and pickup had been towed away, long after the shattered windshield glass had been swept up. What did the picture show? Site of Car Accident. Site of Car Accident? The asphalt equivalent of Doorway to Burgled Apartment. Sigh.

YOU BROKE IT, YOU BOUGHT IT

As noted in chapter 2, the photo editor is responsible for overseeing all equipment in his or her department. Cool. So what happens—as it invariably does—when a photographer comes back from an assignment with a damaged camera or a lost camera? (Um, how exactly does one return with a lost camera?) A policy on liability should be in place, and equally important, the photo editor should be maintaining insurance and warranties and the like on all equipment.

ETHICS AND LEGALITIES

I discuss journalistic ethics in chapter 19, but since photos carry their own special legal and ethical baggage, it seems appropriate to discuss some of that luggage here—especially in connection with topics I've just been discussing.

1. *Enhancement.* The introduction of digital photography meant the possibility of image manipulation as never before. As a result, most news organizations have adopted policies of not using photos that have been altered beyond the normal parameters of cropping, adjusting contrast, enlargement, and so on—the things expected in the old film labs. The principle is to avoid using pictures that have been digitized to the point where they no longer depict reality. Or if newspapers do use such photos—say, for some arty illustration or montage—then the papers should inform the reader of the concoction by means of a little credit line. News organizations are ostensibly in the truth business. As such they eschew publishing untruthful photos as much as they avoid (or try to avoid) printing lies. An excellent set of ethical guidelines—both on photojournalism in general and on digital enhancement in particular—has been established by the National Press Photographers Association. Check its Web site: www.nppa.org (and note that it has a student membership division).

An early and classic instance of manipulation illustrates the point well. In 1997, *Newsweek* decided to run a cover story on a woman named Bobbi McCaughey who gained national attention by giving birth to septuplets. The cover photo was the woman's face; design experts maintain that a nice portrait is usually very helpful for a magazine's newsstand sales. Trouble was Mrs. McCaughey didn't have a glamorous or even an especially appealing face (you go have seven babies all at once and see how glamorous you look). Specifically, the problem was the new mom's wonky teeth, which gave her an unattractive smile. You guessed it. A little orthodontics via the miracle of computer image manipulation and the lady was ready for her close-up. Trouble was the patchwork picture was immediately recognized for what it was. After all, the new multiple mom's face, bad bridgework and all, was appearing throughout the world's media. Only in *Newsweek* did Bobbi McCaughey have a Hollywood smile. The newsweekly's editors accordingly had to wipe the grins from their faces. They had been caught publishing an image from an alternate universe and were universally condemned for it. Since then, when choosing and editing digital photographs, editors remain alert to the ethics of enhancement, as well they should. You should, too.

2. *Taste.* I have an entire chapter, 18, on matters of taste, but because photographs can cause such strong visceral reactions—and because readers tend to be upset more by pictures than by words—I'll say just a few tasteful words

here about taste. In fact, I'll frame my words in the form of a one-question situational exam. Goes like this:

A prominent personality, say, the vice president of the United States, visits your campus to deliver a lecture. A student press photographer gets the requisite pictures of the man at the podium. But the photographer also happens to catch the VP after the lecture, in the wings of the auditorium, vigorously reaming a nostril with his forefinger. Everyone in the newspaper office finds the photo hilarious. The photo is especially appreciated because nobody much likes the vice president—he's pompous, arrogant, nasty, whatever. The decision on printing such a photo is a judgment call. So—what's your call on printing the photo in your newspaper? (Clue: What do you think the National Press Photographers Association's ethical guidelines say?)

3. *Privacy.* The issues discussed above, photo manipulation and taste, are essentially matters of ethics but not of law. This is not true of privacy. In this instance, the right of individuals not to have their pictures published is a matter of state law. Most of these laws will distinguish between photos taken in public and private places, whether the photos are to be used for commercial purposes, if the subjects are private citizens or public figures, and so on. It is important to note, however, that these laws vary from state to state. Photo editors and photographers therefore should know their state laws (usually accessible on state government Web sites) and observe them (more on this in chapter 17).

GRAPHICALLY SPEAKING

Graphics is a la-di-dah, contemporary term with multiple meanings. Essentially it denotes drawing, or the pictorial, and especially the pictorial that is reproducible by some means of printing. For a large portion of its history, drawings were the sole means of illustration in newspapers. Then in the late nineteenth century the photogravure process was invented, allowing the reproduction of photos on newsprint. Nevertheless, drawings are still used in newspapers—even if the drawings today are more likely to be produced by computer programs rather than by the human hand.

Graphic illustrations are useful in a number of ways. For one thing, when you don't have a photo to illustrate a story, you may resort to a drawing. This may sound like a sleazy form of substitution, but it isn't. For example, let's say the university is planning a redesign of the parking facilities on campus. You may not have photos to explain the new plan, but a well-drawn map might do the trick nicely. Let's say a dog has mauled a student, and the cunning canine didn't stick around to pose for a photo. How about a police-artist-type sketch of the suspect based on the victim's description? Or perhaps a sorority has announced plans for constructing a spectacular float for homecoming. Since no picture of the float yet exists, you could help readers get an idea of the structure by doing an artist's impression.

In all three examples above many editors would conclude that, lacking photos, they just have to run the articles without illustration. Yet in all three, illustrations would be of immeasurable value to readers. A little imagination can make up for the absence of photography. And chances are, at least one person on the newspaper staff has some drawing ability. ("Anybody here ever take a life drawing class or graphic design? Yo, Saperstein, you're our new staff artist.")

Off the Charts

By far the most common graphic illustration in print today is the chart or graph. Again, *USA Today* and its then-state-of-the-art Apple computers trailblazed the regular use of computer infographics in newspapers with which we are so familiar today. Many a story—and especially those in which numbers figure prominently—is greatly enhanced by a pie chart, a graph, a table, a diagram, a map, or some other form of visual aid. Indeed, readers have become so accustomed to such aids that articles without them seem incomplete. A chart, for example, is an excellent way to illustrate where a student's activities fees are allocated, while a graph might well explain the demographics of graduation rates or a race for a football division title. The best part is that you might not even need Saperstein to work out such illustrations for you. Certainly newspaper staff members who have studied statistics, social sciences, and other courses where graphic illustration is commonly used might be tapped for these chores. But don't limit yourself to—or be defeated by—a spreadsheet program like Excel. Numerous computer programs and Web sites can either provide templates or walk you through the making of an infographic, or both. Check out, for example, www.mathleague.com or the National Center for Education Statistics at http://nces.ed.gov/nceskids/graphing. The best book on the subject that I know is *A Practical Guide to Graphics Re-*

porting: Information Graphics for Print, Web & Broadcast, by Jennifer George-Palilonis (Burlington, MA: Focal Press, 2006).

And don't take the attitude that charts and graphs and the like must be formulaic, because there is plenty of opportunity here for a creative student at the keyboard. One of my all-time favorite graphic illustrations was a pie chart showing the proportional representation of the fractious Italian parliament's numerous political parties. The kicker was that the pie chart was superimposed over a pizza pie.

12

Design

Although I've seen some intriguing exceptions to this rule, newspapers generally come in two sizes. Readers normally think of these two forms of newsprint as "big pages" and "smaller pages." Being better informed than everyone else, we journalists know those two sizes as broadsheet and tabloid.

Historically the broadsheet has been associated with more serious papers serving higher-class readers, and tabloids most commonly have been thought of as lighter-weight dailies serving working-class folk. Think of it this way: Executives being chauffeured in limos to their offices are more likely to be reading *The Wall Street Journal* and *The New York Times* than *The Daily News* or the *New York Post*. The latter are more commonly read by working stiffs like you and me on the bus or subway. Of course this is a generalization, but in fact the smaller, more easily handled tabloid was invented specifically to appeal to commuters trying to read their papers on crowded public transport to and from work. None of this, however, is to suggest that broadsheets are automatically superior to tabloids. There are excellent and terrible newspapers in each category; the test is how well the individual newspapers serve their readers.

I bring all this up because most likely your newspaper is either (a) broadsheet or (b) tabloid, and perhaps you should ask yourself if (c) you're wearing the right size. And so, a few points to ponder regarding the size of your pages.

SIZE MATTERS

Studies have consistently shown that most readers prefer the tabloid size. The reason is fairly obvious: Being more magazine-like in shape than the broadsheet, the tabloid is easier to manipulate and navigate, making it more reader-friendly. What really surprised many industry insiders was a recent experiment in Britain. In England that perceived class association of tabloid and broadsheet readers was most pronounced—so much so that broadsheets are called "quality papers"—leaving the tabloids as synonymous with what, "non-quality"? Anyway, in an effort to retard falling circulation figures, London broadsheets like *The Times* and *The Independent* a few years back got the idea of publishing in both formats, and the resulting sales figures bore out publishers' suspicions: Readers, even those "higher-class readers," like tabloids. Other "quality" newspapers, meanwhile, like *The Guardian*, descended a half-step to something between broadsheet and tabloid because the editors felt some of that "down-market, low-class" association with the tab persisted among readers.

The British experiments aside, two somewhat contradictory points remain regarding page size. The first is that the shape of your pages sends a subtle signal as to whether you are high class or low. Well, hey, nobody wants to be considered low-class. So broadsheet, right? But wait, the second lesson is that readers, both limo lizards and subways salamanders, like the tab. So that suggests you should perhaps put your class consciousness aside and publish in tabloid format.

But hold on: Tabloid pages have an additional downside. That downside is that smaller pages mean fewer design options. It doesn't take a genius—or a student newspaper adviser—to quickly realize you can put more on a broadsheet page than you can on a tabloid page. In terms of the front page, the broadsheet allows for more stories, more pictures, more of everything. This means a broadsheet can give more important stories the prominence they deserve. It also means that by offering more variety on its front page, the broadsheet can appeal to a wider range of readers.

Okay, so broadsheet? Well, not necessarily. The tabloid may be able to squeeze only three or four stories onto its front page, or perhaps only two, or just one, but if newspapers are indeed functioning as daily magazines—and if that's what readers by now are accustomed to—then maybe the less-is-more approach is more appropriate for a first news page. Give me one eyeball-grabbing headline, one dynamite story, and one excellent photo and I can give you one very effective front page. This is precisely the principle by which so many tabs, like the *Philadelphia Daily News* and London's *Daily Mirror*, publish every day.

Okay, so, tabloid? Well, not necessarily. Look, I've seen excellent tabloid student newspapers and excellent student broadsheet papers, and I've see ugly dwarves and giants as well. (Aren't you pleased I'm clearing this up for you?) All I'm suggesting is that size matters, and whatever size you're publishing in now, perhaps you should give it a rethink (just as I think everything about a newspaper now and again requires a rethink).

THE RETHINK

Newspaper editors generally do review their design every few years, or if they don't, they should. Usually the rethink focuses on two questions: Is our design working and do we look up to date?

Looking up to date is the main reason design changes periodically, because up to date changes, well, virtually with the date. Unless they are unaccountably enthralled by tradition (say, like *The Wall Street Journal*), the press has an understandable horror of looking old-fashioned. Just go through a newspaper's archives and you'll see how quickly design takes on an antique look. It's fascinating to glance back at what newspapers looked like five, fifteen, twenty-five, fifty, and a hundred years ago, and while doing so it's often hard not to ask: What were they thinking? In certain periods, for example, the modular model held: Designers considered it cool to have everything stacked in neat square or oblong blocks. In somewhat modified form this holds in many newspapers today. At other times everything was linear, with columns like so many supermarket cash register receipts. There was a time when *The New York Times* crammed eight solid columns of type on every page. There was a time when headlines bellowed, a time when they whispered. There was a time when British newspapers published nothing but advertisements on the front page (it surprises Americans, but many foreign papers still devote part of their front pages to ads). There was a time—well there was a time when just about everything was tried in newsprint. Even today, the *Financial Times* is printed, heaven knows why, on peach-colored paper. Ain't that peachy? No, I don't think so either.

In any event, student designers and other editors should be doing what all other designers and editors are doing all the time: monitoring other campus papers, mainstream media, and alternative newspapers for design ideas and trends. Numerous instructional design Web sites abound as well, and these are great for raiding (for openers, try www.designorati.com or www.visualeditors.com). If you're publishing in tabloid format, it's always wise to study magazine design, because these days tab newspapers, especially weeklies or semi-weeklies, are as much mags as rags. It's also instructive and indeed often eye-opening to look at the results of campus newspaper design contests, such as those sponsored annually by the Associated Collegiate Press (www.studentpress.org/acp) to see what some students are really capable of. Keep an eye out everywhere for what's new, what looks good, what works, and what doesn't. Then do as everyone else does and steal those good ideas. Just call it adaptation or inspiration. Oh, all right, call it theft. But a little thievery is better than falling behind and looking old-fashioned.

DESIGN OBJECTIVES

Beyond trying to make a newspaper look up to date, good designers are motivated by several basic objectives. These include:

1. *Clarity*. The nearly universal aim these days is to have pages clean, clear, and reader-friendly. This translates into no-nonsense-type fonts, such as Helvetica or Century, abundant white space around text, story and picture placement that the eye and mind can apprehend without conscious effort, and an avoidance of clutter on the page. The idea is that the reader should not look at a page and feel confused, because a confused reader soon enough becomes a nonsubscriber.

This is not to say designers always triumph. Examples of some persistent challenges for newspaper designers aiming for clarity are TV listings and stock tables. I've seen newspapers struggle year after year to find a comprehensible way in which to present TV listings (and certainly the ever-expanding offerings from cable and the like have only compounded the problem). As for the Wall Street numbers, some newspapers have effectively thrown in the towel, saying in so many words, here's a few highlights and if you want to know if you personally gained or lost capital today, get thee to the Internet.

At the same time, it appears even newspapers dedicated to having the latest technology and the sharpest of cutting-edge designers don't always get it right. From its first issue one of the great attractions of that pioneering newspaper *USA Today* was its innovative design—bright, crisp, obviously well

DESIGN 185

planned. Yet over the years the front page and inside pages of *USA Today* have often looked like they were laid out with a shovel—or as if some overenthusiastic interns were turned loose on the page-design software to the point where, well, clarity got obscured.

So—examine your pages. Leave aside content for the moment. Are the pages eye-friendly? Does the design have some rationale behind it? Is the typeface the optimum your printing company makes available? Should your text columns be wider? Should you have more white space on the page? Should you use rules (solid lines) between columns or just leave gutters or alleys of white space? Can the reader navigate your pages painlessly?

2. *Navigation*, or if you prefer, *navigability*, refers to the degree of ease readers have in negotiating their way through the newspaper. Obviously the larger the newspaper the more easily it is to get waylaid or lost, but even if you're publishing an anorexic eight tabloid pages per issue readers shouldn't feel like they need a global positioning system to find their way around.

One of the leading causes of readers losing their bearings in the forests of newsprint is jumps and, oh, I just love this subject. That's because there are fewer things that illustrate the arrogance of print media as sharply as their persistence in printing stories that start on one page and then "jump" to their conclusions on other pages deep inside the paper. Study after study has shown that few aspects of print journalism irritate readers more than having to interrupt their reading of an article to rumple their way through scads of pages or even sections to find the rest of the story. In short, readers *hate* jumps.

But does that stop newspapers from jumping stories? No way. Defending their adherence to jumps, editors point out that advertisers like them, because chasing jumps means readers are exposing themselves to more pages, and hence more ads. Moreover, by running only a portion of a story on, say, the front page, rather than an entire story, editors can place more stories on that front page. Right. *But readers hate jumps!*

And newspapers know that. So doesn't that count for something? Apparently not. In fact, the only major daily that seriously takes this reader preference into account is, again, *USA Today*, which at its founding included among its many innovations the decision not to jump stories. This often meant very brisk and condensed stories, which led to the criticism that the colorful new newspaper was shallow when it came to news. *USA Today* then countered this carping with another innovation: a short version of a news story on the front page and, if merited, a longer, more detailed version inside. Point being the front-page story was TV succinct (and perhaps shallow), but at least it was a complete unit, and didn't jump.

Bottom line: Will you have stories jump from page 1 to the inside? (Oh, go ahead, ignore reader preferences. Who cares about readers?)

Along with jumping continuations of stories from one page to another is the matter of causing the reader's eyes to jump around the page. The possibilities for placing stories on pages are almost endless, but exploit all those possibilities and your reader will get a headache. Avoid extremes: Your pages should not be boring, formulaic, predictable. Nor should they be something out of the funhouse.

Above all, placement of stories and pictures on a page must not be arbitrary, because not every point on a page is of equal importance. For example, the top half of the page obviously carries more weight than the bottom half, and the upper right columns above the fold signal greater significance than the left side. This is because studies supposedly show that our eye falls first at the top right-hand side of a page of print (I don't know what these studies show about the British, whose newspapers customarily have their lead stories on the top left-hand side of the front page, but then again the Brits don't drive on the proper side of the road either).

Point is, where and how you play a story sends a signal. Put an article in the lead position—upper right-hand side—or splash a story over several columns, and you are signaling that the article is important. Downplay the article—down the page, smaller headline and display—and you assert that the story is of lesser importance. Same holds true with page selection. Front page is obviously more prominent than inside pages, first page of a section is obviously more significant than second or third page of a section, and so on. So be alert to the signals you are sending, because the readers are picking up on those signals.

Another important element in navigability is what I call signposts. That is to say, logos or labels to tell readers what they're reading. In the broadest sense, I think it's a good idea to have a signpost at the top of sections, like "Opinions," "Sports," "Arts and Entertainment," "Features," and the like. This helps readers find the pages they want, and it helps to avoid confusion, so that readers shouldn't have to ask themselves, "Hey, is this a news story I'm reading or an opinion piece?"

Of course one needn't stick an identifying label on every article in the newspaper, but those labels do help. In news, for example, when a reporter writes an analysis or a backgrounder on a news event, it's appropriate for such explanatory pieces to be identified as such. In your A&E pages, it's helpful to label previews and reviews, and in that latter category I think it's important to let readers know right at the top just what entertainment medium is under review. I've actually seen reviews in college newspaper A&E pages in which it was unclear if the reviewer was discussing a movie, TV show, concert, or video game.

Normally in the sports pages the headline will indicate what sport is under discussion—but not always, and as I indicated in chapter 10, I've read sports reports in which the writer took it for granted the reader knew which kind of athletic contest was being described. Well, in this life one should take very little for granted. I think a label atop the headline (BASKETBALL, HOCKEY, CLUB SPORTS) doesn't hurt.

Signposts are also very useful on the Op-Ed pages; readers rightly want to know if what they are reading is the opinion of the editorial board (EDITORIAL), a letter to the editor (LETTERS), a personal column (here a columnist might have an individual title for his regular think pieces, something like MY TWO CENTS or MY BIG MOUTH), and so on. This last point reminds us that labels and logos are an opportunity for some creativity. Yes, you can rip some clip art, but you can go beyond clipping a quill pen for LETTERS and have fun coming up with novel phrases and fresh designs.

3. *Harmony and unity* are elements that virtually all designers favor. This does not mean that all typography must be of the same character, font, size, and the like. It does mean that typographic elements should suggest some controlling intelligence behind their selection. With the hundreds upon hundreds of fonts now available via the magic of computers, it can be tempting to sex up every headline, caption, story text, and logo with some wildly off-the-wall typography. You would do well to resist this temptation. The face and font of your editorial matter will be most pleasing if they are of the same family, that is, fairly unified (if not, both readers and printers will curse you). It is, however, perfectly legitimate to have different fonts, say, for news columns and for Op-Ed column texts. Normally one headline font for news is sufficient, with bold and italic variants accepted, and then perhaps different fonts for certain features inside. Designers will also maintain that signposts and logos

should have harmony and unity; that is, even as they are distinct from headlines, they should all have the same identifiable character (font, color, placement on the page, and, depending on the function on the page, probably the same size). The idea is to have signposts that are immediately identified for what they are—and not to be mistaken for a bulletin board full of handmade fliers and note cards.

Beyond harmony and unity, it is common practice to employ variable designs to distinguish news from features, or news from Op-Ed pages. Common ways of making these distinctions include varying column widths, using different size type, or justifying and unjustifying lines. Any of these devices—a ragged-edge column, for example—will subtly but helpfully signal to the reader that a new or different section is under way. But again, don't get carried away. Run type all the way across the page and you'll run the reader out of the room. In addition, it makes sense to suit the style to the substance. Editorial pages usually deal with serious stuff, so a fairly plainspoken and sober design is in order there. Feature pages or A&E may contain fluff 'n fun, so that's where your fluffy 'n funny design is most suitable.

4. *Balance* is another favored feature among designers. Various items placed on a page have various weights. For example, heavy headlines, photos, and dark stuff—say, when you run a story in reverse plate that shows white letters on a black background—will be "heavy" as opposed to regular blocks of type. Hence designers get all in a twist when they see an unbalanced page—too much heaviness in one area, threatening to capsize the boat. Whether or not readers are alert to this matter of balance is debatable, but I suppose that in a subtle, subconscious way they are, and that's enough to take it into consideration. So designers will argue against clustering photos or headlines in a manner that throws off the balance of the page. At the very least, it does not make for an easy read to have photos bumping up against ads, especially if those ads contain photos or art themselves.

5. *Familiarity* is yet another factor in good newspaper design. Newspaper readers are in many ways a conservative lot, and one of the manifestations of this is the comfort they get from knowing what is where in their daily or weekly read. That is, if they are used to the sports being the final section of the paper, that's where they like sports. If they are accustomed to seeing readers' letters placed on the upper right-hand side of the editorial page, that's their comfort zone for readers' letters. Believe it or not, newspaper audiences get

DESIGN   189

upset even when the comic strips are rearranged. Now this certainly does not mean you must stick with the layout you inherited over the years and over the decades. But it does mean if you are shifting things around every few issues you are going to have a lot of discomforted and disgruntled readers who at the very least are going to be asking, "What are these editors doing? Can't they decide where the hell things belong?"

Bottom line: In terms of design, yes, rethink everything. But be on guard against overthinking and overtinkering. Doing so can drive readers nuts—and drive readers away.

RAGEMAKERS AND QUIRKS
Almost all college papers are designed with the aid of such software as Adobe InDesign, QuarkXPress, or similar programs. From what I gather, everybody at one time or another gets enraged by PageMaker or furious at the quirks of Quark, yet we still use their templates and formatting and the like. I'm not going to get into such arcana as composition zones, job jacketing, and kerning, mainly because I don't understand this stuff well enough to discuss it in any clear and useful way. But I will make what I hope are some useful observations.

First, just as computers don't do the reporting in computer-assisted reporting, so too design programs don't do the actual designing. Such programs are only as good as the person using them. Indeed, using design templates is about as original as painting by numbers or as creative as cutting paper dolls according to a Barbie pattern. The best of page design software, like InDesign, do indeed allow for customizing their features, so I say customize away. Otherwise your newspaper will be in danger of looking like every other student newspaper, and where exactly is the glory in that?

Next, even as I urge creativity and originality in design, be wary of going wild. I've seen contemporary campus papers that recall nothing so much as the alternative hippie newspapers of the 1960s—or maybe some of those famous rock concert posters of that era. You know—stunning artwork, but you can't make out a word of the text. (I always wondered how those Grateful Dead fans ever made it to the Fillmore.) Not for nothing did I list *clarity* first and foremost among those design objectives. I don't care how innovative your design is; if readers can't figure out what they're supposed to be reading, your design fails.

Along with at least one good hardware geek, your newspaper would do well to have at least one certified software geek. Every toddler coming out of preschool these days seems to have some familiarity with Photoshop Elements and Baby Quark or whatever, and that's cool. But you will benefit from having a designated design master, a student who not only knows the programs and can handle design but who can also keep everyone else up to speed. Providing additional training for your geek via courses, conferences, and specialized software is a worthy investment, as is having some sort of instruction for the rest of the staff. All staffers should know something about these programs, even if they are not engaged in design. This helps everyone understand the final product all the better. And for heaven's sake, you don't want all of the tribe's design wisdom lodged in one person's head. Lose that one person (the traitor suddenly decides she prefers working on the literary magazine to the newspaper) and you've lost a hard-to-replace asset.

Other points about software. First, you would do well to have copies of your operating, editing, and design software off site and in a secure place. Thus if your office burns down, if an enraged student government or administration suddenly bars you from the premises, or if a faculty strike shuts your campus, you still might be able to put out your newspaper, even if it's in a limited print edition or perhaps merely online (this may sound paranoid, but I know of all the paranoid scenarios of which I speak). Second, although I just referred to "copies" of your software, I trust you realize that all of your discs should be legally licensed. Last thing you need is some industrial gumshoe sniffing around your office and finding ripped-off software; that could be costly to you and to your reputation. Report the news, don't become the news.

GADGETS AND GIMMICKS

No one need be a computer geek—or for that matter, a design genius—to find ways to dress up an otherwise staid newspaper page. A few tried and true devices are readily at hand. One such device is a drop cap—an oversized letter used at the beginning of a story or perhaps at the beginning of each section of a story. These usually look out of place on news stories, where sobriety rules, but add a nice touch to feature articles and the like. Another is a pull quote—an eye-catching sentence or two from the article that is repeated in larger type and set into the text, either in a box or within borders of white space. This serves to break up a thick block of type and is especially useful when you wish you had a photo to go with the story but for whatever reason you don't. A third device is setting a story against a gray background or screen, or perhaps reversing the plate (mentioned above) to have some white letters against black, just for variety's sake. Yet another device is setting the text of a story over a shadowy background drawing—say, a football story superimposed over a football helmet. You might also brighten a Valentine's Day article with clip art, like candy heart emoticons (though with that one you're unlikely to win many points for originality). But my advice is don't do these things just to show you can do them. It's easy to get carried away with these tricks to the point where your newspaper starts to look like a typography sample catalog. I've seen student newspapers that look just like that, and it makes me dizzy.

COLOR

We discussed color photography in the previous chapter, but I'll add a few cents' worth here on nonphotographic color. What I mean is that even if your budget or printing facilities don't allow for full color reproduction, you may still be able to use spot color, a one- or two-color wash, or duotone in your typography. Using one additional color (or even a different shade of your normal black) can add a nice distinguishing touch, whether to the newspaper's nameplate, column rules, or borders or as a background to a boxed story that deserves special attention. If your newspaper doesn't use such a device, check with your printers and see if a splash of spot color can be added at nominal cost. And yes, it's cornball, but printing in green on St. Patrick's Day? Readers can be mighty cornball too. Many will get a smile out of it, few will complain. (Those candy hearts for the Valentine's Day article are another matter.)

Finally, if you do have the wherewithal to print in all color all the time, just my usual word of caution: Use color judiciously. I've seen excellent use of color in campus newspapers—but I've also seen color riots that recall nothing so much as all of last night's pizza and calzones recycled onto paper. So be careful about attempting to blow the readers' minds with your color palette. You just might make them blow their cookies.

LAST POINT

I have one last point on design, which oddly enough I've been saving for last: However you decide to design your newspaper, it should have its own immediately recognizable identity and should not be mistaken for anything published by your college or university. Some institutions of higher learning put out their own newspapers, and almost all also pump out great numbers of bulletins, newsletters, and other public relations mailbox stuffers. Unless your student newspaper is an official college publication (which is sometimes the case), you would do well to distinguish your publication's independent character by its very appearance. This may mean employing a typeface and design markedly different from what the college uses in its publications; it may even mean developing a college logo different from the school's official emblem. And I hope it goes without saying—but I'll say it anyway—I believe your newspaper should look like a newspaper—not a church bulletin, graphic novel, or travel brochure.

End of last point.

13

Copy Editing

Quality control. We'd like to think the tires of that airplane in which we're about to take off have been inspected. Same with the brakes on that rental car. Same with the raisins—at least we hope those are raisins—in our raisin bran. Quality control. We rarely even think about it. Unless, maybe, those raisins are moving about in our bowls.

Copy editing is quality control, and as such it is vital to the newspaper's reputation and to the readers' respect. If a newspaper hit the stands without being copy edited, or without being copy edited well, it would look a poor product indeed. I've seen a few student newspapers that appear as though they haven't been copy edited, and it's not a pretty picture. At the same time, when I read a paper that has obviously been copy edited carefully, I take off my Mets cap to those students who beaver away far into the night, with no recognition from the public and with no thanks from the writers who are collecting all the glory and bylines. Once and only once in my professional life did I observe a reporter thanking the copy desk. "Hey, you guys did a great job on that bomb-threat story I cranked out yesterday," the reporter said. "You really made me look good."

The copy editors were dumbfounded.

Copy editors are the unsung heroes of journalism. So let's sing a song of copy editors.

Who are these people who silently sacrifice their eyesight and their social life in anonymity for the greater good of the newspaper? We often think of them as geeky word nerds or other weird characters who for some ungodly reason memorized the entire *Associated Press Stylebook*. But that is no more accurate or fair than the antique image of pasty-faced editors wearing celluloid eyeshades and arm garters. As with so many other fields of endeavor, I suspect copy editors are drawn to the job because of talent and temperament. And that talent and temperament deserve respect and honor. Copy editors are probably as much born as made. You may decide this after you meet some copy editors at the American Copy Editors Society (www.copydesk.org).

Yes, a good copy editor is strong on spelling, grammar, and newspaper style, but that's only the start of it—and arguably the least of it. Typographical errors, botched sentences, and to a lesser extent stylistic inconsistencies stand out in newspapers, much to the derisory delight of the *gotcha!* crowd. But as I suggested in the Introduction to this book, *typographical and syntactical errors don't upset me in the least*. Yes, I notice them, and yes, I regret them, and yes, I automatically mark them when I'm critiquing a newspaper. But no, typos and such do not bother me; they are simply the result of a hasty or careless eye. That's not to excuse the errors, just to explain them. Mere mechanical slippage is not a firing offense. Mental slippage, however, is something else again.

Which is my central point in this chapter. A good copy editor is neither a human spell-checker nor a walking, talking thesaurus. A good copy editor is not merely the newspaper's stylebook specialist. A good copy editor is not merely a proofreader. A good copy editor is all those things, sure. But more important, a good copy editor is a sensitive and inquiring reader.

SO SENSITIVE

Sensitivity to language cannot be taught—but in good measure it can be learned. It's certainly acquired through practice (plenty of reading and writing), but it's also the product of such innate qualities as being a good listener and perhaps even being endowed with a musical ear.

A Person Sensitive to Language knows the difference between saying "He smiled," "He grinned," "He beamed," and "He smirked."

The PSTL likewise is alert to the difference between "The man said he was innocent" and "The man claimed he was innocent."

The PSTL knows that "presently" is not synonymous with "at present."

The PSTL is aware of the nuances in saying the accountant "misappropriated the cash," "pinched the cash," "embezzled the cash," and "stole the cash."

The PSTL knows that an aircraft can zoom in only one direction—up.

The PSTL realizes that even Albert Einstein wasn't a "very unique" human being.

The PSTL would know which two letters to knock out of the phrase "a secret shared amongst friends."

The PSTL is not bothered by the fact that in the plural we may have two bears chasing two deer, or that while deer have hooves, Rudolf's hooves never clatter upon rooves.

The PSTL isn't necessarily master of such aggravating pairs as *emigrate* and *immigrate, lay* and *lie, effect* and *affect, accept* and *except, capital* and *capitol, principle* and *principal, than* and *then, its* and *it's, flout* and *flaunt*—but the PSTL at least knows always to double-check these bastards when they show up in the copy. (And what about *stalagmite* and *stalactite?* Oh, unless you're a bat, who cares about stalagmites and stalactites?)

The PSTL finally would also recognize that PSTL, an acronym I just invented, is an acronym I should immediately disinvent because PSTL is unpronounceable at best and at worst keeps bringing to mind a handgun. As in "going PSTL."

So, how did you do on the sensitivity training test? Hardly matters, because even knowing what's correct in the above list still doesn't separate the sheep from the goats—or, more precisely, it won't distinguish between the merely competent copy editor and the truly intelligent copy editor. This is where the empathy with the reader comes in.

EMPATHY FOR THE DEVIL

Good copy editors are the public's advocate and as such put themselves instinctively in the place of the typical newspaper reader. As they study their copy, editors will constantly demand on behalf of the readers: Is this story clear? Is the writing comprehensible? Are the sentences well constructed, the diction crisp and precise? Is the article well organized, meaning it flows in a logical manner and can be followed with ease? Does the story anticipate and answer all questions readers might have on the subject, or does the story have holes? Are persons named in the article identified properly? Are all pertinent terms and concepts properly explained or defined? Are the sources of information and quotes fully and properly identified? Is the story balanced and fair, or is the writer's opinion or bias evident? Is the story lacking any necessary background information or explanation? Is there anything in the article that might cause legal problems, such as libel or invasion of privacy? Is the importance of the news in this story made clear—in other words, is it evident why the newspaper is giving the readers this story? And last—but very far from least—is the story interesting?

Now all of these questions presumably were dealt with by the reporter who wrote the story. In addition, the reporter's section editor and perhaps the editor in chief as well went over the story and fielded the very same questions. But, hey, if the reporter and the other editors were doing their jobs, there would be no need for the copy editor, right? Sure, in an ideal newsroom everyone would do his or her job perfectly and we could replace the copy desk with something really useful, say, a tanning bed. But guess what? The ideal world has yet to produce a newspaper. That's why copy editors are so important: Their eyes are the *last* to run over a text before it goes to print. Final check. Buck stops here. Quality control.

HOW TO PROCEED
In an ideal setup copy editors would have their own place to work that is private, quiet, and free of distractions. They would have ready access to all the necessary reference works and online resources. They would have their own espresso machine and popcorn maker. Okay, none of this is going to happen, but let's keep going. Ideally the copy editors would go over each story three times—once for factuality and thoroughness of content, again for construction and presentation, then for purging those unnecessary commas and for making nouns and verbs agree. Throughout these readings the copy editors can make repairs to a story. But two things copy readers should resist doing. The first is overediting. Editors must fight the common temptation to justify their paychecks by altering or otherwise "improving" a story where no alteration or improvement is required. The second thing copy editors should avoid is rewriting a story. This is not a copy editor's job. That's the job of the reporter who wrote the story in the first place.

To realize that last point, the copy editor must consult with the reporter. If a copy editor doubts a statement or a fact in a story, the copy editor should contact the reporter and raise the query. Same with a clarification, a perceived missing piece of information, verification of a name or a statistic, the wording of a quote, identification of the person quoted, and so on. In other words, the copy editor's role is to identify problems in a story, but it is not the copy editor's job to resolve those problems on his or her own. Copy editors should not be doing the fact gathering for the reporters—no more than reporters should be relying on the copy desk to fill in information, check facts, or flesh out vagaries. If editors and writers work together, editors won't be doing double duty as reporters, and reporters won't be surprised by what appears in print.

But guess what? Such a copyediting scenario is about as common as that private space and personal espresso machine. Yes, copy editors should make every effort to consult reporters on matters of substance in their stories, but this won't always be possible. Copy editors are usually swamped with work and racing against deadlines. Reporters, meanwhile, aren't always available for consultation. They're either off somewhere on another reporting assignment or, just as likely, off somewhere goofing off. Or maybe they're catching up on some well-earned sleep, since reporting usually occurs during the day and copyediting is often conducted in the evening, if not somewhere deep into the night.

So there's the dilemma: Copy editors must copyedit, but on their own they shouldn't be messing about with copy, trying to verify facts, filling in holes, and rearranging information with the hope of improving clarity while possibly changing the thrust or emphasis of the story. Yet even as they know they should get back to the reporter on such matters, this isn't always possible. And because the story needs editing, the next day the reporter opens the newspaper and sees an article under his or her byline that bears only a passing resemblance to what the reporter turned in to the news desk. As we noted back in chapter 2, that shouldn't happen—but it does. And everybody's pissed at everybody else.

So what is a poor, harassed copy editor to do? The one thing a poor, harassed copy editor shouldn't do is work in a vacuum (there goes your dreams of that private office with the popcorn maker and the electro-vibe executive swivel chair). On matters of substance—legal concerns, verification of facts or quotes, missing information, and the like—the copy editor should consult with someone, preferably the reporter's section editor, the managing editor, or the editor in chief. Thus, if any changes or additions have to be made to a story, responsibility will be shared; this way, the alterations at least will result from a consensus of authorized parties, and not from one copy editor's personal judgment or predilection. Remember, putting out a newspaper is always a team effort. Forget that and you may as well forget the whole enterprise.

OPEN WARFARE
Having said all that, in many a newsroom there is often a lack of respect, if not downright animosity, between copy editors and reporters. This shouldn't occur, but it does. And if it exists in your newsroom, you should address it. Chief causes of such conflict are (a) a mutual lack of understanding or appreciation of the other guy's role and of the obstacles each faces in getting the job done and (b) a lack of communication between the two warring sides. Regular pow-wows between editors and reporters, presumably conducted by the tribal chiefs, might go a long way to smoothing out your newsroom operations.

Bottom line: A reporter shouldn't have to storm into the office the day the newspaper comes out and demand to know: "Who butchered my story?"

Beneath the bottom line: Copy editors shouldn't be wasting their breath by muttering: "How did these clowns ever get to be reporters? They just can't write!"

Copy editors should bear in mind that if the reporters were perfect, copy editors would be out of a job. By the same token, I've never, *ever* known a reporter (myself included) whose copy couldn't be improved by a good copy editor. So there.

TEST TIME
Okay, grab your blue pencils. Here's a little concert review in raw (very raw) copy form. See how many errors you can catch:

Nine-Inch Zucchinis delight local moshers

SLAVERTOWN, May 10—The British heavy metal band Nine-Inch Zucchinis presented a stimulating setat the Hard Rock Cafe here last night, followed by minor arrests.

Lead heavy metal guitarist Bobby Banshee, 22, opened the program with a tender ballad called "Ice Pick to the Heart" from the Band's latest CD, *Hot Rats Are Eating Your Mother,* which is on Britain's Warning Label. The crowd moshed merrily and cryed for more. The twenty-two-year-old Banshee accordingly followed up with the Band's current hit, "Happy Deathday." Bassist Lew Lewd and drummer Rudy Rude, meanwhile, provided driving rythms which made for charming counterpoint to Marcel Dupont's acoustic harpsicord.

"This is the first time we've had a band from overseas at our club", said Hard Rock manager Marten Smith. ""Its great to hear what's going on in other countries. I believe we've opned a new era for the local music scene. We have the best club in the area."

Opening for the Zucchinis, who is from Edinburgh, was the local techno-industrial-thrash-hip-hop-alternative trio Smashing Puppets. There set failed to ignite the audience and a few impatient Zucchini fans started fistfights which led to 3 arrest for Disorderly Conduct according toSlavertown police leiutenant Sam Spade. When the headliners finally took the stage, the English band played their heartout.

For a encore the musicians crucified a cat.

Not the worst review I've read, but probably in the running. Main problems are spelling, grammar, word choice, stylistics, extraneous stuff—about fifteen slips in all. Get them all? Hmm. I'll only comment that if you tell folks from Edinburgh they're English, you'll be in big trouble.

(Bonus points if you caught the misspelling of *harpsichord*.)

Okay, let's move on to something a bit more challenging. Let's consider what a copy editor should do with the following news story.

Zoning board approves fence

SLAVERTOWN, May 10—The city zoning board yesterday approved the construction of a ten foot high chain link fence around the cemetary behind the Church of Our Lady of Perpetual Exasperation to keep out young teenage vandals. But the Board denied the church's request for razor wire along the top of the fence because the cemetary, which is located at 4400 Epiphany Avenue, is a Residential zone.

"Without the barbed wire, the fence won't keep the little bastards out of the cemetary," Wiliam Jones, a lawyer for the church, complained after the vote last night. Mr. Jones has represented the Church for over 20 years.

Church members have complained that young people is using the cemetary as a shortcut to the nearby Mall and otherwise hanaging out and partying there at night, and that unless an affective fence is built, they fear graves will be dessicated.

A few gravestones have already been damaged, the Reverand John Pious told the zoning board, and just yesterday morning for the first time crack vials and hyperdermic needles had been found in the graveyard. The 51-year-old pastor said that if more parents would take their children to church their wouldn't be such problems in the city.

The Church of Our Lady of Perpetual Exasperation is located one half-mile north of Slaverhundt University.

I trust the reader has discovered that the above story is riddled with errors. Most obvious perhaps are the goofs in spelling, grammar, and stylistics (assuming we are going by *The Associated Press Stylebook*). Of these I will mention now only that *cemetery* is misspelled (did I gotcha?). At least the writer had the good grace to be consistent in that error. But as I remarked at the outset of this chapter, I consider such missteps, while regrettable, far less important than errors in the sense and substance of the story. Mechanical errors are best scrubbed in the final read of the story. The first read should focus on more important matters.

The first substantive matter concerns the story's lead. The reporter built his story around the zoning board's decisions. Normally that's a reasonable practice, even if the zoning board meeting was boring (which such meetings often are) and even if the board's actions were not very exciting. But an alert editor reading this story would likely spot something more intriguing than the votes of the zoning board. The report of evidence of hard-drug use, which is buried in the fourth paragraph, strikes me as more interesting news than the nature of the fence approved for the graveyard. Were I the copy editor on this story, I would likely say to myself, "Mall rats smoking crack and using needles? First time ever found in this nice suburban neighborhood? Whoa, that's interesting. Certainly makes for a more exciting lead on this story. Maybe the zoning board's decision on the fence should be a secondary aspect of the article."

Yes, and I think most editors would agree with me (they'd better). But the copy editor should not just plunge ahead and write a new lead for the story. A good copy editor will bring such concerns to the attention of, say, the news editor or the managing editor. If those editors agree that evidence of narcotics should be the article's focus, then more reporting is required. We need more detail, verification, comments from cops and school officials, all sorts of things, and that's the reporter's job. If the editors can't reach the reporter at this time, or if the reporter can't get the necessary information on this short notice, it's best if the editors agree to hold the story until the reporter can do the job. Journalists hate to hold up news stories, but many times there are compelling reasons to do so. In the end the reporter should end up with a much more interesting story, and everyone—reporter, editors, and readers—should be happy.

A few other matters in this story call for contemplation and consultation. The lawyer's use of the term "bastards" should raise an eyebrow, if not a red flag. We're told, quite gratuitously, that Jones has represented the church for twenty years. If he expects to keep the church as a client, maybe he shouldn't be seen in print using the word "bastards." Your job is not to see that everyone else keeps his job, but you do want to keep yours. Therefore: (a) Did the lawyer really use such intemperate language? (b) Should you substitute dashes or "expletive deleted" for the foul term? (c) What in fact is your publication's policy on putting such words in print? (d) Can you change a direct quote, which you know shouldn't be altered, into an indirect quote, where you may paraphrase your way out of using the curse word? (e) None of the above?

In answer to these questions, I would say: (a) Check with the reporter. (b) Your call, but obfuscating might leave readers thinking the lawyer used an even nastier term than he used. (c) You should know your publication's policy on everything. (d) Yes, you may always paraphrase, as long as you do not alter or distort the substance of the source's remark ("Jones expressed the belief that, lacking the razor wire, the fence would not prevent the young miscreants from accessing the cemetery"). (e) None of the above? Okay, you give me a better alternative. But bottom line: If you're hesitant about what to do in a situation like this—or in any editing situation—consult another editor.

On the technical side, meanwhile, the story has a number of faults—wrong word choice, irrelevancies, miscapitalization, verb agreement, redundancies, all the usual suspects—but one thing is especially suspect. Note that the lawyer's name is given as Wiliam Jones. Now nobody spells *William* like that, not even Willem Dafoe. "Wiliam" is most likely a typing error—but "most likely" is not a good enough reason for a copy editor to change it. Who knows, maybe Lawyer Jones's mother was illiterate. So what to do? Check with the reporter, or if the reporter as usual has her cell phone turned off, check the phone book.

Great, now you're feeling truly professional. Let's look at one last story:

ACE announces new programs

Yesterday Jamie McDougall, program director for Slaverhundt University's Alliance for Campus Events (ACE), announced several new programs scheduled for next semester. ACE is the organization responsible for bringing visiting lecturers and cultural and entertainment programs to the Slaverhundt University campus.

Among the programs Jamie announced will be a production of William Shakespeare's Hamlet by the West Virginia Arts Company, a lecture by the Assistant State Secretary of Commerce George Grump, a performance by the Dave Matthews Band and an exhibition of Tibetan sock-weaving.

Andrea Doria, president of Slaverhundt University Student Government, said the Dave Matthews concert would be in February in Baskerville Hall and that it would be free to all students with a Slaverhundt student I.D. card. She also explained she is a longtime Dave Matthews fan.

Several members of the ACE board are rumored to have resigned in protest over the excessive cost of bringing Dave Matthews to campus. Dave Matthews is the most expensive act on the college circuit. But Bill Overdew, a senior Marketing major, said he was "thrilled" at the prospect of seeing the concert and the cost was worth it.

"We're especially happy that we managed to book Dave Matthews," Jamie replied. "His show is expensive, but we had just enough in our budget to manage it." She added that the Administration had recently allocated ACE a special allocation of extra monetary funds.

All the programs sponsored by ACE promise to be worthwhile, so everyone should come out and support each one.

Along with the usual mechanics I see three main problems with this story, and I trust any copy editor, acting as the reader's advocate, would as well. First, the lead, to use the standard journalistic jargon, sucks. It's not only boring—as is the headline—but Dave has got to be up there at the top, in the lead and in the headline. Dave Matthews is mentioned in the third paragraph, and some might say, "Well, gee, that isn't too long to wait to get to the news about him," but yes it is, it's way too late. The DMB performing at your campus is big news, and big news can't wait even for a split second.

The second problem should be equally obvious: The story is full of discussion about the expense of bringing the DMB to campus—but we have no clue as to how much it's actually costing. Any reader would naturally want to know that. So you get back to the reporter and demand the specifics. And if the reporter tugs his forelock and scuffs the floor and says, "Well, I asked but they wouldn't reveal that," you tell the reporter that's not good enough. ("It's student money bringing the band, and we have a right to know how much, so get the answer, and by the way, are there going to be press passes for the concert?")

If in the end the reporter is unable to wrench from his sources the cost of the concert, the story should inform the reader: "ACE officers repeatedly refused to reveal the cost of bringing the DMB to campus." Beyond that I'd have the reporter surf the Internet to determine how much Dave and his friends normally shake down for a gig.

Finally, something astounding is reported in the fifth paragraph: Members of the ACE board are rumored to have resigned over the cost of the concert? Hello? First of all, newspaper should print facts, not rumors. Either those kids resigned or they didn't, and the reporter should be able to determine that. If the reporter can't confirm it, it shouldn't be reported. Otherwise the reader is going to say, "Hey, either those kids resigned or they didn't, and the reporter should be able to determine that!" And hey, didn't I just say that?

Other matters in the Matthews story: If a definition of the Alliance for Campus Events is needed—and I'm not sure it is—then stick it somewhere lower in the story, not in the second paragraph. Also, is the DMB in fact the most expensive act on the concert circuit? Verify that. And who cares if Andrea Doria is a DMB fan or if some marketing major, apparently selected at random, is thrilled at the prospect of seeing the band? That isn't news, it's filler. And as for the story's final sentence—burn it. That isn't news either—it's cheerleading.

FOR THE RECORD

Finally, it's good practice to keep a record of who is doing what to a story. In the precomputer age, it was customary for copy editors to initial stories on which they worked. Electronically it's possible to do the same. Depending on the programs you're using, you may do edits in an edit mode or make separate edit files and so on and sign off on them—the objective being a record of what changes were made in a story and who made them. All of these versions should be saved for a period, say, a month. (Just make sure the final edit is the one that gets put on the page.) Why all these obsessive precautions? Well, if an error (or a libel) appears in print, the record will show where the goof originated and who let it get by. Saves a lot of shouting and pointless finger-pointing later on. I can recall several occasions in which articles I wrote appeared in print with errors and even nonfactual insertions, all thanks to careless and overzealous copy editors. Fortunately the record showed who was responsible, so I could catch the filthy saboteurs and beat the living—

Well, no. But I prefer to create my own errors and nonfacts, thank you very much.

14

Headlines and Cutlines

Writing headlines is an art—at least as much an art as writing anything else for a newspaper and quite possibly more. In fact, writing good, effective headlines seems to require as much skill as writing an artful haiku. Some people simply have better heads for heads than other people do. But before we get too deeply into the Zen of headlines, let's consider a few practical matters.

Along with inheriting every other aspect of your newspaper, you also inherited a legacy of headline principles and practices. Accordingly, along with giving everything else a rethink, you would do well to cast a critical eye over those headlines.

As they do with general newspaper typography and design, art directors and production editors these days very much tend to favor headline fonts that look crisp and clean. Some day soggy and dirty (or the young and the restless) might come into fashion, but until then you would probably do well to stay with the majority; otherwise your paper risks standing out in ways you really don't want it to stand out. So staffers should weigh your current headline style, look at other papers, and come to a consensus on what you think looks good for you.

Designers will normally seek a harmonious marriage between body type and headline type; these don't have to be in the very same font family, but feudin' families should be avoided. If you have doubts about how your text and heads seem to be getting along, you might consult someone from the graphics department at your university, or the outfit that does your printing. The matter does get confusing, because these days there seem to be endless choices in styles and fonts. A recent study of American newspapers found the most popular typeface families are the very sharp Franklin Gothic, Poynter, Futura, Helvetica, Century, Utopia, and Times, but several newspapers have created their own individual fonts. You can lift many useful ideas (and fonts) from such Web sites as www.designorati.com, www.desktoppub.about.com, and www.visualeditors.com, among many others. Before you go surfing (come back here!) I'll offer just three pieces of advice in settling on a choice:

1. The typography should be readable (there goes all that cool lettering from your favorite heavy-metal albums).
2. The typography should be distinctive enough that readers, even at a distance, will not mistake your newspaper for other publications on display and distributed around campus (PR newsletters, shoppers, rental listings, other newspapers).
3. As noted in chapter 12, one or possibly two headline fonts, perhaps with bold, light, or italic variants, are normally enough for news pages. For features pages you can have more latitude, but as Mom and Dad cautioned you when they shipped you off for freshman year, don't take your freedoms to an extreme (oh, well, you didn't listen to them, either).

Having cleared up all your typographical questions, I'll turn to some general principles and practices regarding headlines. The following are not laws; rather, they are conventions based on what experience has shown to be useful in writing clear, effective headlines. Exceptions are always possible. But in general, these principles make sense and will help you avoid pitfalls. The first deals with display on the page.

DISPLAY'S DA THING

1. This point should be dead obvious, but I mention it because I've seen more than a few student newspapers whose editors apparently wouldn't recognize the obvious if it bit them on the ankles: *Big stories should have big headlines, small stories should have small headlines.* Doggone it, if you've got hot news ("College president moons trustees"), don't underplay it. By the same token, if you overplay insignificant news ("New trash can in student union"),

you're (a) looking silly and (b) informing the readers you don't have any better news—or at least any better news judgment. As with every other design element in a newspaper, headlines send signals to the readers. The size of a headline requires several judgment calls: What point size should this head be? How many lines? Across how many columns? Should it have an overline (kicker) or secondary head (deck)? If you weigh the news properly, you should be able to choose the right weight for your headline.

General headline size advice: Don't scream, because overuse of the huge headline weakens its effect; something like crying wolf. But don't whisper, either. My tabloid heart says, when in doubt pump up the volume a bit.

2. The next point is also in the obvious category, but sometimes it's not obvious until the newspaper comes back from the printers and it's on the racks: Heads of the same size and column width should not be placed next to each other. This is called "tombstoning," because such heads stand shoulder to shoulder like so many grave markers. This isn't a problem out there in the cemetery, but it is a problem on the page. The effect would be something like this:

College president   New trash can
moons the trustees   in union bldg.

3. You've heard it said that consistency is the hobgoblin of little minds, but if you actually heard it from Emerson as I did you'd know he was talking about *foolish* consistency. There's really nothing foolish about keeping headline style consistent, because oddly enough readers notice these things. So, for example, do you set your headlines flush left, or do you center them? Justified or ragged edged? If you don't know the answer to these questions without checking, you're in trouble. Actually, many publications will use one such setting—say, flush left—for the bulk of their headlines, and then another—say, centered—to offset a special story like a backgrounder or news analysis. But they will be consistent in their use of these options.

Likewise with capitalization. Capitalize all main words ("College President Moons Trustees"), or just the first word ("College president moons trustees"), or all caps ("COLLEGE PRESIDENT MOONS TRUSTEES")? Or one capitalization system for news stories and another for feature stories? In such matters the choice is yours. Just be hobgoblin—I mean, consistent.

4. Some modernists are playing with the next concept, but in general, headline writers still tend to favor lines of heads having equal numbers of characters and spaces. This is both asthetically appealing and tidy, and it's indicative that you care about such matters. One or one and a half characters' difference in line lengths, most headline writers say, is about all you should allow. Poor example:

Newspapers declare Britney
woman of the year

Better example:

Press names Britney
woman of the year

Best example:

Britney selected as
woman of the year

Computer programs may let you fudge out the character count or point size to match up the length of your lines, but it's still good practice to seek out the words that will approximate that match as best you can. That's one area in which the Zen poets on your staff come into their own.

5. Each line of a head should read as a complete unit. That is, don't split names, titles, idioms, or adjective/noun or preposition/noun phrases from one line to the next. The following "split heads" simply do not read properly:

SU to host UN
chief next week

Theater casting Man of
La Mancha for next term

Bears meet Nittany
Lions on Saturday

College dean in
trouble with law

Student sticks
up local bank

*Madonna declared woman
of the year by newspapers*

Since readers, even if they don't know it, expect lines to be complete units, the so-called bad splits above create disconcerting pauses where pauses aren't wanted; the effect is perhaps more psychological than cognitive, but it's there and it jars. All of the above splits, of course, can be easily fixed. Examples:

Student robs
nearby bank

and

*Press names Madonna
the woman of the year*

Easy, wasn't it? In fact, thanks to the rich possibilities of the English language, you can *always* find a way to reword a headline. I don't know if that holds true for, say, the Tagalog language, but hey, that's not our problem. Above all, don't waste time twisting yourself into knots trying to find a better word or structure. You don't work in a vacuum. Don't be ashamed to turn to the Zen poet next to you and ask: "What's a shorter word for *excretion*?"

The matter of bad splits, meanwhile, involves not just the appearance but also the comprehension of heads, so let's now move into discussing what makes headlines readable and what they should contain.

READ ALL ABOUT IT

1. News headlines will most often strive to convey the news. If a traditional news lead is the story in a nutshell, then the headline will be the nutshell in a nutshell. Example:

Dean steals petty cash

That's telling it straight—in a nutshell. You could of course put a brighter head on this:

Dean's sticky fingers
get caught in cookie jar

But you want to be careful about getting too cute. I'm all for cute ... but I tend to favor cute for feature story heads. With features you can break all the rules, be funny, flip, frivolous. News, and especially serious news, deserves serious headlines.

2. Heads should be clear and concise, with simple, short, punchy words. Words of three or more syllables should be avoided whenever possible. Consider this head:

Administration contemplating undergraduate revenue enhancement

First of all, what the hell does it mean? Second, the words are long and unwieldy. Third, it has no impact on the reader. Compare with:

SU may hike fees

Instantly comprehensible. Punchy and to the point. You won't always be able to reduce headlines to blunt monosyllables. But it's worth trying.

3. Heads generally have more impact when they are in the active rather than the passive voice. Compare:

Suspect apprehended in break-in

That's passive. The active subject-verb-object construction hits much harder:

Cops nab burglary suspect

Careful readers will have observed that in our Madonna headlines above, the first example ("Madonna declared woman of the year by newspapers") is in the passive voice, while the second ("Press names Madonna the woman of the year") is in the active voice. But that doesn't automatically make the second superior to the first. (Note I said "heads *generally* have more impact in the active voice." Generally doesn't mean always; hey, I thought you were among the careful readers.) Headline writers may well favor the active Madonna over the passive Madonna (hah?), but headline writers will also favor getting the story's key name up front. This is why headline writers are so frequently found wrestling on the newsroom floor. Meaning that every head is a judgment call—with clarity and impact the criteria for your judgment.

4. Meanwhile, there's little ambiguity or floor-wrestling about this: A well-chosen action verb is worth a dozen flowery adjectives and adverbs:

> Bears maul Lions, 56-0

or:

> *Hackers shatter myth*
> *of Internet security*

Those are good, strong verbs that need no amplification by modifiers.

5. Somebody mention ambiguity? Here's a cardinal rule: Always reread and test heads for possible ambiguity, unintentional humor, or anything else that might be misunderstood. Example:

> Teachers raise issue
> to be discussed today

Is *raise* a verb or a noun?
How about:

> Stolen painting found by tree

And I've always liked:

> Red tape holds up new bridge

Even a little, misplaced, two-letter word can be disastrous. Here's a recipe headline that appeared in *The Washington Post* written by a friend of mine:

> *You can put pickles up yourself*

What the writer meant was:

You can put up pickles yourself

You don't even have to know that "to put up pickles" means to preserve cucumbers in vinegar and spices (in other words, to pickle them) to understand that inserting "pickles" between "put" and "up" would be a cause for giggles—and may be in certain states a cause for arrest.

6. Don't use an unknown name in a head. Unless we know who the hell Herkimer is, and we don't, this is meaningless:

Herkimer to speak at
Slaverhundt in April

This is less specific, but still better:

Newsman to speak on campus

This is better still:

CBS reporter John Herkimer
to discuss Iraq at Slaverhundt

7. What you think is cute often makes readers groan. Especially avoid that creaky old attempt for headline wit, alliteration:

President ponders Peterson as possible provost

Positively pukey. Likewise, don't make puns of people's names, like "Tumbleson fumbles" or "All that glitters isn't Goldberg." Most people quite rightly don't like to see their names joked with or otherwise jerked around.

Also, being frivolous about death is considered bad taste:

Six teens greased
by huge oil truck

If you must be clever, save it for features and sports. But remember, there's a yawning gap between being cute and being bright.

8. Sometimes you can't get everything you want into a headline. So you might consider writing subsidiary heads. These are lines that go either above or below the main headline.

Example of a headline with an overline, or kicker:

Lost leg to car bomb
CBS reporter John Herkimer
to discuss Iraq at Slaverhundt

Example of lines, usually called a deck or deck head, under the main head:

College president
moons the trustees

Hangdog declares
he has had enough

Overlines and underlines are customarily half the point size of the main headline and perhaps even less than that; it depends how it looks on the page. These lines will also normally take a different member of your font family—light or italic or perhaps all caps, something to distinguish them from the main head and to keep them from all mooshing together. By the same token, you don't want to overdo the page with all sorts of additional headline apparatus; your page will look like more headlines than anything else. These headline devices give you a chance to get creative . . . but don't go overboard.

9. Some headline conventions. These are purely conventional, but they seem to work.

The first is the avoidance of all forms of the verb *to be*. Headlines seem to consider "is," "are," and the like mere clutter and get along nicely without them. This is why we write:

Liberal Arts dean
in trouble with law

and not

Liberal Arts dean is
in trouble with law

The second convention is that headlines are almost always in the present tense. Even past events are headlined in the present (e.g., "Dean steals petty cash"). This idiomatic usage is oxymoronically known as the historical present; it doesn't mean that the dean is pilfering from the coffee fund at the very moment the reader is perusing the paper; it means that the dean was up to no good some time ago (and presumably got caught, because otherwise how would the newspaper be reporting it?). In other words, even if the home team beats the visitors on Saturday and you don't publish the news until the following Wednesday, your headline still reads: "Bears maul Lions, 56–0."

Just to confuse matters, however, some things can be headlined in the past tense. For example, if a report comes out showing the results of an investigation, the head might read: "Dean covered up cash theft."

Yet another headline convention is the avoidance of definite and indefinite articles, as in: "Dean swipes Hershey bar." Why? Probably for concision. In any case, like all the other conventions, readers accept the missing articles without a second thought. Unless the missing article is a Hershey bar, in which case . . . oh, forget it.

Another convention is to use single quotation marks rather than double quotes:

President says, 'I quit!'

Why single quotes? I dunno. Saving space? Seems doubtful, but there it is.

A final headline convention is skipping conjunctions. That is, instead of

Dean swipes money and
escapes from SU campus

standard headline style would have it:

Dean swipes money,
escapes from campus

To reiterate, all these are customary practices, but you're not bound by them. Some newspapers somewhere, for example, still probably use the old tabloid imperative headline style: "Steal cash, flee campus!" Some may use the articles ("Dean swipes the petty cash"). Some may ignore the other conventions. Do as you like; I simply advise being consistent, and not looking too weird.

10. Your final step. After you've written your head, always read over the story to make sure the head accurately reflects what the story says. For example, if the story reports that the administration is *considering* a tuition rise, your head better not say: "SU to hike tuition." Likewise, if the story says that the cops are holding a burglary *suspect*, don't convict the guy by writing: "Cops nab burglar." That's not only inaccurate . . . it's libelous.

TESTING, TESTING

Now you pasty-faced newsroom denizens look like you could use some exercise. So—write good heads for the following stories:

> Actor Brad Pitt will be unable to accept in person his Man of the Year Award, which was to be presented this Saturday on campus by the *Slavering Hound* staff, his press agent announced in Hollywood yesterday.
>
> "Mr. Pitt is thrilled by the award," the press release said, "but unfortunately prior commitments prevent him from. . . ."

> Tuition fees will be reduced by 10 percent next year, President Harrison Hangdog announced yesterday.
>
> Student activity fees however will be raised to $3,000 per semester, the president added.
>
> "We think this new system will save our hard-working students a good deal of . . ."

CAPTIONS COURAGEOUS

Now a word, or a couple of hundred words, about photo captions, aka cutlines.

1. Captions, commonsensically, should indicate what is in the photo. For example, if the picture shows two students donating blood at a blood drive, the caption should identify both students and state what they are doing and when and where; it should not name, say, just one student or leave it to the story to explain why these kids are writhing in agony. The caption won't tell the entire story—that's what the story is for—but it should be complete enough in and of itself, like a capsule of the story.

Similarly, if three students were arrested at a demonstration, the picture should show students being arrested and not students quietly listening to a speaker on a stage. If your photographer got only the speech and not the bust, the caption should describe what's depicted—although the information about the arrests may be added ("After the rally, three students were arrested for burning a police car").

2. Captions come in a number of styles, but aesthetics suggest they should be consistent. For example, are your captions full sentences or more like labels?

Example of the first:

> President Harrison Hangdog presents a good citizenship certificate to freshman Suzie Kew at yesterday's awards ceremony in the Student Union.

Example of the second:

> Good citizenship certificate for freshman Suzie Kew.

Either style is acceptable; it's just best to choose one and stick to it. Readers notice such inconsistencies (or subconsciously sense them) and are made somewhat anxious by them. Of course, you may allow variations. For example, full sentences under pictures, and labels (like just a name) under mug shots. Or you may have full informational captions under news pix, but allow flights of fancy under non-news pix. An example of the latter would be labeling a photo of students shivering under umbrellas with a caption that reads: "April is the cruelest month." (That will work, unless of course you're running the photo in September.)

3. Tell the reader who is who by putting "(*left*)," "(*center*)," "(*right*)," and so on in the caption. Normal practice is to identify people left to right "(*from left*)." But use common sense. If the photo shows the college president and a freshman coed, it's clear enough which is which without wasting space by indicating who's on the left and who's on the right.

4. Keep open the option of the extended caption, aka the caption story. You might use this when the picture tells the story well enough without an accompanying article; an extended caption of, say, three of four sentences might be sufficient to cover the subject. Rule it all off in a nice box and—*voila*, picture/caption story.

5. Finally, don't forget to check your caption against the reporter's information for accuracy . . . and to give the photographer a credit line.

15

The Online Edition

Online editions have long been standard supplements to print editions of campus newspapers. Indeed, it won't be long before the word *supplement* won't apply. I don't think "hard copy" newspapers will ever disappear—history shows that for all their impact new media tend to take their place alongside current formats rather than to displace them. But who knows? Maybe some day pulped pine trees will become the supplement to pixels.

Until that occurs, however, if your campus newspaper isn't already accompanied by an electronic edition you are not only in the minority but also way out of date. In fact, even publishing on the Web is starting to look somewhat dated. Just as some college yearbooks are now being produced on DVD, so student papers are already podcasting their content. By the time my passel of pulped pine trees is in your hands heaven knows what additional technology will be available: Maybe text piped right into our brains, or bubbled into our beer (no, college students certainly wouldn't go for that).

So it's a fair assumption that you not only already have an online edition up and running but that you've had one for some time now. Therefore I won't go over the how-to of online editions. Instead, I'll mention (a) a few words about design, (b) some principles and practices you may not have considered, (c) some operational options you may not have considered, and (d) some features you may be neglecting or underexploiting.

A FEW WORDS ABOUT WEB PAGE DESIGN

Just two points on design, actually. The first is that, having monitored in recent years on a fairly regular basis about a hundred online editions of student newspapers, as well as not a few Web sites of other sorts, I no doubt will not exactly be breaking news when I report that cyberspace contains an awful lot of the good, the bad, and the damn near unreadable. I won't offer guidelines on what makes for an aesthetically pleasing homepage—cyberpretty is probably in the mouse of the beholder. But I can say that the central principles of attractive and reader-friendly print design (see chapter 12) seem to translate wholesale into Web design: clean and readable typography, coherent layout, lack of clutter, allowance for white space, thoughtful use of color, ease of navigation.

My second point is that even in the relatively young universe of cyberspace, it's interesting how quickly a Web page can look old-fashioned. Experts can no doubt pretty well date when a page was designed just by perusing it, but even to lay surfers it's usually evident when a page looks dated. So, too, when a page looks designed on the cheap.

All of this is something for you to consider as you cast you eye over your online edition. Which is what you should periodically do—not as a writer, photographer, or editor but as a casual reader or surfer. It also wouldn't hurt to look at a hundred other online student newspapers in your spare time to see how you measure up.

IN PRINCIPLE

Aside from the fact that everyone else is doing it, there are basically three reasons why newspapers maintain electronic editions: geography, advertising, and interactivity.

1. *The geographic factor.* The printed paper gets distributed around campus, maybe dropped off at a few points off campus (local merchants who advertise, gathering spots like diners and barbershops), mailed to the odd subscribers (retired professors, alumni, parents of students), and exchanged with other student newspaper offices. An online edition by stark contrast is distributed globally and is accessible by everyone on earth and in neighboring galaxies. You know all that already—but have you thought about its implications for what you publish?

For example, should the content of the print and electronic editions be identical, considering that the audience for the former is mainly right there on campus and that a large portion of the audience for the latter is elsewhere? You might well say the online edition should repeat the print edition in its entirety as a matter of record and leave it at that. That's a valid viewpoint. Before embracing such a conclusion, however, you would do well to read your online edition through the eyes of an outsider. Would everything in your online edition be comprehensible to, say, a student's uncle living out of state? Would everything that interests your student readers be of interest to nonresident, nonstudent readers?

If you answer in the negative to these questions, maybe the manner and the matter of your online texts need some serious tweaking. In terms of manner, such tweakage might mean some rewriting of print stories for clarity in their online versions. For example, everyone on campus likely knows that ACE means Alliance for Campus Events or that SUB stands for Student Union Building; spelling out those terms for campus readers is unnecessary, but for off-campus global readers it seems in order. Similarly, a news story about "the investigation into last semester's riot" will likely require more backgrounding for those online but off-campus readers than it does for your local print readers who witnessed (or participated in) the burning of the school's ROTC office.

Tweaking content for the Web site may go well beyond just rewriting for clarity. As you prepare your online edition, ask yourself what material seems germane solely to your campus readers and what content "has legs." For example, news of a proposed rise in tuition costs is relevant both to off-campus readers (like parents who pay the tuition) and to on-campus readers (like students who waste the tuition). Likewise, lots of off-campus readers (alumni, parents, professional gamblers) presumably are interested in the fortunes of your varsity sports teams. Yet most likely those distant online readers have little or no interest in coverage of club sports. Same with many other news items: a cancelled class field trip, the reassignment of lecture venues due to repairs on certain lecture halls, an alteration or addition to the campus shuttle bus route—these are all solid public service news stories that affect your immediate audience but most likely have no effect (and no interest) for many online readers. Alternately, you may receive a PR handout that interests alumni; little reason perhaps to put it in your paper, but good reason perhaps to include it in your online edition.

Thus simply duplicating online what you print on paper, while having the virtue of completeness, may not be the best service to your online readers. To be sure, editing print stories specially for the Web, or adding or eliminating stories, requires both numerous judgment calls and more than a tad more work. But if you want to maintain your online edition properly (you do! you do!), then just bunging in stories from the print newspaper seems both lazy and inappropriate.

Online publishing, meanwhile, offers a whole different landscape of opportunity for photography. Normally, in-print space limitations will allow you to illustrate a story at most with one or two photos; on rare occasions you can spread out to a photo spread. In your online edition, however, you have the space to mount every good picture your photographers have snapped. And you don't have to clutter up the homepage with this cornucopia of images; instead, you can create "albums" or "slide shows" through which interested readers can browse at their leisure. Now of course such devices are the equivalent of last season's baseball hat to many student Web masters, and I wouldn't even mention them were it not for the fact that I still see countless student newspapers that apparently have never heard of the clickable photo gallery. For shame, because the album is a boon to both readers and photographers, and it serves that aim of getting more student names and faces into the newspaper—albeit online.

2. *The money factor.* Ever since newspapers started giving away their content over the Internet, publishers have been asking themselves two questions. The first is: Why are we doing this? The answer to that one is as compelling as it is simple: Because everyone else is doing it. The second question is: Well, can't we somehow make some money out of this? The answer to that is still up in the air—or somewhere out there in cyberspace.

From an informal survey that I've conducted—a couple of years' worth of monitoring those hundred or so online editions of student newspapers—I estimate that about half of the sites carry advertising, with that percentage increasing, but glacially, as the months go by. This means that all of the papers are investing some time, personpower, and money (if your staffers are paid) into producing online, but that only some 50 percent are earning some financial return on that investment. Well, I admit I'm prejudiced: I believe in gaining money and not losing it. If you share this prejudice, you'd do well to ask yourself why your online edition isn't at least generating contributions to your pizza fund.

The mere fact that your online edition never carried ads in the past isn't sufficient reason for carrying on that policy into the future. I advise checking into it. It could be that the founding mothers and fathers of your online edition envisioned a commercial-free Web site as a purer, nobler form of college journalism. Cool—and I'll see you in the monastery next time I'm in the neighborhood. More likely some technical, contractual, or even legal reasons prevent an online student newspaper from including advertising. If, for example, the electronic edition is hosted on the university's Web site, the university may be bound by its bylaws to eschew certain forms of commercial enterprise (if that's the case, you may want to explore prying yourself off the university Web site and finding an independent host). Alternately, your site may be part of a host network that limits or bans advertising—or at least advertising solicited by its individual clients. Numerous permutations of these scenarios exist.

In addition, chances are your online setup was established so long ago that no one on the current staff remembers why or how such a decision was made. That's all the more reason to give your arrangement a critical reexamination. It's quite possible, for instance, that when your newspaper first decided to go electronic, only a few options for doing so were available. Today, knowing how Internet technology and commerce have expanded, you almost certainly have many more options to choose from. Some of those options may allow you to generate advertising revenue that not only bolsters your pizza fund but that allows, say, more staff members to attend more national collegiate press conferences.

Advertising revenue can reach you in a number of ways. Your ad staff can of course solicit your print advertisers to cough up for additional exposure on the World Wide Web. Another route is to link up with a national outfit, such as www.alloymarketing.com or www.CollegeMarketPlace.com, that brokers advertising specifically for college newspapers. I am not, of course, endorsing any particular advertising firm. I am recommending that you carefully check them out, both in concept and in execution, to see if such a partnership may benefit you. If you do find something that sounds promising, check it with current clients (other student newspapers). If all goes well, you'll be ordering additional topping for the pizzas.

3. *The interactivity factor.* Interaction with readers is a third reason for maintaining an online edition. We know it's good to be the king, but a

monarch (albeit to his peril) normally doesn't care about feedback from his subjects. You, however, should care about feedback, because your readers aren't your subjects, they are your electors. Fail to serve your readers well and you'll find them voting you out of office; well, not quite, but you'll find more unread papers in your distribution boxes, which are clearly negative votes. Therefore, the more feedback you get, the more insight you should gain into how and why you're pleasing—or displeasing—the peasants.

In discussing readers' letters back in chapter 7 we made the point that readers love reading other readers' letters. What we didn't mention is that ninety-nine out of a hundred letters to the editor are bitching about something—usually something the paper has printed. Well, the bitching and moaning come with the territory. Moreover, complaints and criticism don't detract from the overall good—it's good to know readers' sentiments and it's good that readers have the opportunity to express those sentiments. Providing a readers' forum for sharing views on your online edition enhances that opportunity. Fact is, for a reader perusing your print edition to sit down and pen a letter, or even to write an e-mail message, takes a certain amount of effort. But the chore is less onerous for readers of your online edition who have a mechanism right there on the screen for tapping in their thoughts. Electronic readers also have more options: They may post their letters on a general message board, address their letters to the editor, or send them directly to individual reporters or columnists. All of this spells increased reader feedback, which is good for you. It furthermore means an enhanced sense of involvement, which is good for the readers. And since electronic publication has no space limitations, it means more letters can get aired, which is satisfying to readers.

A couple of caveats, however. One is that while newspapers consider it prudent to check the identification of letter writers (see chapter 7), such ID checks are more difficult over the Internet. That's because e-mailers can easily disguise their identities. A second problem is that while you'd like to keep your online forums and blogs and letters sections democratic and free-flowing, the sheer volume of submissions might require your spending enormous amounts of time scrubbing profanities, expunging libels, and simply editing to make barbaric English readable. Indeed, I have seen so many online newspapers—both collegiate and mainstream—featuring so much reader gibberish that I can only wonder why the newspapers post these things (or for that matter why anyone reads them).

CONTENT

Having discussed the whys of online editions, let's consider the whats.

Foremost among the online edition's content should be a replication, to greater or lesser degree, of your print edition's editorial matter. We discussed above whether or not the entirety of the print edition should be posted online and whether or not that material needs editing. Those are your calls—but the next one is mine: Nothing seems more detrimental to an online newspaper than failing to keep it up to date. I mention what should be such an obvious point only because I've seen far too many online editions of student newspapers with far too much lag in keeping up with the print version. Few things are more discouraging to readers than picking up a newspaper and facing . . . old news. Same holds true with logging on to a newspaper Web site.

But consider this: Printing on a weekly basis means you're updating your printed newspaper on a weekly basis. Same principle with twice-weekly or bi-weekly or whatever. But hey, does updating your Web site once or twice a week make sense—especially when the cyberworld lets you update moment by moment? Indeed, if you're presenting an online edition, you are obligated to keep it fresh. This might require a single staffer solely assigned to that chore, or it might mean a corps of designated staffers, or it might involve input from all staffers. Different newspapers will have different configurations of personnel for getting their content onto the Web; there's no one-size-fits-all formula that I'm aware of. But if your Web site seems stale or staid, or if keeping the site bright and timely is proving problematic, you might need to reexamine the way your Web work is being handled.

BEYOND CONTENT

News, features, and photos, of course, are the meat, potatoes, and veggies of online newspapers—but hey, you can get all that served in print editions, right? Right, the true glory of electronic newspapers is what they can offer that dead trees cannot.

Let's return, for example, to the matter of interactivity. Conducting surveys via your Web site is, as the British say, a doddle, or to put it into real English, a snap. At a minimum, polls are simply fun, and readers enjoy them because, after all, it's readers reading the work of readers. To this end you can post a survey question on your site to the effect of: "Which band would you most like to see perform on campus?" Or "Pick a new name for the school mascot." Polls might ratchet up the seriousness with a question like: "What requirement would you like to see eliminated from the general education curriculum?" (Actually the most user-friendly and easiest-to-score surveys are multiple choice; the questions in the first few examples above could easily be tweaked in that direction if you prefer by offering choices. Yes-or-no questions are also a doddle all around: "Do you favor the reinstitution of the military draft?") Meanwhile, the neatest thing about many polls is that the results might serve as the source of a good news story. Seventy-five percent of your survey respondents favor dropping lab science as a gen ed requirement? A reporter could follow this up with some research and a series of interviews and produce an excellent article.

Among the appealing characteristics of Web site surveys are that (a) they are easy to manage, (b) they provide the readers a means of participation, and (c) they stimulate repeat visits because readers will seek out poll results the next day—which is a good argument for running surveys on a daily basis. On the negative side, you should bear in mind that online polls are far from scientific. For one thing, your poll respondents are not necessarily a cross-section of the student body; you are getting, after all, responses only from online readers and only from those weirdos who have nothing better to do than to voluntarily answer survey questions. There is also no more effective control, or at least none that I know of, over Web site survey respondents than there is, say, for *American Idol* voters. Which is to say that there may be no way to screen out a teenager from Osaka, Japan, voting for your football team mascot—and voting a hundred times. So should your poll be open to anyone surfing the Internet who gets cast up on the shores of your Web site? Or should your survey be open just to your students? And what control have you over respondents casting multiple votes? Or do all the multiples balance out each other and should you care?

Another factor to consider is that if you're featuring polls on your Web site—and especially if you're going to feature them on a daily or weekly basis—it ain't all that easy coming up with good survey questions. More than that, it is all too easy to come up with lame questions. "What do you plan to do on your summer vacation?" strikes me as uninspired in the extreme. And how about: "Who is the most obnoxious/unfair/least qualified faculty member at Slaverhundt University? Sounds provocative? Sure. But it also sounds like possible grounds for a defamation suit.

Bottom line: Polls offer wonderful opportunities on your Web site, and readers love 'em. But as with everything else, craft 'em with care.

ANIMATE

Another feature that can add sparkle to your Web site is some synergizing with other media. Audio and video are obvious examples. Nine-Inch Zucchinis performed on campus and you're running a review in your print edition. How about accompanying the online version of the review with some audio and video of the concert? Movie review? How about a trailer or film clip? President gave an important speech to the university senate? An audio tape of the speech might be more digestible than all that printed text.

Based on my monitoring of campus newspaper Web sites, only a minority of online editions are exploiting audio and video as fully as they might—and those happen to be the overall best Web sites. But I can already hear you protesting: "Hey, audio and video? We have enough trouble putting out a newspaper and getting some respectable text up on the Internet. Now you want us to get into shooting and editing film and all that?" To which I respond, Oh, behave. First of all, there's no good reason (aside from budgets) to prevent you from arming your reporters and photographers with audio and video recorders.

Beyond that, consider the outside resources at hand. Does your campus have a radio or TV station? Do you ever engage in any interchange with them? Can you pool resources and synergize—say, the newspaper supplying the reporting or background research on a news event, while the electronic media nerds handle the video? What about your campus arts magazine? Have you ever considered buddying up on your Web site—like offering some of the mag's poetry, short stories, art, or video? If you've never explored such cooperative efforts, I'd advise looking into them. Your Web site just might start looking a lot more lively. Similarly, just about anyone engaged in public relations these days is pumping out as many VNRs (video news releases) as they are printed handouts. This includes everyone from your campus PR department to movie studios, record producers, and other commercial enterprises, as well as noncommercial interest groups (governmental, political, environmental, charitable, health and science, etc.). Some material is available free or at nominal cost from the Web. Point is, a lot of worthy stuff for animating your Web site is out there. If these sources are not finding you, it's incumbent on you to find out about them.

Yet another feature most online readers appreciate is links. I've seen online campus papers that provide a judicious selection of links—and I've seen online campus newspapers that apparently have never heard of links (or perhaps their Web masters haven't figured out how to create them). Whatever the case, if your site lacks links, I think you're not exploiting one of the key capabilities of the Internet.

One obvious set of links your site might provide is to other campus sites. For philosophical reasons you might wish not to do this; perhaps you're protective of your independent identity and would like to keep your distance from the "official" university realm. I can understand that. But I can also understand readers of your online edition who would be grateful for a handy link to the school's academic calendar, final exam schedule, semester bulletin, course selection process, basketball schedule, descriptions of graduate programs, and a host of other information to which you might serve as go-between host via homepage links.

Staying close to home yet going off campus, you might consider, if you haven't yet, a link to your community's Web site. Such a site might give your readers info on events in town, community services, church services, recreational facilities, job and internship opportunities, procedures for appealing parking tickets or lodging complaints about off-campus landlords, and on and on. I think students also appreciate links to neighboring colleges and to their student newspapers: What better way to learn about concerts, lectures, and keg parties in the area? After all, there's *never* anything to do on your campus on the weekend.

Then there are general information links your readers will appreciate. It's astonishing, for example, how many weather junkies are out there. Long before the establishment of The Weather Channel, it was axiomatic among media folk that if a newspaper failed to print the daily forecast, the newspaper was going to hear about it—in spades. So, do your online readers care about the weather? Sure they do, just as they care about local movie listings, bus and train schedules, and the like. In addition, your print version news stories are enhanced online when accompanied by links. Story on Earth Day? Why not include environmental Web site links? Special programs for Martin Luther King Jr.'s birthday? How about some MLK links? A story on student aid? Readers will appreciate links for loan information and application forms. Running a book review? How about links to the author's Web site, or to barnesand noble.com or amazon.com? Finally, Web links are a cool way to serve your readers' interest in the wider world of state, national, and international news. You may cover these minimally or not at all in your weekly or semi-weekly print editions, and you may be perfectly right in that choice. But if your Web site has links to the Associated Press, British Broadcasting Corporation, CNN, Yahoo! News, or any of the many other excellent Internet news services out there, you're providing a useful service. And if you're not, you're not, and so what is all that about?

16

Finances and Advertising

From what I've gathered in consulting other student newspaper advisers, their publications are managed and financed in a great many ways. Some newspapers, primarily those at private institutions, are essentially owned, published, and financed by the colleges themselves. At the other extreme, some student newspapers, usually dailies, are maintained by for-profit corporations, with salaried publishers, managers, and even advisers, and published with only the most tenuous connection to the university administration. Still other papers, and this includes a great many, are published in a sort of proprietary limbo of quasi-institutional status. In such cases it may not be precisely clear who the owner of the newspaper is, or who is its publisher, or who is responsible for exactly what aspect of the publication's operations or even its existence. Sometimes the overseer of a student newspaper is a student media board, which may comprise representative administrators, faculty, and students, as well as outside parties, possibly from the worlds of business and journalism. Whether this board is appointed or elected or hails from Mt. Olympus also varies from institution to institution. None of these differences in management or proprietorship may really matter much . . . until a problem arises. Like a law suit or a tax audit.

The same multiplicity of possibilities exists for financing college newspapers. Funding may come from the university itself, from some foundation connected to the university, from the student government, from student activity fees, or from all or none of the above. Advertising revenue is almost always added to this mix, but where that revenue is deposited may vary (e.g., in accounts held by the newspaper, by the university, by the student government, etc.). Ad money may be funneled into a certain fund in its entirety or it may be sliced and diced among a number of hungry parties. Sometimes student advertising managers and sales personnel earn commissions on ads, sometimes they do not, and sometimes commissions depend on the kind of ad.

Along with who may or may not get ad commissions, means of compensating staff members also differ widely from campus to campus. Some reporters and editors receive reductions in tuition fees in recognition of their service to the publication. Some receive salaries, with that money coming either from the newspaper's general fund, from the student government, or from some other source. In other instances newspaper staffers may be employees of the university (and get paid the same minimum hourly wage as the kids mopping up the vomit in the cafeteria). At some campuses student reporters and editors may earn academic credit or internship points for their labors. In yet other cases student newsies may be compensated with nothing more than bylines and glory and maybe a year-end dinner at the local all-you-can-eat Chinese buffet.

With all these variations on a theme it is difficult if not impossible to generalize about the business and financial sides of the student press. Still, I do have some general advice.

A GOVERNMENT AGENCY

Many student newspapers receive all or part of their funding from the student government. Many times there may be no alternative to such an arrangement, and many times it's a perfectly amicable system. Yet if we can assume that few Americans would favor mainstream newspapers being controlled in any way by government, I wonder if it is desirable on the college level. For one thing, the student newspaper is placed in the position of reporting on that hand that feeds it. For another, student governments in many instances have proved more troublesome to—and censorious of—student newspapers than college administrations have. I know of one instance, for example, in which a student government suddenly declared that the student newspaper must use PCs instead of Macs—a change of platform in which the newspaper had no say whatsoever. In another case, the student government single-handedly reduced the newspaper's office space, glomming part of the editorial offices for some other purpose. At the very least, it appears unseemly if not ignoble for the newspaper to appeal to the student government each year, hat in hand, for its funding. If such is your situation, you might do well to explore other funding options. For example, if a dollar of each student's activity fee were designated as a subscription to the newspaper, you might find yourself in a happier budgetary circumstance—and be free of "government sponsorship" in the bargain.

KNOW THYSELF
When you take over the editorship or business managership of a student newspaper you inherit a financial framework and a series of business procedures. If you're lucky your predecessors will stick around and explain all the requisite procedures and practices. If you're unlucky, they won't, and if you're really unlucky they'll have disappeared along with all the petty cash, movie passes, and pizza discount coupons. But let's say you're lucky. At best, your former business and ad managers can explain what's to be done. But most likely they won't explain much of why it's done that way because they won't know. That's because they inherited the system just as you are doing now. Advisers also probably won't be much help in this regard because the system likely predates their coming on board and they don't understand these financial things anyway because they were liberal arts majors.

What I'm getting at of course is that following a set of business practices simply because they exist may not be a good enough reason for following a set of business practices. Are there more efficient procedures for running your railroad? Are there ways of enhancing your revenue? Is there a means of improving the compensation for your overworked staff (and your overworked selves)? Do you fully understand where your funding is coming from, where it is going, and why? Are your contracts with printers, advertisers, and advertising agencies at optimum advantage? Is your distribution system the most efficient and economical? Is there sufficient control and oversight of your accounts? Are financial records being kept properly?

If you don't know the answers to these questions—and I'm betting many of you don't—then it is incumbent upon you as responsible folks to find the answers. Finding those answers may be tedious and time-consuming, but this isn't exactly like deciphering Signor Da Vinci's code. After all, you're journalists, and you should know how to flex your investigative skills. More than that, the answers should be right there on your campus. The campus business, payroll, and accounts offices and the student government should be able to fill you in on most of these matters. The big fun occurs when you ask questions that no one knows how to answer ("Why must purchase orders be done on paper, in triplicate, instead of electronically?" "Um, er, well ...").

What you may discover of course is that the wise old men and women obscured back there in the mists of prehistory established an excellent system of business practices and everything is cool. You may also find fixed reasons for why you must do the things you do. Certain powers and responsibilities invested in the student government, for example, may control how you may manage your finances. Similarly, the university may be limited by its charter, or by state or federal law, in regard to how it oversees and funds student organizations and how it compensates or otherwise rewards students for their service to those organizations. By nosing afield, you might also learn that student newspapers at neighboring campuses have financial setups that in some respects are better than yours.

Point is, you might learn a lot of things. You might learn you're getting a good deal. You might learn you're getting screwed. You might learn that while you suspected you were getting screwed you really aren't. You might learn of ways of improving the newspaper's situation. And you might learn of things that can't be changed, meaning you have to go on getting screwed or at least feeling like you are. Whatever the case, the more you know the better off you'll be able to judge your business and financial picture. I liken it to knowledge about what's under the hood of a car. You can certainly drive a car year after year without even knowing where the hood latch is located. But come that day when the smoke starts pouring out of your engine ... Even without a fire, I think the more informed you are about automobiles and how they work, the better off you are. Such knowledge should enhance your ability to judge if things are performing at their best.

THE BUDGET

Whatever the newspaper's financial setup, the business staff is probably required by whoever holds the purse strings to prepare and submit for approval an annual or semi-annual budget. Even if for some peculiar reason you were not required to prepare a budget, doing so is to your benefit, since your financial health (like your physiological health) should not be a mystery to you. Same holds true if for some reason the budget is out of your hands. If some other authority is determining and tracking your cash flow, expenditures, and the like, you should be in the picture; I cannot imagine any valid reason for withholding this information from you.

Depending on the size of your operation, you likely have some sort of internal budgets as well—or if you don't, you should consider instituting a budgeting system. You could cover all of your expenditures out of a general operating fund, but that's potentially inefficient in terms of tracking your cash flow. Do you know precisely how much your photo staff is spending on supplies? Can you keep track of how much the arts and entertainment editor is compensating reviewers for concerts tickets and the like? Should the sports editor be billing the newspaper for transportation costs to away games when she could have traveled with the team?

Guidelines on budget design, bookkeeping, management, and more may be obtained from College Newspaper Business and Advertising Managers, Inc. (CNBAM; www.cnbam.org), an outfit very much worth knowing about.

COMMERCIAL ADVERTISING

Along with inherited business practices and so on, you also most likely inherited commercial advertising rates. These should be monitored regularly; after all, everything else in the economy (with the exception of computers) steadily goes up in price. Many college newspapers publish their rate cards on their Web sites, so one way to see if your rates are in line with reality is to check ("price check!") the sites of colleges of comparable size and location. CNBAM may be helpful here as well. And don't overlook your own campus resources; faculty over at the school of business administration, for example, may have some valuable input for you.

Back in chapter 1 I discussed policies on the kinds of ads you may or may not choose to accept, so I won't reiterate those here except to say that if you have no established policies, you should, and if you do have them you should subject them to the periodic rethink. In chapter 17 ("Student Press Law") I also discuss legal concerns and advertising.

The advertising principles in chapters 1 and 17 largely deal with ads that may violate university, state, or federal regulations or that may be objectionable for reasons of taste or community harmony. Here I'll mention an additional matter of concern: dubious come-ons and outright scams. I'm always skeptical of offers that sound too good to be true, and I think you should be as well. Such offers in campus newspapers run to the order of cheapo, "all-inclusive" spring break vacations, certain credit card deals, and ads promising information on overseas employment. I've even seen come-ons telling attractive coeds they can make big bucks as artists' models or as casino greeters. What if the travel agency offering that bargain trip to Cancun takes the money and runs? What if that credit card broker is concealing the fact that its interest rates for students are the same astronomical levels made available to felons just getting out of prison? What if those lists of overseas jobs were drawn up before the Korean War? What if the model or hostess job is a front for a prostitution ring?

You're chuckling? Stop chuckling. All of these examples are based on actual cases. Depending on a number of factors (e.g., state legislation, how the ad was placed), your newspaper could be held liable for printing such ads or for publishing them on your Web site. But even if you faced no legal consequences, do you want to be responsible for seeing a fellow student get ripped off—or worse? In journalistic terms, it is as wrong to publish a misleading advertisement as it is to print a misleading news story.

Now you can't check out every ad submitted to your newspaper any more than the elves at eBay can test drive everything they post for auction. And you shouldn't be held responsible for a classified ad in which a student is selling a used CD player that's no longer useful for playing CDs. But doggone it, when any ad looks the least bit suspicious, you have the moral if not the legal obligation to check it out. You would do the same with a fishy news story, would you not? You are, for example, perfectly within your rights to demand bona fides from a dubious advertiser and to check out the experience of other newspapers that have taken those ads. The Better Business Bureau can also let you know if it has received any complaints about the advertiser. Your state's attorney general's office, consumer advocacy agency, and other state regulatory offices can also be helpful in this area.

CLASSY?

Classified ads are almost as much a public service as a generator of revenue. Accordingly, both mainstream newspapers and their readers have traditionally valued classifieds greatly. In recent years, of course, such advertising has largely drifted to the Internet, but the question remains: Should you offer them? Subsidiary questions: Do you run them free as a readers' service, do you charge for them, and if the latter, how much? And do you accept ads for anything (bongs?)? Do you allow "romance" ads ("Man seeking tall blonde foot fetishist with interest in Wittgenstein")? Do you devote space to classifieds in your printed pages, or just in your online edition? Whatever you decide, it's good to work out guidelines and put 'em on paper.

PUBLIC SERVICE ADVERTISING

Strange as it may sound, people like advertisements. Well, maybe it isn't so strange; ads after all are by far the best thing on TV. Ads are likewise one of the main reasons people read newspapers. Readers want to know what's on sale, what's at the movies, what new products are available, and how to get that impossibly cheap trip to Cancun. In this sense when you publish advertisements you're not only helping someone hustle goods and services, you're also performing a public service.

Some advertisements, however, are not hustling goods and services at all. Such an ad might be a solicitation for volunteers to spend their spring break helping hurricane victims rather than sunning themselves on the beaches of Mexico. Another such ad might announce auditions for an open mike cabaret. The rock climbing association might want to place a condolence notice for one of its less talented members. A fraternity might want to congratulate a brother for finally passing a course. Blood drives, voter registration drives, sweatshop boycotts, HIV testing, charity bake sales—the list of causes that various advocates and activists may seek to advertise is endless, and the newspaper quite rightly would view running such ads as a public service. Question is, should your advertising manager charge these advertisers the commercial ad rate? Many of these noncommercial outfits won't have much budget for display advertising. You can offer them a free line or two in your Kampus Kalendar or Wha's Happenin' column; some student newspapers also offer free classified ads or swap n' shop bulletin boards as a public service. But such ads obviously have limited exposure—and I am talking worthy causes here.

There's no completely satisfactory formula for dealing with public service ads, but I think in the true spirit of public service a newspaper does well by its readers if it affords a certain amount of space to publicizing good causes. Of course, determining what constitutes a good cause is a judgment call, as is how much space to give away in each issue. Don't be a Scrooge, but don't be overgenerous either; remember, every inch of advertising space you give away costs you, because it's an inch not bringing in revenue.

There's a further reason to keep your generous impulses in check: Once you grant free advertising space to one group, ten others will request the same. Give the Hillel group a free ad for its Hanukkah latke sale, and the Roman Catholics, Greek Orthodox, Copts, Armenians, Baptists, Methodists, Lutherans, Mennonites, Episcopalians, Christian Scientists, Latter Day Saints, Secular Humanists, animists, Wiccans, Shiites, and Sunnis will be beating down your door demanding free ads for their latke sales too. How can you pick and choose without picking a fight?

THE FIREWALL

While you're busy beating back all those competing confessionals, let's consider another knotty problem arising from advertising, namely the advertiser who seeks to encroach on your editorial columns. The typical scenario goes something like this: The manager of, say, a new sporting goods store in town tells your ad manager he'd be happy to purchase advertising space in the newspaper. But the merchant says this is conditional on the newspaper running a nice feature story on the shop. Let's say the problem is compounded when the advertising manager comes a'courtin' the features editor with a song and dance about how the paper really needs the ad revenue and the sporting goods shop really is special and the owner is a really neat guy and it will all make for a story that will really interest the readers and a new and struggling business really deserves the publicity and on and on to the point where the features editor would really rather be sorting out the Shiites and the Sunnis than listening to this sales pitch.

Well, like so many other things at the newspaper, a decision on assigning a reporter to a feature on the new shop is a judgment call. Such a story, after all, might be considered newsworthy and is likely of interest to many readers. It might even be considered community service to give local independent merchants some publicity. But under no circumstances should an ad manager promise editorial coverage of an advertiser, and under no circumstances should the editorial side encourage advertisers in the notion that they have access to your editorial space. The principle is that the editors, and absolutely no one else—not a shop owner, not a charitable organization, not the college president—should decide what goes into the newspaper. Reason: Nothing less than your journalistic credibility and integrity is at stake.

This is a significant matter because news organizations are frequently pressured to stroke advertisers with feature stories. The media like to insist that they maintain firewalls between the business and the editorial sides of their operations. But the truth is, those firewalls are often mighty porous. The concert promoter inquires about placing a full-page ad, which promises beaucoup bucks for the newspaper. But the promoter also lets it be known he'd like a nice big preview of the concert on the features page tossed in to clinch the deal. A local supermarket finds itself up to its ass in avocados; it will run a big ad, contingent on the "coincidental" publication of avocado recipe ideas in the newspaper's food pages; the supermarket will even supply the recipes and attendant copy extolling the glories of the fruit. The ad department has no problem with such propositions, but the editorial side of the firewall should. Yet many times the editorial side will justify such invasions of its space. Well, hell, people want to read a profile of the Nine-Inch Zucchinis, don't they? Well, hell, avocados are in season, aren't they? The smaller the newspaper, the more dependent it likely is on every advertising dollar. But even bigfoot media like *The New York Times* are not immune to such deals. Economic necessity may sometimes trump editorial integrity. If a news organization isn't vigilant, however, it may find itself selling off more and more of its news and feature holes. Even a single sellout is compromising, and readers can smell it (you know, the damage done to reputation and self-respect from just one one-night stand lasts a lot longer than one night—hey, what am I talking about?).

Oh, yes, firewalls. Do you have 'em? Are they intact? Bottom line: Business and editorial should be kept as far apart as possible. In this regard, some student newspapers, in contrast to what is suggested in our model newspaper constitution (chapter 1), do not even allow the business manager to be a member of the newspaper's editorial board. That's worth considering.

YOUR CORPORATE SPONSOR

A special category of advertiser is found within the college or university itself. The career services office may want an advertisement for its upcoming job fair. The painting and design department wishes to promote its annual faculty exhibition. The outdoors club is hustling tickets to a rock climbing competition. The administration is hosting a forum on alcohol abuse and wants all booze heads to know about it. The athletic department wants to publicize an upcoming exhibition game with the Harlem Globetrotters. A sorority is holding a special event to raise money for a battered women's shelter. The campus bookstore is having a hoodie sale.

Some of these ads are commercial in nature, some are not, but all are emanating from some corner of your campus. So, do you charge them your normal advertising rates? Best to have at least a general policy in place, then weigh each ad individually against those guidelines. And just like the off-campus advertisers mentioned above, these campus advertisers may also seek to breach your firewall by requesting a news or feature story on what they are advertising.

SELF-PROMOTION
Built into your business plans and budgets should be a certain amount of self-advertisement and self-promotion. Most likely you periodically run ads to the effect of "Wanna grow your portfolio, have fun, and get free pizza? Join *The Slavering Newshound* staff today!" Such notices are called house ads, and you are right to run them. For one thing, they are great for filling those holes on the page you discover right at the end of a long, hard layout night. More important, you should let readers know about opportunities for working on the newspaper. Many times, students view the newspaper as a closed shop staffed by some secret, self-selected cabal. So it's good to disabuse readers of that notion. It's also good to run recruitment ads because student newspapers rarely have enough good staff.

Bedsides, those ads don't cost you anything, right? Wrong. Those ads take up space, and in the print world, space, not time, is money. So you're blithely filling holes or half-pages with recruitment ads all the time, eh? Cool. But every inch devoted to a house ad is an inch denied to editorial matter or to paid advertising. So somebody, presumably your advertising manager, should be keeping track of just how many ad inches the newspaper itself is consuming. Some newspapers even bill themselves for house ads, and there is good sense in that.

Aside from using your own pages and Web site for recruitment, other forms of outreach should be budgeted. This may include the costs of participating in campus activities fairs, buying promotional pens or key chains (or, most desirably, bottle openers) with the newspaper logo, advertising in other media outlets, mounting promotional posters, erecting eye-catching distribution boxes for the paper, arranging links to your Web site on other Web sites, and maybe even outfitting staffers with cool T-shirts, sweatshirts, or hats bearing the newspaper's logo (one T-shirt I've seen sported by more than one college newspaper staff has emblazoned on its back: "We Put Out on Thursdays"—awful, but awfully amusing).

Retention, meanwhile, is as important as recruitment, which is why I believe that once you've obtained your staffers, you should spend a little money to reward them for good work (and to keep them working.) Bonuses for story-of-the-week or reporter-of-the-month might take the form of a simple certificate of appreciation (and even better if accompanied by a gift certificate from a record or book shop), but these little treats may go a long way to keeping reporters on the job.

All of these promotional tactics and self-serving activities cost money. Spend it. You couldn't devote your money to a more deserving cause.

17

Student Press Law

Two central points must be made right at the start in regard to legal problems and the student press:

1. A campus newspaper is a genuine newspaper. It may be produced by a bunch of beer-sodden amateurs—no, wait, that sounds too much like the mainstream press . . . I'll rephrase that. A student newspaper may be produced by underage journalists, it may be under the patronage of an institution of higher learning, it may be distributed free, it may be the most ragged of rags, but none of that contradicts the fact that a student newspaper is still a real newspaper. As such, the people producing the student newspaper share the same duties and responsibilities of professional journalists, largely enjoy the same freedoms and First Amendment protections (more so at public institutions, less so at private colleges), and for the most part face the same legal consequences if they violate the law.
2. The law concerning the press is a bit of a mess. For openers, the First Amendment to the U.S. Constitution guarantees freedom of the press. Historically, however, that freedom has rarely if ever been judged in any courtroom as absolute, and certainly the U.S. Supreme Court has never ruled to that effect. Congress has rarely passed any legislation regarding the press, but in those instances when it has, such as the Espionage Act of 1918, the Supreme Court has recognized that Congress may limit some kinds of expression. The various states also have statutes that affect the media. For

example, while there is no federal libel law, the individual states have their own libel laws. To make the matter more complex, state and federal circuit courts with great frequency hear suits and appeals on media issues and pronounce rulings. These rulings may set precedents that in turn may, in lieu of existing legislation, have the force of law until contradicted by rulings of other, usually higher, courts. What all this means is that media law is constantly subject to change. What that means in turn is that student journalists (a) should be knowledgeable about their newspaper's legal responsibilities and liabilities and (b) should keep up to date with developments in media law, and especially those concerning the student press.

RUNNING SCARED
None of the above means that student journalists should have to work in fear of the law. It simply means that you should operate with respect for the law. When you're commuting to work or to class, are you driving in fear of the law? If you're accustomed to speeding, running stop signs, ignoring your seat belt, and tippling wine behind the wheel, yes, you should be worried about being caught. If you respect the laws of the road, however, you've no reason to turn pale every time you pass a patrol car (unless you're passing it on the wrong side).

Extending our motoring metaphor, I'd say it's a bit on the immature side if you think that, in the event of being ticketed for a traffic violation, "Daddy will take care of it." Same with violating the law by something you print. You can't assume that the college—or the college's legal team—will take care of your legal problems. It is hoped that the college will be sympathetic to your problems and perhaps offer some assistance. But the liability may well be yours and yours alone. This depends on your newspaper's degree of independence. As indicated in the previous chapters, some colleges (in the main, private institutions) are considered the proprietor and publisher of the student newspaper, while other colleges may have only a technical relationship with the student newspaper. Therefore, in the face of, say, a law suit, the newspaper may share the defendant's dock with the college. Or the newspaper may be entirely on its own.

LIBEL
I'm not going to offer here anything like a comprehensive review of media law; for that you have your journalism classes and books like *The Associated*

Press Stylebook and Briefing on Media Law. Instead, we'll look at a few central media law issues, especially as they affect the student press.

The most commonly cited legal problem the press faces is libel. As noted, libel law is state law, and the definitions of *libel* therefore vary from state to state. But in general, libel is *published material that falsely defames or otherwise harms the reputation or standing of a person or, in a few instances, a group of persons*. Each of the elements in that definition is defined and refined further in law: what exactly *published* means, for example, or *material*, or *falsely* (which may or may not be part of a state's libel statute), or *defames*, or *person*. *Published*, for example, now includes stuff posted on Web sites. *Material* includes articles, photos, cartoons, letters to the editor, headlines, captions, and advertisements. *Defame*, in one of its earliest incarnations in English law, included suggesting that someone had a "loathsome disease," like leprosy, and while that sounds quaint you could well find yourself on the wrong end of a lawsuit after suggesting in print someone has AIDS or a sexually transmitted disease. Even the defamation of *people* has been extended; recent libel suits have dealt with the alleged defamation of corporations and, get this, hamburger and fruits.

Now that I've defined *libel*, albeit it not definitively, I will make a few pertinent observations on the topic.

PERTINENT OBSERVATIONS

1. Libel laws indirectly restrain the press. The press is still free to print harmful lies, but libel laws give individuals recourse to penalize the press for its false defamations via lawsuits. As a result, the press normally enacts safeguards—restrains itself—against wrongfully libeling people.

2. Libel laws are a good thing. The press is powerful, and since the harm it does can have long-lasting effects, people need protection from the damage the press can wreak.

3. The press very frequently publishes material that injures the standing of individuals in the eyes of the community. If you report, for example, that the president of your university has phony credentials listed on his resume, your article makes the president look bad. If you publish a review that says a student grunge band is amateurish and unoriginal, that makes the band look bad. If your newspaper prints a story revealing that a student has been convicted of serial urination on Main Street, your story makes that student look

bad. All of these things are defamatory and may have serious and material consequences for the individuals. The president may be forced to resign, the band may lose bookings, the urinator—I don't know, he may be required to attend meetings of Flashers Anonymous. But that doesn't mean any of these individuals can successfully sue you for libel. That's because:

4. The press has three basic defenses against libel suits. The first is *provable truth*. If you have evidence that the college president's resume has been treated with steroids, then he can't win a suit against you. (An important concept here is *provable*; it's not enough that a thoroughly trustworthy source told you the resume was padded, you have to have the evidence to prove it.) A second defense is *fair comment and criticism*, which basically says that the performers and others who put their work out there before the public have to accept criticism—as long as the criticism is directed at the artistic offering itself and not at the artist as an individual. (Fair comment also applies to criticism of the official duties of public officials.) A third defense against libel is *privilege*, meaning that the facts are a matter of official public record; in this case, the fact that the weak-bladdered student was convicted in court means that you may publish that information.

Many important nuances figure in all of these defenses against libel, such as different levels of protection for public officials, public figures, and private citizens. Other factors that may come into play include the intent evident in the libelous material, if the newspaper knew the defamatory material was false but printed it anyway, whether or not the material in question was of public concern, and whether or not it was newsworthy. These and other issues may also vary from state to state. But what I've outlined in the above paragraph is what at the very least student reporters and editors should keep in mind.

5. Most instances of libel result from sloppy reporting, writing, editing—and thinking. Simple as that. Courts may view some libels as resulting from "honest mistakes," and even deadline pressure may be taken into account. In some instances that may get you off the hook. But don't count on it.

6. In all but seventeen of our fifty states as of this writing, libel is solely a matter of civil, not criminal, law. This means that if a court found you guilty of libel, in most states you won't face jail time. Instead, you might be required to publish a retraction of or apology for what you published. You might be sentenced to community service. You might be sentenced to taking a journalism course (I once had just such a hapless reporter in one of my news writing classes). Not least, you might have to pay the plaintiff damages.

Paying damages can be mighty damaging, and this brings up a host of issues. First of all, a person suing over something that appeared in, say, a news article, most likely will not sue only the reporter. Most often the plaintiff goes after what are called the deepest pockets. Out there in the real world, the most reporters have in their pockets at any given time is lint. Likewise, student reporters are prone to have more debts than assets (who wants to sue a kid saddled with student loans?). Plaintiffs seeking damages therefore may go after anyone connected with the publication of the allegedly libelous material, and anyone so connected may be so liable. This could include the editors who assigned and edited the story, the newspaper adviser who read the story, the printing company that printed it, the trucker who distributed it, and the university that funded or otherwise hosted the newspaper. Who actually may be accountable will vary from campus to campus, depending on that relationship between newspaper and college administration. Point is, committing libel may not spell trouble just for the author of the libel; you may be taking down a lot of other folks with you.

7. Should a libel case go before a jury, you should know that juries tend to sympathize with plaintiffs against the press. The reason is that plaintiffs are individual citizens and the press is, well, it's the press, an institution the public does not greatly esteem. That appeals courts (which have no juries) tend to overturn decisions on libel rendered by juries is of some comfort, but remember, you're paying lawyers' fees and going through months and years of aggravation to get through that appeals court. So even if you ultimately win, you still lose a lot. Best advice: Don't print something that will get you dragged into court in the first place.

8. Damages in libel suits have steadily grown over the years to astronomical proportions; the payoff for a plaintiff in a libel suit can even be bigger than that given to the klutzy plaintiff who spilled McDonald's coffee on her lap. Some libel damages are so big that they can put a news organization out of business. As a result, much as physicians carry malpractice insurance, news organizations customarily carry libel insurance. As with the doctors' insurance, however, libel insurance has become very expensive. Despite this, you should check out the matter. First, does your newspaper currently have libel insurance? If it does, how much and is it adequate? If not, does the university have some indemnity for your iniquities? Good advice on libel insurance is available from the Student Press Law Center (www.splc.org).

9. None of the above is calculated to drive you out of student newspapering and into a lower-profile campus activity, like the backgammon team. Two things to bear in mind: First, you are not alone. Help is available from such organizations as the Associated Collegiate Press (www.studentpress.org/acp), the American Civil Liberties Union (www.aclu.org), the First Amendment Center (www.firstamendmentcenter.org), the Media Law Resource Center (www.medialaw.org) (I love its "panic book"), and the invaluable and aforementioned Student Press Law Center. The latter organization will even give you phone numbers of lawyers in your area who can usually give you some free assistance. Aside from seeking help, keep point number two in mind: While it's important to know the law, it's arguably more important to know your job and to do it properly. Do your job and you shouldn't wind up in court.

PRIVATE, KEEP OUT
After libel, the next large concern in media law is violation of privacy. While the notion of libel has been enshrined in law for hundreds of years, privacy is a relatively new legal concept. As with libel, privacy is largely a matter of state law (privacy is implied but not directly mentioned in the Bill of Rights). Thus, you would do well to know your state's privacy statutes. In general terms, violation of privacy includes unauthorized use of a person's name or picture for commercial purposes, disclosure of private information (a person's medical or financial records) which is not of legitimate public interest, and intrusion into an individual's private domain. So, for example, you might think you have a hot item when a reporter brings in photos and a story showing that a male philosophy professor likes to dress up at home like Little Bo Peep, complete with crinolines, high heels, nail polish, and, well, I suppose, sheep. Interesting story perhaps, but it probably runs afoul of privacy issues in several ways. Is the story newsworthy? Does the public have a compelling need to know this information? Does the professor's behavior at home have anything to do with his academic performance? Will publication of the information impact him negatively? Did the photographer invade the prof's property when he got the pictures? So—hot item? Or will it plunge you into hot water?

The above example deals with likely privacy violations off campus (the philosopher's private sheep ranch), but on campus you have an additional set of concerns. These mainly arise out of the 1974 Federal Educational Rights and Privacy Act (FERPA), also known as the Buckley Amendment (named for its proponent, New York Senator James Buckley). Among other things, this law safeguards the privacy of student records. At its most benign level, this is why you cannot publish a student's grades without the permission of that student or of the student's parents. Cool. But colleges have also used FERPA to withhold or to limit access to disciplinary records and to deny student reporters access to campus police records and judicial proceedings. Although federal laws may insist that colleges make public campus crime statistics, colleges don't like to admit that crime occurs on their campuses. This is why they also like to keep a lid on campus judicial proceedings. In at least one instance, a student newspaper editor was handcuffed and taken into custody by police for trying to attend a campus judicial hearing. On many campuses—certainly not all, but on many—student journalists have to wage constant battle to get the facts on campus crime. Reporters wail about the right of readers to know, administration and campus police cry about the need to safeguard students' records, and the war goes on.

FREEDOM OF INFORMATION
As mentioned in chapter 6 (Investigative Journalism), federal and state laws provide mechanisms for reporters and other citizens to gain access to public records that in their apparently innate zeal for secrecy some thick-skulled government bureaucrat or police desk sergeant withholds. You can't legally access everything, but neither can officials legally conceal records the law says must be made public. The federal law designed to aid the public in this regard is the Freedom of Information Act (FOIA). The individual states have laws with the same name, or they may be called the Open Records Law or the Right to Know Law or the Sunshiney Government Documents Act or some such promising designation. The requisite government Web sites will inform you of how to file a request for information. Not all requests will be honored, or perhaps not completely fulfilled. In such cases there is usually a means of appeal. Even with an appeal you may not get all that you need. But then again, you may—so keep that in mind.

NAUGHTY, NAUGHTY
The U.S. Supreme Court has ruled the First Amendment does not extend to filthy speech but, with its deference to "community standards," lets the

individual states determine what exactly is filth, that is, obscenity, profanity, pornography, and the like. We'll discuss these matters in more detail in the next chapter, which deals with taste. But for the moment, just be alert to the fact that depending on the state in which you publish, you can get your mouth washed out with legal soap.

CENSORSHIP

The worst-case scenario regarding conflicts over student press freedom is outright censorship. This is when the college administration prevents publication of a story or of an entire issue of the newspaper. Such censorship, also known as prior restraint, is normally considered un-American. In the tradition of the U.S. Constitution, the press is free to publish unhampered. Then, having done so, the press may face legal consequences (e.g., a libel suit) for something it has published. This however is not quite the situation that obtains on all campuses.

As recently as February 2006, for example, the U.S. Supreme Court let stand a judgment (*Hosty v. Carter*) by the Seventh Circuit Court that held that newspapers published at public universities with school sponsorship (academic supervision, funding, the granting of office space, etc.) may be subjected to prior review and censorship by the university administration. (Administrations at private institutions already had that power, though they have usually been reluctant to exercise it.) The exercise of administrative prior restraint has been deemed lawful at high school newspapers ever since the 1988 landmark *Hazelwood School District v. Kuhlmeier* case, but *Hosty* was the first time the principle was extended to public college newspapers. The implications and interpretations of *Hosty* are still being thrashed out. For the present the judgment affects only public institutions of higher learning in Illinois, Indiana, and Wisconsin (the district in which the ruling was made), but with this precedent similar rulings could be made elsewhere.

Another factor coming into play is whether or not the student newspaper serves as a "public forum." According to the courts, if the student newspaper is written and edited by students outside of the classroom and is open to all contributors, it should have full First Amendment protection; if conversely the newspaper is considered a closed, non-public forum, the college administration evidently has the right to determine what does or does not get printed. Just to complicate matters, how the newspaper is funded may determine its "forum" status. (Who pays the bills may decide who calls the shots). As you might imagine, with the myriad ways in which student newspapers are financed and operated, at many campuses it may not be clear if the newspaper is an open or a closed forum.

Against all this fuzzy legal background, the Student Press Law Center in 2006 began urging student newspaper staffs everywhere to cut to the chase by getting written statements from their college administrations that run like this:

"J. P. Slaverhundt University recognizes and affirms the editorial independence and press freedom of all student-edited campus media. Student editors have the authority to make all content decisions free from censorship and advance approval and consequently they bear the responsibility for the decisions that they make."

A similar statement is in our model newspaper constitution (chapter 1). If the student government and the college administration approve your constitution with such a defining clause, all to the good.

EVEN WORSE

Worst of the worst-case scenarios? How about the administration confiscating all copies of the newspaper before the readers can get their hands on them? Bad enough when groups of unhappy students resort to such action, as they have done on scores of campuses, but on a number of occasions even the administrators have been subject to such seizure fits. In one instance, a court in 1995 upheld Kentucky State University's decision to confiscate the entire run of the college yearbook, lock it up, and throw away the key. A federal appeals court later overturned that decision, ruling in favor of the student editors. But in light of the more recent *Hosty* case, it is unclear where student journalists now stand in regard to such censorship.

College administrators have other means of censoring the student press. One way is by replacing a pro-First Amendment adviser with someone who is, well, more pro-administration than pro-free speech. Another method is by reducing or eliminating funding for the student newspaper. Such actions are rare, and they are usually camouflaged as being inspired by something other than censorship (the old adviser is needed elsewhere, all budgets must be cut). Such actions may or may not hold up in court. But the point is, they can and do occur.

Both public and private college administrators in the main support the First Amendment and an unhampered student newspaper. Yet the possibility of being hampered still hangs over the heads of student journalists. How then should student journalists respond to this possibility? By never publishing anything that might upset the administration? Certainly not. Overly timid journalism is just as bad as purposely provocative journalism. No, the answer is—do your job properly, thoroughly and well.

OTHER LEGAL PROBLEMS

The student press faces a host of other legal challenges faced by the professional press. Let's consider a quick ten scenarios:

1. A coed has been raped. In your news story do you use her name? You should know what the law in your state permits in such cases. But even if the law permits publishing the name, should you?

2. An eager cub reporter bursts into the newsroom and excitedly announces she's got a star athlete to admit he regularly cheats on exams. The reporter proudly adds the fact that she's got the jock's confession on tape, because she recorded her phone conversation with the miscreant without his knowing it. Question: Who's the miscreant here? What does federal law say about recording phone conversations? What does the law say in your state about same?

3. Another eager young reporter (where are you getting all these eager young reporters?) says he's got the goods on health-code violations in the campus cafeteria kitchens. The reporter says he took a job as a busboy with the purpose of working undercover and has documented evidence, including photos, of unhealthy practices and unnatural acts behind the scenes at the caf. Do you have a scoop—or a possible lawsuit claiming deception?

4. Several reporters have covered a recent anti-war demonstration on campus and the resulting clash with the campus cops. Now the police have come to the newspaper office demanding the reporters' notebooks, photographs, and interview tapes regarding the demo. The cops say the material may be important evidence in criminal cases against violent demonstrators. How do you respond to the cops' demand? Does it make a difference if the cops have a search warrant?

5. Several students tell you, on condition of confidentiality, that Professor X (not his real name) is invariably drunk when he shows up for class—that is,

when he bothers to show up at all. You don't like to use anonymous sources, but these sources seem thoroughly credible. They've spoken to you individually and you are certain they have no axe to grind against the professor. Their only beef is they're not learning anything in this important class. You get further confirmation of the professor's alleged problem with alcohol from several other sources, including his fellow faculty members. You think it's wrong for a faculty member to be so wayward in his duties. You bring the allegations to the attention of the dean of the college in which Professor X teaches. The dean also thinks it's wrong for a faculty member to be so wayward in his duties, but he can't believe the charges against this professor. He wants to know the names of the sources who made the allegations. What do you do? What do you do if you run the story and the dean then threatens to get a court order for the names of the sources? What does the law say about all this?

6. A student drowns in the college's swimming pool. (Sorry for all these grotesque examples, but journalism has to deal with a lot of unhappy news.) Your photographer gets a terrific close-up shot of the dead body. The drowning victim's family is outraged that you ran such a picture and threatens to sue you. You laugh in their faces, confident you have committed neither libel nor invasion of privacy. The family's lawyer laughs back that courts now recognize the right to sue over outrageous behavior of the press. You stop laughing. How do you deal with this non-laughing matter?

7. You'd like to run a photo with your review of the new Nine-Inch Zucchinis album. You find a photo on the Internet. May you legally download and use it?

8. You run a photo of a dude wearing a sweatshirt with an Abercrombie and Fitch logo. Is it a violation of copyright to run that photo without the company's permission?

9. In your interview with a retired professor you suggest he is a pennypincher. The emeritus prof then says he'll sue you for depicting him in a "false light." Has he got a case?

10. A bunch of slackers is arrested buying dope from an off-campus dealer. The dealer is an enterprising fifteen-year-old from the nearby junior high. Can you print the name of this minor?

What do you do in any of these cases? First of all, know the law and be careful that you don't violate it before you publish. And if you do publish something and find yourself in legal hot water, remember that you are not alone. Seek advice from the student press organizations mentioned earlier, and seek out friendly campus sources. (Law professors, journalism professors, and administrators dealing with judicial procedures are often very helpful.) Who knows, even your newspaper adviser might have some advice.

18

Taste

An old joke says that the shortest chapter in any journalism textbook is the one dealing with journalistic ethics. The shortest chapter more realistically might be the one on taste. That's because increasing evidence suggests that taste no longer exists. Or if taste does exist, the concept has become so obscured and diminished that I can no longer detect it. Someday I expect to see journalism's chapter on taste to run something like this:

"Taste (n. *archaic, obsolete*): The sense of what is proper, seemly, or least likely to give offense in a given social situation."

End of chapter.

I mean, after MTV, Howard Stern, Jerry Springer, Madonna, *Desperate Housewives*, hip-hop lyrics, slasher films, *South Park*, traveling exhibits of peeled cadavers, artists exhibiting crucifixes pickled in urine, front-page newspaper articles on penile implants, and the most recent crop of political candidates, can anything truly be said to shock the public any more? Forget shock—does anything even mildly upset people?

Amazingly enough, some things still do offend. And the matter is of particular concern in the student press, which in some respects has traditionally enjoyed more latitude in matters of taste than has the mainstream press. We tend to cut student journalists more slack because—well, you know, you're young, it's all a learning experience for you, and we don't want to slap you down because in response you might burn down the library and hold the college president hostage. Thus, some student newspapers airily print profanities that would not normally appear in mainstream papers. You sometimes run cartoons that are crude and offensive. You publish satire that would embarrass Alexander Pope. You do all sorts of things that violate fuddy-duddy standards of taste and we normally let you get away with it because you pay tuition . . . I mean, because you're students and because we want you to develop independence of mind and because we love you.

That said, there are still a number of things you might publish that could upset or offend readers. Now newspapers frequently publish things that shock or disgust: a photo of a particular grisly car accident, a description of starving African children, the details of an especially hideous crime. The question is, do you want to offend readers or turn their tummies unnecessarily? That's my question. The answer is yours.

FEELTHY PICTURES

The Federal Communications Commission is empowered to police sexual language and images in broadcast media, but in regard to print, few matters of taste are regulated by law. As noted in the previous chapter, the U.S. Supreme Court ruled (as long ago as 1973, in *Miller v. California*) that there is such a thing as obscenity and that the states have the right to decide if printed material violates their community standards. Fact is, we don't have many busts these days concerning obscenity or pornography; those that we do have generally concern the Internet and protecting children and so on. Still, college newspapers can and do occasionally overstep the boundaries into the pastures of obscenity.

Let's take a totally wild example (one that has occurred on only a few dozen campuses). Let's say you get the brilliant idea of creating a photo montage that attaches the dean of women's head to the nude body of a porno queen. Such a photo could be deemed defamatory, and, depending on how explicit the photo is, it could be judged as violating your community's definitions of obscenity or pornography. In your defense you might claim satirical intent ("Come on, it was our April Fool's issue!"). You might get all sorts of experts to testify on your behalf regarding free speech, the perceptions of pornography, and the like. And the public prosecutor or the person suing you might lose the case.

But all that is law; our real topic is social acceptance. Regardless of what the law says, and putting aside whether or not you get a court summons, was publishing the photo a clever thing to do? Were some people offended by the picture? Does it matter how many or how few of your readers were offended? If only 1 percent of your readers was outraged, you might well say, "Well, hey, some people are always offended by something. We can't cater to everyone's sensibilities." To which I might say, Well, why not? Who's to decide that the feelings of 1 percent of your readers are too small in number to be considered? Why should you offend even one reader? Especially if the photo or story is published for amusement or titillation, and not for news value.

Remember, we're talking about gratuitous offense. A photo of dead bodies lying in the rubble of a building bombed by terrorists might be judged a necessary photo—even though it is bound to disturb and possibly sicken some readers. But it's harder to make a case for the overwhelming newsworthiness of photos of nude bodies engaged in obscene acts.

LANGUAGE POLICE

As we noted back in chapter 11, readers are more commonly outraged or disgusted by photos than by words; photos have that immediate, visceral impact, and some readers, for some obscure reason, don't particularly like looking at pictures of, say, a pack of coyotes eviscerating a Cub Scout while they (the readers, not the coyotes) are about to dig into their cornflakes at the breakfast table. So consider the *yuck!* factor. If a photo passed around the newsroom or from computer monitor to computer monitor elicits one or more "yucks!," that might be a clue that publishing the picture will offend.

But bad taste extends beyond photos, drawings, and other graphics. Words still have the power to sting. Now it is true that profanities abound in our daily speech, in the entertainment media, in magazines, and in some newspapers. But in fact some people really don't relish constantly hearing or reading about alleged Oedipus Jocasta relationships, or about what goes on in the bathroom or the bedroom. How seriously should you be concerned about this weird minority? Your call.

But there are other minorities you might be even more concerned about. Racial, ethnic, and religious slurs are classified as hate speech in many states, and purveyors of same may be prosecuted. In addition, most college campuses these days have codes of civility and other means of discouraging disrespect for minorities, women, gays, and others—and mechanisms for punishing those who violate the rules. Even where no written codes or contracts exist, groups of students may still be so upset by what is published in the newspaper that they picket the office, or gather up and burn all copies of the paper, along with an effigy of the editor if the actual editor is not available for immolation. Although I indicated above that "[w]e tend to cut student journalists more slack," a case may be made that college campuses enjoy less free speech these days than does the society at large. You all know about campus language police and political rectitude. You may agree or disagree with these phenomena. Just be aware that what you publish may violate someone's notion of what is politically or socially acceptable to utter or print—it will be strange if you never do—and be prepared for the consequences.

BLASPHEMY

Did he say "blasphemy"? The term sounds quaint, like something out of the seventeenth century. That's precisely why I'm mentioning it. You may get away with publishing the f-word. You may print a gruesome accident picture with no reader complaint. But mess about with God, or with people who are dedicated to their religion, and yes, even here in the twenty-first century, you may well offend an awful lot of people. If you don't think so, just consider the case of *Jyllands-Posten*. Don't recognize the name? It's the Danish newspaper that published those satirical Muhammad cartoons. Consider too the American student newspapers that reprinted those cartoons; some had their papers stolen; at another, the editor was fired.

You don't have to go far afield to offend the sensibilities of the faithful. Joke about Jesus, mess about with Moses, be flippant about the Bible or abortion or the death penalty or sex or intelligent design or any number of other hot-button issues and you will offend some readers. You want to discover how many Catholics, Jews, Evangelicals, or Muslims you have on campus? Easy. Just print something denigrating their beliefs.

Bottom line: Campus news stories, photos, columns, editorials, editorial cartoons, and features will offend some of the people some of the time. You can't please everybody. But that truism is no license to ignore the potential offense to somebody.

Below the bottom line: It's usually a judgment call. Exercise your judgment. But don't neglect expert opinion. For guidelines, consider such sources as the Associated Collegiate Press (www.studentpress.org/acp), the National Press

Photographers Association (www.nppa.org), and the Student Press Law Center (www.splc.org).

Beneath the line below the bottom line: I told you this would be a short chapter.

SURPRISE QUIZ

Well, I don't know how much of a surprise quiz it is when it comes labeled as a surprise quiz. But since this is a short chapter, I'll emulate the professor who makes up for a shortfall in his lecture by ordering you to close your books and put on your thinking caps. So—how would you handle the following?

1. A reviewer turns in an article about a university production of *The Vagina Monologues*. The review contains numerous four-letter words, the kind of vocabulary the newspaper normally does not publish. The reviewer argues vehemently that since the play used the f-word, the c-word, and so on, her review should be allowed to use these words as well. Agree?
2. A sports reporter covers an altercation that occurred during a basketball game. Players hurled epithets at each other, including the n-word, the s-word, and the twelve-letter compound referring to incest. Direct quotes?
3. A reporter does a story on how the local park and playground have turned into a giant outdoor canine toilet. The reporter supplies photos that prove same. Print photos?
4. A photographer gets incriminating photos of fraternity brothers illegally hazing pledges. The pledges are naked; the photos show full nudal frontity, I mean, full frontal nudity. Everyone on the newspaper staff naturally hates fraternities. Do you use the photos?
5. One of the residence halls on campus has been spray-painted with racial slurs. You have pictures. Do you print them?
6. A local stream has been polluted with industrial waste. Would you print pictures of mounds of poisoned fish? The carcasses of poisoned squirrels and chipmunks? Poisoned dogs and cats? Poisoned children?
7. A group of students disrupted an outdoor graduation exercise by streaking naked across the stage. Use pictures?
8. An antiabortion group wants to place an ad in the paper that shows mutilated fetuses. Take the money and run?

9. Revolting evidence of binge drinking at an off-campus apartment is seen in the photos of vomit-covered floors. Print?
10. A coach and an underage athlete are arrested on charges of engaging in gay sex in the locker room after hours. A campus police spokesman tells the press in explicit detail exactly what the two men were doing. Do you quote completely?

19

Ethics

All of the professions operate according to codes of ethics, whether such codes are formalized or not. Unethical physicians can lose their licenses to practice medicine, sleazy lawyers can be disbarred, corrupt accountants and teachers can be thrown out of their respective professions. It's not universally agreed that journalism constitutes a profession—no journalist, after all, has to undergo special training or otherwise qualify for a license. Nevertheless, news organizations customarily maintain professional codes of ethics—guidelines of acceptable and unacceptable behaviors and practices—that their employees are required to observe. Most news organizations use the ethical code established by the Society of Professional Journalists (www.spj.org) or some adaptation thereof. Some news organizations have written their own codes of ethics (*The New York Times*'s "Handbook of Values and Practices" runs to nearly sixty pages and may be downloaded from www.nytco.com/pdf/NYT_Ethical_Journalism_0904.pdf). Other media outlets, often the smaller and independent ones, will have a code of ethics that consists of the Ten Commandments posted on a bulletin board and a series of ethical do's and don'ts lodged in the head of some gruff old managing editor.

Since a student newspaper is a real newspaper, it too would do well to have a code of ethics and, as we argued in chapter 1, it would do well to have those ethical guidelines in written form so that reporters and editors don't have to wonder about what's journalistically right or wrong. Before we get into individual problems, let me establish two central points about ethics, and journalistic ethics in particular:

1. Ethical problems are usually distinct from legal problems. The law says what is lawful or unlawful. Ethics deals with matters of right and wrong, but those matters may not be covered in the law books. In this sense resolving ethical problems is often more difficult than determining a legal course of action. A cop or a court can tell you if you are in violation of the law. You might be more or less on your own when it comes to deciding if you have violated ethical standards.
2. Sartre and Camus aside, being on your own regarding right and wrong is not a cause for existential despair. Even if you have no written code of ethics to serve as a guide, you do have your own conscience. If it doesn't feel right, it's probably wrong. Moreover, they don't call it the Golden Rule for nothing. The Golden Rule offers a good test: If you wouldn't like someone to do it to you, should you do it to someone else?

Having established those two points, let's consider the ethics of the business.

GOTTA SERVE SOMEBODY

One of the key principles of journalistic ethics is keeping one's eye on whom one is serving. When you're in the information business, your business is informing the public. When you're out there gathering the facts, writing your articles, editing those articles, you're working for the good of the readers (i.e., the public). This means you're not working to satisfy the wishes of the editor in chief, you're not working to please the advertisers, and you're not working to promote the university.

Holding fast to the principle of keeping your eye on your objective also means avoiding conflicts of interest. This means you don't publish material with the purpose of promoting your boyfriend's theater production, your girlfriend's sorority event, an advertiser's products or services, this person's charitable activities, that person's political agenda, the other person's pet project. And you certainly don't use the newspaper to boost your own cherished causes. You may write about all of the things listed here, but you do so only if publicizing them is first and foremost in the readers' interests, not in the interest of anyone else, including yourself.

FAIR PLAY

If you publish material that benefits a source as much or more than it does the readers, then you are violating the unwritten contract between journalist and reader to play fair. Publishing an encomium studded with exclamation points on that new sporting goods store; printing a stenographic interview in which, without the reporter's verification or confirmation, the alumni office boasts about what a great job it is doing; allowing a source to criticize another source without the reporter seeking reply or rebuttal—all of these things are examples of unbalanced and therefore unfair journalism. We discussed these matters in chapter 5 ("Reporting") in terms of fairness. Now I'm stressing the view that unfair journalism is unethical journalism.

INFLUENCE

Journalists who allow their reporting to be influenced to the point where balance, objectivity, and truth suffer are acting immorally. That influence may be emotional. Some of the examples above (friends or favored people as sources) suggest emotional influence; a journalist's own biases (political, social, artistic, whatever) may also emotionally slant a reporter or editor's work. Keeping free of emotional blackmail, which may be difficult even to recognize, is a psychological struggle; good luck in your battle. Material influence is a more substantive matter. Journalists are frequently offered material inducements and privileges by sources seeking positive coverage in the press. Currying favor may take the form of gifts from sources (a carton of CDs, a gift certificate for dinner at a nice restaurant), junkets (free trips), or the promise of inside information, scoops, or access to highly placed newsmakers. Some gifts are sent to journalists as rewards for articles the sources liked. Some goodies are presented as innocent tokens of appreciation, or simply as business-as-usual (and tax-deductible) swag. Others are thinly disguised bribes. How can you tell the difference between a present and a bribe? I'm not sure—by the smell?

Two points about influence, both emotional and material:

1. You must always be alert to the fact that people out there seek to exploit journalists. They want to use you, either to get publicity for themselves, their offices, and their activities or to publicize a point of view, or maybe even to see that certain news doesn't get publicized. These people are not evil; the means of disseminating their desires exists and they would like

access to it. You may allow yourself to be exploited in this way (and you may exploit these sources in return for your own journalistic needs). Example: A physics professor calls you with news about her new research grant. This is a legitimate news story. It also just happens—even as this is not your intent—that the story makes the prof look good, and the publicity might even help her or her department get additional grants. Even without these subsidiary consequences, by your publishing the story, we might say the prof now "owes" you, so that when you need information later on for a story that has to do with physics, you may call on the prof for help. All that's cool. What you must guard against is this tit-for-tat mutual exploitation pushing you into unfair journalism. You don't want to be a source's mouthpiece. You don't want to give a source unfair coverage at the expense of parallel or competing sources. And you don't want to accept anything from a source that might even be perceived as a bribe or a reward. (Remember, it's not enough to *be* honest, you also have to be *seen* as honest.) If all the readers see is stories month after month about this prof and her projects, and nothing, say, about what's happening over in the biology or chemistry departments, something is not going to smell right. An even worse odor arises when the prof gives you an A you do not deserve in her course.

2. We know you'll take the A in physics without argument (after all, it's physics . . . *just kidding*). But can you accept that material gift (the concert tickets, the dinner for two at Red Lobster), even if it appears tendered in the most honest and open manner? Well, what is your newspaper's policy on such gifts? If you don't know, ask the editor in chief. And even if you are permitted to accept—can you take these things and remain free of undue influence from your benefactors? Will accepting a free DVD player from an electronics firm or a hotel room paid for by the athletic department while you're covering an away game interfere to any degree with the fairness and objectivity of your reporting?

THE PUBLIC GOOD

In the immortal words of columnist Finley Peter Dunne (1867–1936), journalism at its most high-minded "comforts the afflicted and afflicts the comfortable." In campus terms, the afflicted of course are the students, and the comfortable are everybody else in the world, beginning with your faculty and administration. But seriously, what percentage of the material you publish in each edition is doing your readers good? You might instinctively say all of it, and you might instinctively be wrong. Look over recent issues of your paper. How much of what you published benefits certain individuals, certain factions, but less certainly the majority of your readers? How much of what you print is primarily fulfilling the desires—and perhaps satisfying the egos—of the writers and editors? How much of what fills your pages is fluff? How much is strictly fun and games? I don't minimize the importance of fun and games. But if we need fun and games, maybe that's why God invented Nintendo. What I'm really asking is how much of what you publish is truly useful or important to your readers? How much of what you write and print might actually help your readers? How much enlightens them about how the world, or at least their collegiate world, works? How much might improve their lives?

Journalists are not social workers. It is not their mission to improve society or to save the planet. But it is their job to cast light and to spread knowledge, and if they can do so in a way that stimulates awareness of problems and motivates people to seek solutions, that's all to the good—the public good. So, how much of what you have published recently is to the public good?

Simple examples. You might run a story reporting the results of a survey on the most popular cartoon characters on campus. Who rules—SpongeBob or Bart? Such a feature could be full of bright quotes and even enlightening information on how many hours the average student spends watching TV or downloading animation onto their cell phones. Fun story. Everybody will read it. Nobody will benefit from it.

Alternatively, a team of reporters might go out and examine the safety devices on campus. When were the elevators last inspected? Are the requisite fire extinguishers in place and do they work? How about the fire hoses? Are building evacuation instructions posted prominently? Are there sufficient smoke alarms on campus, and do they work? What's the state of the emergency telephones around campus? Does the campus have emergency medical personnel on duty round the clock?

Get my point? A campus safety story is as interesting as the cartoon survey—and a lot more vital.

Now I'm not suggesting that everything in a newspaper must be medicinal or therapeutic. Yuck. Like most people, I appreciate some sweetener sprinkled over my oat-bran flakes. The question is, how much nutrition are you serving your reader, and how much high-fructose corn syrup? And what does any of this have to do with ethics? I'm glad you asked. For every time you neglect the nobler forms of journalistic enterprise, you are ethically compromising.

Now you might argue, Hey, why single out the student press on this issue? Everybody knows all the news media, including newspapers, have increasingly become infotainment outlets. To which I reply, you're right. But my brief isn't the mainstream media, it's you guys. And must you guys emulate your elders? Surely you know by now that your elders aren't *always* your betters.

WHAT, ANOTHER QUIZ?

Anyway, that's my basic overview on journalistic ethics. Let's see how you would handle the following situations in our quiz:

1. A faculty member's wife calls the newsroom and says that a recent profile of her husband published in the campus paper had a number of errors: the man is fifty-two years old, not fifty-three; he earned his Ph.D. in 1995, not 1985; the couple has four children, not three. The woman would like you to print a correction in the next edition. You think the errors are minor, you don't like to admit mistakes in print, and the professor himself didn't call to request the correction. Should you run the correction?
2. A student who works in the bursar's office says she can get you copies of internal university memos showing that a dean has been repeatedly reimbursed for trips to Atlantic City casino hotels. Do you ask to see the documents?
3. A reporter for the campus paper also works as a paid stringer for a small newspaper in a neighboring town. The reporter amasses information on pending real estate acquisitions by the university. May she use the information to write stories for both newspapers for which she works?
4. The business manager of the student newspaper is offered a free cell phone from the phone company that advertises regularly in the paper. May the business manager accept the call?
5. A reporter is having lunch in the cafeteria and overhears students at an adjoining table planning some campus redecorating: They are plotting to go out one night and paint the statue of the college founder, J. P. Slaverhundt, in hideous Day-Glo colors. Can the reporter join in the conversation to learn exactly when this mischief is to take place and who is involved . . . without revealing he is a reporter?

6. An editor of the student newspaper is elected to the student government board. May the student serve both organizations?
7. A student calls to tell you that next day at noon he will set himself on fire in front of the campus flag pole to protest the war in Iraq. How do you respond to this call? Would you alert the police, line up a photographer, or take some other course of action?
8. For an article of alleged prejudice and discrimination on campus, you interview numerous sources. Some African-American students have a lot of specific complaints, but they don't want to be quoted by name. Same with some gay and lesbian students. Same with some faculty members who have complaints about the academic abilities of minority students, especially those who graduated from inner-city high schools. How do you handle these requests for anonymity?
9. A student who works at a local family planning clinic tells you the facility has received a number of bomb threats. You ask the local police chief about this and he confirms the threats. He also asks you to keep this news out of the newspaper, as the police have the abortion clinic under surveillance and he believes publicity will harm the investigation. How would you respond to this request?
10. You have an exclusive interview with a noted actor who is making a film in your area. During the interview the film star rolls and smokes a hashish cigarette. He makes no comment on this and neither do you. After the interview, however, the actor's manager takes you aside and asks you not to mention the dope in your article. Do you?

I could supply answers to these questions in the back of the book, but it might be too tempting for you to peek—and I figure tempting you wouldn't be ethical.

Final note: The very comprehensive Associated Collegiate Press Model Code of Ethics may be obtained via www.studentpress.org, free to association members and $7 for nonmembers.

20

The Joy of Journalism

Joy? Joy? After all that sober and solemn discussion of legal and ethical concerns is Grumblestiltskin now actually going to discuss joy?

You bet. Because putting out a student newspaper—any newspaper, for that matter—should be terrific fun. And if you're not experiencing terrific fun in your newsroom, I think you have a terrific problem that deserves immediate scrutiny.

Journalistic joy comes in a variety of forms. Let's look at some of these.

CREATIVITY

Creativity is a word we've hardly ever used in this book. Mea culpa—which is Latin for "I guess I was saving it until the end." Anyway, what's creativity got to do with newspapers? Just this: Don't ever let anyone—especially those snobs over at the literary magazine—tell you that journalism is not a creative enterprise. All writing is creative, and that even includes news accounts of those boring student government meetings. The meeting may be boring, but in the hands of a good writer and editor the article can sparkle. Good reporting is never formulaic, and good editing is an art. Creativity is required in discerning the potential stories lurking out there in the world around you. Talent is required in finding the right verbs and nouns and in putting them in the right places. Ingenuity is required to solve journalistic problems, such as how to explain a complicated issue in seven hundred words, where to place those seven hundred words on the page, how to write an accurate but attractive headline for that story, and how to express that headline with just so many characters per line. Artistry is needed to illustrate that story, either with an information-laden photograph or with a concise and readable graphic.

And guess what? All of this creativity generates pleasure. Some folks will tell you writing is agony, a matter of staring at the blank page or computer screen until drops of blood form on the forehead. Cool. If that's the way those fey creatures over at the lit magazine would have it, well, good for them. Journalists haven't time either for posing or for poeticizing. Journalists are too busy producing what Matthew Arnold labeled "literature in a hurry." Okay, it's not literary fiction and it's not poetry. But good journalism does require imagination, resourcefulness, and originality. And when you do it well, it makes you feel great.

Literature in a hurry? In both senses of the term, practicing journalism is a rush.

JOB SATISFACTION

Newspapering and ditch digging: They're both dirty jobs but somebody has to do them. They also have something else in common: At the end of the day on each job you can see exactly what you've achieved. Unlike many other endeavors (teaching comes to mind) ditch diggers and journalists are presented with the material results of their labors. The diggers can measure precisely how much ditch they excavated that day, determine if they achieved their goals, evaluate their techniques and equipment, and so on. Journalists get to hold a product in their hands. If they did the job well, they deservedly feel proud. If they did less well, they have the opportunity to analyze their weaknesses and learn from them. The ditch diggers go to bed at night comforted by the knowledge of how much progress they made during the day, which bolsters their belief that the job can be completed, the nut can be cracked. The journalists, likewise, know that the challenge of another day full of news is just around the corner. If they did well today, they can smile. If they did badly, at least they have the consolation that today's paper soon enough will be lining bird cages and that tomorrow the news staff gets to start all over again on a whole new slate, and who knows, maybe this is the day they'll publish that Pulitzer Prize–winning story.

If all this sounds romantic and sentimental, well, beneath their crusty exteriors journalists are frequently a romantic and sentimental lot (I don't know if that obtains for ditch diggers). Truth be known, in my innumerable years in journalism I've worked with reporters and editors who glumly carried out their duties in a routine and joyless manner, punching in and out of the clock with barely a smile and who might just as well have been digging ditches as filling columns of newsprint. But these sourpusses were decidedly in the minority. Far more common were the newsmen and newswomen who day after day labored long over their hot telephones and notebooks and keyboards, who did not grumble about working nights or on weekends, who did not rush home after the paper was put to bed, and who on top of a long and deadline-pressured day in fact couldn't wait to get back next morning to the office or to their beats. I've known journalists who accumulated so much vacation time they had to be *ordered* to go on holiday—and when they did finally go they hated every minute they were away from the newsroom. Why? Because they enjoyed their journalism. They were having fun.

This fun factor is something that spouses, significant others, and other others often can't comprehend. Maybe this is where journalism departs from ditch digging. The road crew might get satisfaction from a job well done, but who's to say they wouldn't jump at the opportunity to do any number of other jobs? Journalists, particularly veterans, may be lured away from the newsroom by the regular hours and better pay of public relations work or teaching, but if they yield they'll often feel like traitors to themselves. And they know they'll never have such fun again.

A student newspaper is unlikely to replicate all aspects of the professional press, but if you're not having fun, something is desperately wrong. As noted earlier, the student newspaper is one of the most demanding of student activities. It cuts into your social life, interferes with your studies, possibly alienates you from certain sets on campus (the Greeks, the jocks, the art crowd, the media-sneering literature professors). It limits the time you might devote to better-paying employment, gives you lawsuit anxieties, and wreaks havoc in all sorts of other ways. It is also a very high-profile activity, which means your successes will be widely known—as will your failures. Man, there's got to be something to offset all these liabilities, right?

REPORTORIAL JOY
We tell reporters to get it first, but first to get it right. There is a deep pleasure in both. The satisfaction of the scoop is difficult for a nonjournalist to

appreciate, but let me tell you, one of the most satisfying things a student journalist can experience is getting an important story first, a story so important that it has reporters from the mainstream press calling your newsroom begging to be filled in on your scoop. How often does this happen? As often as you come up with such stories. But know that such stories rarely fall into your lap; they usually result from your own enterprise. And that only increases your satisfaction.

Major or minor story, enterpriser or not, there is also the joy that comes from getting it right. When you've written an article that is clear and bright and interesting, that covers all the bases and answers all the questions, that is fair and balanced and accurate, and that truly serves the readers, then you are perfectly justified in feeling good about yourself and your skills.

That's joyous. That's fun.

THE JOY OF TEAMWORK

Writing is essentially a solitary pursuit, but as I have mentioned many times in this book, journalism is a team effort. Being part of a team can be a gratifying experience. This is obviously true of membership in a winning team, but it's also true of any team that strives to work well together. Think of that rock band in its backstage huddle before it goes on stage. Think of the teammates hoisting a big scorer on their shoulders. There's individual glory to be earned in any team pursuit, but there's also shared glory. A good team player knows this for a fact and revels in it. A newsroom will always have its prima donnas. There will always be jealousies, rivalries, and personality clashes. But a good newsroom, one that has good leadership and the right people in the right positions, can be a joy to behold. Putting out an edition of the newspaper is a matter of problem solving (one damn problem after another). Having a good team on your side all dedicated to solving the same problems is a wonderful feeling; that's one of the reasons you can go home at night exhausted but smiling. A reporter is like that wide receiver carrying the ball on a frantic dash to the goalpost; he's pumping away as hard as he can, and he's confident because he knows his teammates are behind him doing their best as well. Likewise, when the reporter gets that terrific story in print, everyone who had a hand in it—the assigning editor, the copy editor, the design editor, the photographer—justifiably can bask in the moment.

If your newsroom is a friendly, well-oiled aggregation of parts and personalities, then you have something that warms the heart. But people all doing their jobs is not enough. If you aren't experiencing a sense of comradeship you should address this problem immediately—even if it means the staff going on retreat and devoting an entire day to thrashing out ways to improve teamwork. No good teamwork—no joy in the newsroom.

THE JOY OF MENTORING
A zillion years ago when I was a freshman just starting out on my college newspaper, I learned a profound lesson that stuck with me far longer than just about anything I learned in my classes. After a few months of rewriting press releases and covering not terribly important stories, I screwed up the courage to submit a piece to the Op-Ed editor. I distinctly remember surreptitiously placing the article on his desk while he was at lunch and scurrying back to my cubbyhole. Some hours later he came into the newsroom looking for the author of this submission. He was delighted with the piece. He praised me—very publicly, much to my great pleasure—and slapped me on the back and invited me into his office. Then, with his door closed, he proceeded, word by word and line by line, to show me how to make an almost good article truly good.

This instruction went on for well over an hour and left me doubly astonished. First, I was amazed that an essay I had labored over for many days, an essay that I was convinced was darned good, an essay the Op-Ed editor himself had just praised aloud in the newsroom before all those within earshot . . . I was amazed, I say, that this essay needed so much editing. Yet phrase after phrase, sentence after sentence, paragraph after paragraph, this upperclassman gently worked with me to show how the piece could be strengthened, sharpened, made more coherent, have more impact, flow more gracefully, strike the ear more felicitously, develop its argument more logically—in short, how a merely promising sow's ear could be turned into a silken piece of prose.

The second thing that astonished me was this guy's devoting so much time and effort to helping a clumsy freshman writer get his article into shape. More than that, he was carrying out what could have been a humiliating experience for me in such a caring and sensitive manner. *Why is he doing this?* I kept asking myself. *What's in it for him?*

Indeed, up until this point, I had always thought of journalism as being all about me. My sole objective in getting a piece on the Op-Ed page was getting my byline in 12 point Bodoni bold caps. Why would this editor, a senior, older, fairly remote figure with one foot already tapping toward the professional world, be so keen in helping this fuzzy-cheeked freshman satisfy his own ego?

The answer to these questions would come to me only after more time at the newspaper. One thing I eventually figured out was that the time and effort the Op-Ed editor devoted to my article wasn't primarily for my benefit; it was for the benefit of the newspaper as a whole. The editor knew that a major part of his job was bringing along younger, less experienced writers, training them as he had been trained, seeing to it that the traditions of good journalism at our college would continue. In this sense, helping me was simply part of his payback for all the help the newspaper had given him over the years.

But I would learn that there was even more to it: If there is satisfaction in applying one's skills to improve a piece of work, there is genuine pleasure to be derived from helping others. Heaven forbid I should sound like Mother Teresa here; nor do I mean to suggest that people work in leper colonies because it's fun. But doggone it, there is fun in teaching a young pup the tricks of the trade. That's why your dad teaches you to ride a bike and why your older brother shows you how to place your fingers on the pigskin. It is also, although it is sometimes hard for them to recall this, why teachers teach. Yes, it's all bound up in duty and responsibility, but there's pleasure in it for the teacher as well. Put it this way: Have you ever had a really good coach on your soccer or softball team? Have you ever had the experience of coaching yourself? (That sounds like self-coaching; let's try that again.) Have you ever coached a younger player? If you have, then you know there's a lot of labor and frustration in coaching—yet there's satisfaction and reward as well.

So strange as it may sound, there is also satisfaction, reward, and pleasure to be had in even the humble, behind-the-scenes role of an editor.

All part of the joys of journalism.

THE JOY OF KNOWING

It's a cliché to say that knowledge is power. Here's a noncliché: Knowledge in and of itself is a source of deep satisfaction. Understanding your campus, comprehending the world, grasping the whys and the wherefores and the how-it-works, and not incidentally knowing more than the next guy over is a good feeling, and the more you know the better you feel. We don't tell you this when you go to college, but it's in the subtext of higher education and it's there between the lines of journalism as well. The pursuit of journalism is the pursuit of knowledge; do it well and you'll be amazed at what you'll learn. And the more you learn the better you'll be able to make your way in this wicked world.

It's the difference between being in the know and being in the dark.

THE JOY OF JUSTICE
Last but very far from least, there is deep gratification in helping to see wrongs righted and justice done. Journalists don't pursue their craft with the objective of improving the world, but publishing does have its consequences, and sometimes, just sometimes, those consequences are highly satisfying. Your journalism reveals that pricing policies at the campus bookstore are not as advantageous to the students as they might be. As a result of your story the bookstore revises its policies. That's good for the students—but that's enormously pleasing for both you and your newspaper. Your investigation shows that a contract for repaving campus walkways did not go to the lowest bidder, as required by law. As a result of your story, the university's auditors launch an investigation into the matter. You and your editors deserve extra toppings on your pizza. Your series proves that numerous entrances and exits on campus are not wheelchair accessible, which is both a matter of distress to disabled students and a violation of federal law. Because of your story, the university president vows to redress the situation immediately. You're perfectly right to share in the happiness of the disabled students. Your reporting proves that much of the organic produce supplied to the college's food service is not in fact organically grown. The food service changes to a fully authenticated organic supplier. The students benefit, and you and your newspaper can claim a victory.

Having a hand in seeing justice done is especially heartwarming, I hope you get to experience it.

TWO (JOURNALISTIC) LIFE LESSONS
Two true stories:

1. I once wrote an article of which I was inordinately proud and which in fact would eventually win me a small prize. But before that little prize came my way—indeed, just a few days after my dazzling article was published—I

happened to be in the fish market buying some fresh tilapia and—did you see this coming?—yep, I was handed my fish wrapped in my article. That was a great lesson. It really put me, my journalism, all journalism, and later even my prize in perspective. It's a perspective I have never abandoned.
2. On another occasion I was riding on a bus and noticed a man across the aisle reading an article I had written for that day's paper. The man was beaming. It was all I could do to keep from grabbing his lapel and shouting, "Hey, buddy, me, I wrote that!" But before I could embarrass myself that way, the man folded the paper very carefully, tucked it into his attaché case, and got off at the next stop. I was doubly gratified. A reader had smiled at my writing. But even more important, he had preserved the paper carefully in his bag, because there was more in the paper that he wanted to read.

Journalism—yes, and I include journalism devoted to covering a campus—can be a joy. I hope you're experiencing it. All those other students don't know what they're missing.

Bibliography

BOOKS

Aamidor, Abraham. *Real Feature Writing.* 2d ed. Hillsdale, NJ: Lawrence Erlbaum, 2006.

———. *Real Sports Reporting.* Bloomington, IN: Indiana University Press, 2003.

Alderman, Ellen, and Caroline Kennedy. *The Right to Privacy.* New York: Knopf, 1995.

American Society of Newspaper Editors. *Best Newspaper Writing.* St. Petersburg, FL: Poynter Institute for Media Studies, 2005–2007.

Andrews, Phil. *Sports Journalism: A Practical Introduction.* Thousand Oaks, CA: Sage Publications, 2005.

Associated Press Stylebook and Briefing on Media Law. New York: Basic Books, 2004.

Auletta, Ken. *Backstory: Inside the Business of News.* New York: Penguin Press, 2003.

Bagdikian, Ben. *The Media Monopoly.* Boston: Beacon Press, 2004.

Baughman, James L. *The Republic of Mass Culture: Journalism, Film and Broadcasting in America since 1941.* 2d ed. Baltimore: Johns Hopkins University Press, 1997.

Bernstein, Carl, and Bob Woodward. *All the President's Men.* 2d ed. New York: Simon and Schuster, 1994.

Boynton, Robert S. *The New New Journalism: Conversations with America's Best Nonfiction Writers on Their Craft.* New York: Vintage, 2005.

Bradlee, Ben. *A Good Life: Newspapering and Other Adventures.* New York: Simon and Schuster, 1995.

Breslin, Jimmy. *The World According to Breslin.* New York: Ticknor and Fields, 1985.

Brooks, Brian S. *Journalism in the Information Age.* Boston: Allyn and Bacon, 1997.

Campbell, Douglas S. *The Supreme Court and the Mass Media.* Westport, CT: Praeger, 1990.

Clurman, Richard M. *Beyond Malice: The Media's Years of Reckoning.* New York: NAL/Meridian, 1990.

———. *To the End of Time: The Seduction and Conquest of a Media Empire.* New York: Touchstone Books, 1993.

Cohen, Elliot D. *Philosophical Issues in Journalism.* New York: Oxford University Press, 1992.

Craig, Steve. *Sports Writing: A Beginner's Guide.* Shoreham, VT: Discover Writing Press, 2002.

Ehresmann, Donald L. *Fine Arts: A Bibliographic Guide to Basic Reference Works, Histories and Handbooks.* 3d ed. Littleton, CO: Libraries Unlimited, 1990.

Epstein, Edward Jay. *Between Fact and Fiction: The Problem of Journalism.* New York: Vintage, 1975.

Fedler, Fred, John R. Bender, Lucinda Davenport, and Michael W. Drager. *Reporting for the Media.* New York: Harcourt, 2001.

Ferguson, Donald L. *Journalism Today.* 6th ed. New York: McGraw-Hill, 2001.

Fink, Conrad. *Strategic Newspaper Management.* Boston: Allyn and Bacon, 1995.

———. *Writing Opinion for Impact.* Ames, IA: Blackwell, 2004.

Freedman, Samuel G. *Letters to a Young Journalist.* New York: Basic Books, 2006.

Friedlander, Edward J., and John Lee. *Feature Writing for Newspapers and Magazines.* New York: Harper and Row, 1999.

Garrison, Bruce. *Professional Feature Writing.* Hillsdale, NJ: Lawrence Erlbaum, 1989.

George-Palilonis, Jennifer. *A Practical Guide to Graphics Reporting.* Burlington, MA: Focal Press, 2006.

Halberstam, David. *The Powers That Be.* New York: Knopf, 1979.

Hart, Jack. *Writer's Coach: An Editor's Guide to Words That Work.* Pantheon: New York, 2006.

Houston, Brant, Len Bruzzese, and Steve Weinberg. *The Investigative Reporter's Handbook: A Guide to Documents, Databases and Techniques.* Boston: Bedford/St. Martin's, 2002.

Johnson, David. *No Ordinary Lives: One Man's Journey into the Heart of America.* New York: Warner Books, 2002.

Jones, Lois Swan. *Art Information on the Internet: How to Find It, How to Use It.* Phoenix: Oryx Press, 1999.

———. *Art Information: Research Methods and Resources.* 3d ed. Dubuque, IA: Kendall/Hunt, 1990.

Kanigel, Rachele. *Student Newspaper Survival Guide.* Ames, IA: Blackwell, 2006.

Kennedy, George, Daryl R. Moen, and Don Ranly. *Beyond the Inverted Pyramid.* New York: St. Martin's Press, 1993.

Kershner, James. *The Elements of Newswriting.* Boston: Allyn and Bacon, 2004.

Knudson, Jerry W. *In the News: American Journalists View Their Craft.* Wilmington, DE: Scholarly Resources, 2000.

Levin, Mark. *The Reporter's Notebook: Writing Tools for Student Journalists.* Columbus, NC: Mind-Stretch Publishing, 2000.

Lewis, Anthony. *Make No Law.* New York: Random House, 1992.

Liebling, A. J. *The Press.* New York: Pantheon, 1981.

McCoy, W. U. *Performing and Visual Arts Writing & Reviewing.* Lanham, MD: University Press of America, 1992.

Missouri Group. *News Reporting and Writing.* 8th ed. Boston: Bedford/St. Martin's, 2004.

Pember, Don R. *Mass Media Law.* 15th ed. New York: McGraw-Hill Humanities, 2006.

Plotnik, Arthur. *The Elements of Editing.* New York: Collier, 1991.

Reston, James. *Deadline.* New York: Random House, 1997.

Robertson, Nan. *The Girls in the Balcony: Women, Men and The New York Times.* New York: Vintage, 1993.

Stein, M. L., and Susan Paterno. *The Newswriter's Handbook: An Introduction to Journalism.* Ames, IA: Iowa State University Press, 1998.

Stephens, Mitchell. *A History of News.* New York: Penguin, 1988.

Talese, Gay. *The Kingdom and the Power.* New York: Random House, 2007.

Titchener, Campbell B. *Reviewing the Arts.* 3d ed. Hillsdale, NJ: Lawrence Erlbaum, 2005.

Tifft, Susan E., and Alex S. Jones. *The Trust: The Private and Powerful Family Behind The New York Times.* Boston: Little, Brown, 1999.

Wilstein, Steve. *Associated Press Sports Writing Handbook.* New York: McGraw-Hill, 2001.

Wolfe, Tom, and E. W. Johnson, eds. *The New Journalism.* London: Picador, 1975.

Wolseley, Roland E. *The Black Press USA.* Ames: Iowa State University Press, 1990.

WEB SITES

About: "Type Anatomy: Terminal Trivia"

www.desktoppub.about.com

Alloy Media and Marketing

www.alloymarketing.com

American Civil Liberties Union

www.aclu.org

American Copy Editors Society

www.copydesk.org

American Society of Newspaper Editors

www.asne.org

Associated Collegiate Press

www.studentpress.org/acp

Association for Education in Journalism and Mass Communications

www.aejmc.org

College Market Place

www.collegemarketplace.com

College Newspaper Business and Advertising Managers Inc.

www.cnbam.org

Designorati

www.designorati.com

First Amendment Center

www.firstamendmentcenter.org

Freedom Forum

www.freedomforum.org

Investigative Reporters and Editors, Inc.

www.ire.org

Math League

www.mathleague.com

Media Law Resource Center

www.medialaw.org

National Center for Computer-Assisted Reporting

www.nicar.org

National Center for Education Statistics

www.nces.ed.gov/nceskids/graphing

National Press Photographers Association

www.nppa.org

Poynter Institute

www.poynter.org

Society of Professional Journalists

www.spj.org

Student Press Law Center

www.splc.org

U.S. Copyright Office

www.copyright.gov

U.S. Department of Justice (Freedom of Information Act)

www.usdoj.gov/04fopia

Visual Editors

www.visualeditors.com

PERIODICALS

American Editor

6 issues/12 months

American Journalism Review

6 issues/12 months

College Student Journal

4 issues/12 months

Columbia Journalism Review

6 issues/12 months

Copy Editor

6 issues/12 months

Editorial Eye

12 issues/12 months

News Inc.

48 issues/12 months

Index

ACLU. *See* American Civil Liberties Union
Adams, Ansel, 174
advertising, 230–39; classifieds, 234–35; ethics, 260–61, 264; firewalls, 236–37, 238; public service, 235; rates, 233; scams, 233–34; self-promotion, 238–39; and the university, 237–38
advertising policy, 22–23
advice columns, 140–41
All the President's Men, 110
al-Qaeda, 52
alternative newspapers, 9
American Civil Liberties Union, 246
American Copy Editors Society, 194
American Journalism Review, 50
American Society of Newspaper Publishers, 24
Americans with Disabilities Act, 112
anonymous sources. *See* sources
AP. *See* Associated Press
Arnold, Matthew, 268
arts and entertainment, 145–53; advances, 150; art news, 150–51; ethics, 151–53; interviews, 149–50; legal concerns, 151–53; publicity, 148–49; reviews, 146–49. *See also* Fair Comment and Criticism
ASNP. *See* American Society of Newspaper Publishers
Associated Collegiate Press, 184, 246, 256
Associated Press, 57, 136, 227
Associated Press Style Book, 49, 125, 194, 200, 242–43
astrology, 142
athletic scholarships, 111
attribution, 95

balance, 93, 97, 196, 261. *See also* fairness, objectivity
beat, 81
Beeton, Mrs., 140
Bernstein, Carl, 110, 113
Better Business Bureau, 234
Bill of Rights, 246

blasphemy, 256
bookstores. *See* textbook prices
Bradlee, Ben, 41
Breslin, Jimmy, 122
bribes. *See* ethics
British Broadcasting Corporation, 227
broadsheet, 181–83
Buckley Amendment. *See* Federal Educational Rights and Privacy Act
Buckley, James, 247
budgets. *See* financing
bylines, 99, 172

campus crime, 68–76, 112, 247
Capote, Truman, 78
captions, 171, 215–16
Carlin, George, 138
cartoons, 139–40, 254, 256. *See also* editorial cartoons
censorship, 248–50
charts. *See* graphics
chilling effect, 114
Chronicle of Higher Education, 50
circulation, policy on, 20
CNN, 227
College Newspaper Business and Advertising Managers, Inc., 233
color, 174, 191
Columbia Journalism Review, 50
Columbia University Graduate School of Journalism, 79
columns, 122–24
comic strips. *See* cartoons
compensation, 230, 239
confirmation, 114, 261
confiscation, 249, 256
conflict of interest. *See* ethics
constitution (of newspaper), 12–17, 249
contributors, 124–25; policy on, 18–20

copy editing, 193–204
copyright, 21–22, 251; and the Internet, 171–72, 251
corrections, 172, 264
creativity, 267–68
credibility, 3
crime. *See* campus crime
Crimson, 45
cutlines. *See* captions

Daily Mirror, 183
Daily News, The, 181
deception, 250, 264
Deep Throat, 110, 113
defamation, 20, 95, 125, 151–53, 156, 224, 243–44
design, 181–92; balance, 188; clarity, 184–85; color, 191; familiarity, 188–89; harmony and unity, 187–88; identity, 191–92; navigability, 185–87; software, 189–190
Dowd, Maureen, 122
drop caps, 190
Dunne, Finley Peter, 262

Earth Day, 226
eBay, 234
Economist, The, 50
Editor and Publisher, 50
editorial cartoons, 128–29
editorials, 121–22
editors: choosing, 41–42; as mentors, 29–33, 271–72; as organizers, 34; responsibilities and qualifications, 42–43; as story generators, 28
Emerson, Ralph Waldo, 207
Entertainment Weekly, 48, 50, 62
Epstein, Joseph, 98
Espionage Act, 241

ethics, 82, 259–65; and arts and entertainment, 151–52; bribes, 261–62, 264; codes of, 23–24, 259; conflict of interest, 260, 261–62, 264, 265; influence, 261–62; 264; and photography, 170, 175–77, 265; and the public good, 262–64
etiquette, 82–85

Fair Comment and Criticism, 151, 244
fairness, 93, 261, 262. *See also* balance, objectivity
false light, 251
FCC. *See* Federal Communications Commission
features, 61, 131–43
Federal Communications Commission, 254
Federal Educational Rights and Privacy Act, 246–47
FERPA. *See* Federal Educational Rights and Privacy Act
Financial Times, 183
financing, 229–33: and budgets, 232–33; and student government, 230–31
Finnegans Wake, 42
First Amendment, 23, 119, 241, 247, 248, 250, 251. *See also* freedom of speech
First Amendment Center, 246
FOIA. *See* Freedom of Information Act
fonts, 187, 205–6
Fox News, 119
Franklin, Benjamin, 140
Freedman, Samuel G., 79, 80
Freedom of Information Act, 104–5, 247
freedom of speech, 96, 162, 241, 256; in advertisements, 23
Freud, Sigmund, 138

George-Palilonis, Jennifer, 179
GQ, 91
graphics, 177–79
Guardian, The, 182

Habitat for Humanity, 6
hate speech, 255–56
Hazelwood School District v. Kuhlmeier, 248
headlines, 205–15, 267; accuracy, 215; ambiguity, 211–12; capitalization, 207; clarity, 210; consistency, 207; conventions, 213–15; cuteness, 210, 212; fonts, 205–6; overlines and underlines, 213; size, 206–7; spacing, 208; split, 208–9; tombstoning, 207
Herblock (Herbert Block), 128
historical features, 136–38
homophobia, 5–6
Hosty v. Carter, 248
human interest, 133–35
humor, 138–40

Independent, The, 182
influence. *See* ethics
insurance: equipment, 175; libel, 243–46
interviewing, 1–2, 77, 82–83, 85–92, 149–50, 265; and athletes, 161–63
intrusion, 246
investigative journalism, 101–17; and computers, 102–3; and privacy, 112; and public records, 103–5; in sports, 164; and surveys, 115–17, 263; and teams, 109–10
Investigative Reporters and Editors, Inc., 112
Iraq, 59–60

job descriptions: advertising manager, 39; adviser, 40–41; arts and entertainment editor, 38; business manager, 39; copy editor, 36; design editor, 40; editorial page editor, 38–39; editor in chief, 35; features editor, 36–37; importance of, 34–35; literary editor, 38; managing editor, 35–36; news editor, 36; online editor, 40; photo editor, 37; sports editor, 37
Johnson, David, 133
joy of journalism, 267–74
jumps, 185–86
Jung, Carl, 138
justice, 273
justifying, 188
Jyllands-Posten, 256

Kennedy, John F., 94
Kentucky State University, 249
King, Martin Luther, Jr., 226
Kishon, Ephraim, 123

language. *See* writing
language police, 256. *See also* political correctness
letters, 20, 120, 125–28, 222
Letters to a Young Journalist, 79
Lewiston Morning Tribune, The, 133
libel, 242–46; in advertisements, 20, 243; and copy editing, 204; damages, 244–45; defenses, 244; in headlines, 215, 243; insurance, 245; in letters, 20, 125, 243; in quotes, 95; in reviews, 151–53; and sports, 156; as state law, 242
logos. *See* signposts
Los Angeles Times, 146, 150

Madonna, 53, 209, 211, 253
Malraux, Andre, 29
Maxim, 91
McCaughey, Bobbi, 176
Media Law Resource Center, 246
MediaNews Group, 63
Mencken, H. L., 123
mentoring, 271–72
Miller v. California, 254
Miller, Judith, 114
mission statement, 17–18
Modern English Usage, 49
Monroe Doctrine, The, 167
morgue, 51
MTV, 253

National Association of College Auxiliary Services, 109
National Center for Education Statistics, 178
National Collegiate Athletic Association, 112, 161
National Press Photographers Association, 176–77, 256–57
New Hampshire, 58
New Orleans, 57, 58, 59
New Republic, The, 50
news: boosterism, 64–67, 158, 260–61; as information and public service, 61–64; localizing, 57–61; page placement, 185; and the public relations office, 65–76; scoops, 269–70; sense for, 29; special interest, 55–57
newspaper office: access, 52–53; configuration, 46–49; equipment inventory, 51–52; insurance, 52; reference materials and archives, 49; security, 51, 190. *See also* morgue

INDEX

Newsweek, 50, 176
New York City, 94
New Yorker, The, 46
New York Post, 181
New York Times, The, 19, 50, 60, 61, 62, 66, 114, 116, 122, 128, 151, 173, 174, 181, 183, 237, 259
New York Times "Handbook of Values and Practices," 259
New York Times Manual of Style and Usage, The, 49
Nixon, Richard, 128
note-taking, 1, 78–79

objectivity, 95–97, 158
obscenity, 247–48, 254–55
online edition, 217–27; and advertising, 221–22; and design, 218; and geography, 218–20; and interactivity, 221; and links, 226–27; and multimedia, 225; and surveys, 223–25; and timeliness, 223
operations guidelines, 25, 26
opinion, 119–29; in reviews, 147–48
outrage, 251, 258

parking meters, 106–8
partisanship. *See* objectivity
People, 50
Philadelphia Daily News, 183
photography, 167–77, 268; and credit lines, 172, 216; and obscenity, 254, 258; and online editions, 220; and outrage, 215, 255, 258; and sports, 162, 164–65. *See also* copyright
political correctness, 251
polls. *See* surveys
Pope, Alexander, 254

pornography, 254–55. *See also* obscenity
Powell, Colin, 171
Practical Guide to Graphics Reporting, A, 178–79
Pravda, 18
prior restraint, 248
privacy, 112, 177, 246–47, 250
profanity, 253–54, 255
public forum, 248–49
Pulitzer Prize, 101, 132, 268
pull quotes, 190–91
puzzles, 141–42

Q&A, 91–92
quoting, 89–91, 201, 258

Rand McNally, 50
reading, 98
recording: devices, 78–80; legality of, 250
Reik, Theodore, 138
reporting, 77–97
retreats, 25
Rice, Anne, 59
Rolling Stone, 50, 62
Roper (Center for Public Opinion Research), 116
Rosenthal, Jack, 116
ROTC, 59
Royko, Mike, 123

shield laws, 114
Sierra Leone, 86, 87
Sigma Delta Chi, 24
signposts, 186–88
Singleton, William Dean, 63
slurs. *See* hate speech
Smith, Red, 123
Society of Professional Journalists, 24

source list, 80–81
sources: and agendas, 68, 261–62; anonymous, 112–14, 250–51, 265; multiplicity of, 92–93; and pseudosources, 75–76; and public relations professionals, 68–76
South Park, 253
SPJ. *See* Society of Professional Journalists
SPLC. *See* Student Press Law Center
sports, 155–65
Sports Illustrated, 50
Springer, Jerry, 253
Star Wars, 91
Stern, Howard, 253
student media board, 229
student press law, 241–52
Student Press Law Center, 112, 245, 246, 249
submissions policy. *See* contributors, policy on
surveys, 5–6, 115–17, 223–25, 263

tabloid, 181–83
taping. *See* recording
taste, 253–58; in headlines, 212; in photography, 176–77; and word choice, 201
tattoos, 114–17
teamwork, 270–71
Texas A&M, 57
textbook prices, 108–10
theft (of newspapers), 20–21, 256. *See also* confiscation
Time, 50

Times, The (London), 182
trend stories, 135–36
Trudeau, Garry, 129
typographical errors, 3, 194, 201
typography, 184, 187, 191, 205–6

undercover reporting. *See* deception
United Nations, 86
University of Illinois, 57
USA Today, 60, 61, 62, 173, 178, 184–85
U. S. Congress, 241
U. S. Constitution, 248
U. S. Copyright Office, 21–22. *See also* copyright
U. S. Justice Department, 104–5
U. S. News and World Report, 50
U. S. Supreme Court, 241, 247, 248, 254
Us Weekly, 50

verification, 93–94, 261
Village Voice, The, 146

Wall Street Journal, The, 50, 60, 61, 167, 181, 183
Washington Post, The, 41, 128, 211
Watergate, 104
weather, 143, 226
Weather Channel, The, 226
Weekly Standard, The, 50
Who's Who, 49
Woodward, Bob, 110, 113
Wright, Steven, 46
writing, 97–99, 156, 194–95, 267

Yahoo! News, 227

About the Author

Matt Nesvisky is a veteran reporter and editor who has written for such publications as *The New York Times*, *The Philadelphia Inquirer*, the *New York Daily News*, and *The Jerusalem Post*. He holds a doctorate from Carnegie-Mellon University and teaches journalism at Kutztown University of Pennsylvania.